T0018260

LLEWELLYN'S
2025
MOON
SIGN
BOOK

Plan Your Life
by the Cycles of the Moon

- COMPREHENSIVE GARDENING GUIDE
- WEATHER AND ECONOMIC FORECASTS
- NEW AND FULL MOON HOROSCOPES

Llewellyn's 2025 Moon Sign Book®

ISBN 978-0-7387-7196-0

Cover design by Kevin R. Brown
Editing by Hanna Grimson
Interior photographs: Getty Images
Stock photography models used for illustrative purposes only and may not endorse or represent the book's subject.
Typography owned by Llewellyn Worldwide Ltd.

Weekly tips by Penny Kelly, Lupa, and Shelby Deering.

Any internet references contained in this work are current at publication time, but the publisher cannot guarantee that a specific location will continue to be maintained.

A special thanks to Beth Koch Rosato for astrological proofreading. Astrological data compiled and programmed by Rique Pottenger, based on the earlier work of Neil F. Michelsen.

You can order Llewellyn annuals and books from *New Worlds*, Llewellyn's catalog. To request a free copy of the catalog, call toll-free 1-877-NEW-WRLD or visit our website at www.llewellyn.com.

Moon Sign Book® is registered in U.S. Patent and Trademark Office.
Moon Sign Book is a trademark of Llewellyn Worldwide Ltd. (Canada).

Published by Llewellyn Worldwide Ltd.
2143 Wooddale Drive
Woodbury, MN 55125-2989
www.llewellyn.com

Printed in China

FSC
www.fsc.org

MIX
Paper | Supporting
responsible forestry
FSC™ C007683

Table of Contents

The Methods of the
Moon Sign Book

Whether we live in simple, primitive times or a time of high technology and mass communication, we need our connection to Mother Nature and an understanding of how all of her systems work together—soil, sun, wind, water, plants, animals, people, and planets.

The connections among elements of nature become especially relevant when we recognize that many energies—both subtle and obvious—flow through our world and affect all things. Ancient civilizations knew about these changing energies and were much more attuned to the subtle effects that they had on us.

In the world of unseen energies, it has long been accepted in many quarters that the position of the planets makes a difference in the energy flowing around planet Earth. Those who question these energy flows are often sadly divorced from nature.

Imagine placing a large rock in the waters of a flowing stream or creek. Immediately you would notice numerous changes in the flow of the water moving over, around, and past the rock.

It is no different with our solar system. We live on a planet that floats in a solar sea of energies and frequency waves. As the planets move around the sun, the currents of energy flowing through the solar sea change in the same way that flowing water changes around the rock placed in a creek or stream…and we are affected by those changes at every level—physically, mentally, emotionally, and spiritually.

The ability to detect these changes and their effect on us has long been organized into knowledge systems, and the *Moon Sign Book* has always been a stable anchor in maintaining this knowledge and recognizing its importance. We call these organized methods of gaining knowledge *astrology*, and ancient cultures around the globe used this as their science. It was how they found and maintained a sense of prediction, control, and security, something we are still striving for even today as we try to anticipate the cycles and events of our daily lives.

Although there are several ways of organizing and assessing these energy flows based on planetary positions, the *Moon Sign Book* uses the tropical system, which says that spring officially begins when the Sun is directly over the equator at noon, something that occurs around March 20 to 21 every year. Once that moment has been determined, the rest of the zodiac calendar is laid out at thirty-degree intervals. This allows us to be precise, but also flex with the changing nature of all things, including our solar system. We support a knowledge base that upholds the ancient wisdom and teaches it to all who are interested. We invite you to read what we have written here and to celebrate the interactions of these energies with the plants, animals, earth, and stars that share this time and space with us.

Weekly Almanac

Your Guide to
Lunar Gardening
& Good Timing for Activities

♑ **January**

December 29–January 4

Love keeps the cold out better than a cloak.

~Henry Wadsworth Longfellow

Date	Qtr.	Sign	Activity
Dec. 29, 11:37 pm– Dec. 30, 5:27 pm	4th	Capricorn	Plant potatoes and tubers. Trim to retard growth.

Even though your kitchen might be your family's headquarters, you can set aside part of it just for yourself. Create your very own coffee or tea bar, where you can take a few moments to sip and reflect each morning. Include a coffee maker, favorite flavors, cream, sugar, and bits of decor if you like. Tuck everything away in a cabinet or place it on an unused portion of your countertop.

_____

_____

_____

_____

December 30
5:27 pm EST

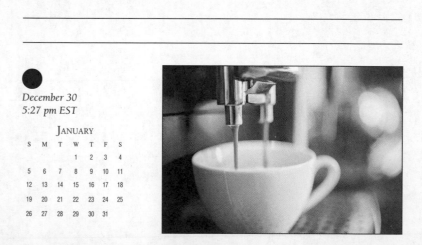

JANUARY

S	M	T	W	T	F	S
				1	2	3	4
5	6	7	8	9	10	11
12	13	14	15	16	17	18
19	20	21	22	23	24	25
26	27	28	29	30	31	

January 5–11   ♑

The secret of a happy life is respect. Respect for yourself and respect for others.   ~AYAD AKHTAR

Date	Qtr.	Sign	Activity
Jan. 7, 5:11 pm– Jan. 9, 8:07 pm	2nd	Taurus	Plant annuals for hardiness. Trim to increase growth.
Jan. 11, 11:24 pm– Jan. 13, 5:27 pm	2nd	Cancer	Plant grains, leafy annuals. Fertilize (chemical). Graft or bud plants. Irrigate. Trim to increase growth.

Getting a few minutes of walking or other light activity in before pre-workout stretching can warm your muscles up and prevent injuries. Pause periodically throughout your workout to stretch again, especially if you have certain muscle groups that like to give you trouble. And get one more good set of stretches in as you're cooling down. All of these stretch breaks can increase flexibility while reducing the chance of injury.

◐

January 6
6:56 pm EST

JANUARY

S	M	T	W	T	F	S
			1	2	3	4
5	6	7	8	9	10	11
12	13	14	15	16	17	18
19	20	21	22	23	24	25
26	27	28	29	30	31	

♑ January 12–18

Snow flurries began to fall and they swirled around people's legs like house cats. It was magical, this snowglobe world.

~Sarah Addison Allen

Date	Qtr.	Sign	Activity
Jan. 13, 5:27 pm– Jan. 14, 4:12 am	3rd	Cancer	Plant biennials, perennials, bulbs and roots. Prune. Irrigate. Fertilize (organic).
Jan. 14, 4:12 am– Jan. 16, 11:46 am	3rd	Leo	Cultivate. Destroy weeds and pests. Harvest fruits and root crops for food. Trim to retard growth.
Jan. 16, 11:46 am– Jan. 18, 10:33 pm	3rd	Virgo	Cultivate, especially medicinal plants. Destroy weeds and pests. Trim to retard growth.

Make this the year to rediscover good, natural, homemade food. At your local bookstore find a small but good cookbook for soups or salads, perhaps casseroles, or maybe breakfast meals. Buy just one, take it home, and start at the beginning, experimenting your way through the entire book. You will learn a lot, expand your tastes, and enjoy some fabulous food.

○
January 13
5:27 pm EST

JANUARY

S	M	T	W	T	F	S
				1	2	3	4
5	6	7	8	9	10	11
12	13	14	15	16	17	18
19	20	21	22	23	24	25
26	27	28	29	30	31	

January 19–25 ♑

It's much more fun to succeed and fail with other people.

~AMY POEHLER

Date	Qtr.	Sign	Activity
Jan. 21, 11:20 am–Jan. 21, 3:31 pm	3rd	Scorpio	Plant biennials, perennials, bulbs and roots. Prune. Irrigate. Fertilize (organic).
Jan. 21, 3:31 pm–Jan. 23, 11:29 pm	4th	Scorpio	Plant biennials, perennials, bulbs and roots. Prune. Irrigate. Fertilize (organic).
Jan. 23, 11:29 pm–Jan. 26, 8:43 am	4th	Sagittarius	Cultivate. Destroy weeds and pests. Harvest fruits and root crops for food. Trim to retard growth.

Who says you have to go to a spa and empty your wallet so that you can feel relaxed? Instead, create the experience at home. Whip up a homemade mask with avocado and honey, soak your feet in Epsom salts before giving yourself a pedicure, and then lay on your bed with cucumber slices on your eyes. You'll be feeling tranquil in no time.

◑

January 21
3:31 pm EST

JANUARY

S	M	T	W	T	F	S
			1	2	3	4
5	6	7	8	9	10	11
12	13	14	15	16	17	18
19	20	21	22	23	24	25
26	27	28	29	30	31	

≋ February

January 26–February 1

We are who we know ourselves to be, and we are what we love. That's OK.
                                                    ∼Laverne Cox

Date	Qtr.	Sign	Activity
Jan. 26, 8:43 am– Jan. 28, 2:31 pm	4th	Capricorn	Plant potatoes and tubers. Trim to retard growth.
Jan. 28, 2:31 pm– Jan. 29, 7:36 am	4th	Aquarius	Cultivate. Destroy weeds and pests. Harvest fruits and root crops for food. Trim to retard growth.
Jan. 30, 5:52 pm– Feb. 1, 8:10 pm	1st	Pisces	Plant grains, leafy annuals. Fertilize (chemical). Graft or bud plants. Irrigate. Trim to increase growth.

Make the inside of your car or truck smell wonderfully fresh and invigorating by putting a few drops of lemon oil, tangerine oil, or spearmint oil on a cotton ball and putting that cotton ball in the center console or the glove compartment. You will be greeted by a pleasant smell every time you open the car door.

_____

_____

_____

_____

●
January 29
7:36 am EST

FEBRUARY

S	M	T	W	T	F	S
						1
2	3	4	5	6	7	8
9	10	11	12	13	14	15
16	17	18	19	20	21	22
23	24	25	26	27	28	

February 2–8 〜〜

Well, I'm not here to live up to anyone else's expectations—
I'm here to live up to mine.   ～JEREMY LIN

Date	Qtr.	Sign	Activity
Feb. 3, 10:33 pm– Feb. 5, 3:02 am	1st	Taurus	Plant annuals for hardiness. Trim to increase growth.
Feb. 5, 3:02 am– Feb. 6, 1:44 am	2nd	Taurus	Plant annuals for hardiness. Trim to increase growth.
Feb. 8, 6:04 am– Feb. 10, 12:01 pm	2nd	Cancer	Plant grains, leafy annuals. Fertilize (chemical). Graft or bud plants. Irrigate. Trim to increase growth.

Starting a collection can be such fun, especially if you frequently shop flea markets and secondhand shops. From matchbooks to antique silver to old radios, think of a collection that will bring beauty and personality to your home. Do your homework and learn which items you should particularly look out for. Then get shopping!

◐
February 5
3:02 am EST

FEBRUARY

S	M	T	W	T	F	S
						1
2	3	4	5	6	7	8
9	10	11	12	13	14	15
16	17	18	19	20	21	22
23	24	25	26	27	28	

≋ February 9–15

When it's really cold, the snow makes a lovely noise
underfoot, and it's like the air is full of stars.

~KATHERINE MAY

Date	Qtr.	Sign	Activity
Feb. 12, 8:53 am–Feb. 12, 8:07 pm	3rd	Leo	Cultivate. Destroy weeds and pests. Harvest fruits and root crops for food. Trim to retard growth.
Feb. 12, 8:07 pm–Feb. 15, 6:45 am	3rd	Virgo	Cultivate, especially medicinal plants. Destroy weeds and pests. Trim to retard growth.

Did a bird fly into your closed window? It needs veterinary help immediately! Though it may seem uninjured, it may have internal injuries that could be fatal if untreated, and adrenaline may cause it to fly away even when badly hurt. If you can catch the bird, wear gloves and a filtered mask and put it in a box in a dark, quiet place outside. Then contact your nearest wildlife rehabilitation facility or veterinarian. The sooner the bird receives professional help, the better.

○
February 12
8:53 am EST

FEBRUARY

S	M	T	W	T	F	S
						1
2	3	4	5	6	7	8
9	10	11	12	13	14	15
16	17	18	19	20	21	22
23	24	25	26	27	28	

February 16–22 〜〜〜

Transformation is not accomplished by tentative wading at the edge.   ~ROBIN WALL KIMMERER

Date	Qtr.	Sign	Activity
Feb. 17, 7:19 pm–Feb. 20, 7:55 am	3rd	Scorpio	Plant biennials, perennials, bulbs and roots. Prune. Irrigate. Fertilize (organic).
Feb. 20, 7:55 am–Feb. 20, 12:33 pm	3rd	Sagittarius	Cultivate. Destroy weeds and pests. Harvest fruits and root crops for food. Trim to retard growth.
Feb. 20, 12:33 pm–Feb. 22, 6:09 pm	4th	Sagittarius	Cultivate. Destroy weeds and pests. Harvest fruits and root crops for food. Trim to retard growth.
Feb. 22, 6:09 pm–Feb. 25, 12:40 am	4th	Capricorn	Plant potatoes and tubers. Trim to retard growth.

Feeling anxious or blue? Help combat this with good nutrition, especially things like vitamin B complex, SAMe, and the full spectrum of amino acids. There's no need to let that messy world out there get the best of you.

◑

February 20
12:33 pm EST

FEBRUARY

S	M	T	W	T	F	S
						1
2	3	4	5	6	7	8
9	10	11	12	13	14	15
16	17	18	19	20	21	22
23	24	25	26	27	28	

♓ March

February 23–March 1

*It's amazing. Life changes very quickly, in a very positive
way, if you let it.*   ~LINDSEY VONN

Date	Qtr.	Sign	Activity
Feb. 25, 12:40 am–Feb. 27, 3:46 am	4th	Aquarius	Cultivate. Destroy weeds and pests. Harvest fruits and root crops for food. Trim to retard growth.
Feb. 27, 3:46 am–Feb. 27, 7:45 pm	4th	Pisces	Plant biennials, perennials, bulbs and roots. Prune. Irrigate. Fertilize (organic).
Feb. 27, 7:45 pm–Mar. 1, 4:52 am	1st	Pisces	Plant grains, leafy annuals. Fertilize (chemical). Graft or bud plants. Irrigate. Trim to increase growth.

Biophilic design is becoming popular in today's interiors. It's
the idea that you're bringing the outdoors into your home,
creating a soothing, natural environment. Embrace this approach
through natural-wood furniture, colors drawn from the outdoors,
houseplants, and collections of shells or stones.

February 27
7:45 pm EST

MARCH

S	M	T	W	T	F	S
						1
2	3	4	5	6	7	8
9	10	11	12	13	14	15
16	17	18	19	20	21	22
23	24	25	26	27	28	29
30	31					

March 2–8 ♓

Being a fish out of water is tough, but that's how you evolve.
~Kumail Nanjiani

Date	Qtr.	Sign	Activity
Mar. 3, 5:37 am– Mar. 5, 7:29 am	1st	Taurus	Plant annuals for hardiness. Trim to increase growth.
Mar. 7, 11:29 am– Mar. 9, 6:59 pm	2nd	Cancer	Plant grains, leafy annuals. Fertilize (chemical). Graft or bud plants. Irrigate. Trim to increase growth.

Mercury retrograde comes three times this year and is a perfect time for reading, reflection, and reassessment of your life. Each time it comes around, select one or two books to read that will help you become more aware of yourself and your life. Then read, meditate, and reflect. When retrograde is over, implement changes!

◑

March 6
11:32 am EST

March

S	M	T	W	T	F	S
						1
2	3	4	5	6	7	8
9	10	11	12	13	14	15
16	17	18	19	20	21	22
23	24	25	26	27	28	29
30	31					

March 9–15

By March, the worst of the winter would be over. The snow would thaw, the rivers begin to run, and the world would wake into itself again.   ∼NEIL GAIMAN

Date	Qtr.	Sign	Activity
Mar. 14, 2:55 am– Mar. 14, 2:59 pm	3rd	Virgo	Cultivate, especially medicinal plants. Destroy weeds and pests. Trim to retard growth.

I f you have an aquarium, put the dirty water you remove when you clean your tank into your garden. The nitrogen and other elements in the waste from fish and other animals will give your plants a boost! Check for tiny snails, fish, and other animals before you pour the water. (If you've had to treat your tank with antibiotics, other medication, or water treatment chemicals, dump the water down the drain instead.)

_____

_____

_____

Daylight Saving Time begins March 9, 2:00 am

○

March 14 2:55 am EDT

MARCH

S	M	T	W	T	F	S
						1
2	3	4	5	6	7	8
9	10	11	12	13	14	15
16	17	18	19	20	21	22
23	24	25	26	27	28	29
30	31					

March 16–22

Go find your joy. Whatever that is, go find your joy.

~SANDRA BULLOCK

Date	Qtr.	Sign	Activity
Mar. 17, 3:30 am– Mar. 19, 4:17 pm	3rd	Scorpio	Plant biennials, perennials, bulbs and roots. Prune. Irrigate. Fertilize (organic).
Mar. 19, 4:17 pm– Mar. 22, 3:29 am	3rd	Sagittarius	Cultivate. Destroy weeds and pests. Harvest fruits and root crops for food. Trim to retard growth.
Mar. 22, 3:29 am– Mar. 22, 7:29 am	3rd	Capricorn	Plant potatoes and tubers. Trim to retard growth.
Mar. 22, 7:29 am– Mar. 24, 11:25 am	4th	Capricorn	Plant potatoes and tubers. Trim to retard growth.

Learn to use herbs and spices in your food. They add a depth of flavor and nutrition that is unmatched! Add parsley to your potatoes or rice, basil and cilantro to your salads, oregano and cumin to your spaghetti sauce, and summer savory to your bean dishes and soups.

◑

March 22
7:29 am EDT

MARCH

S	M	T	W	T	F	S
						1
2	3	4	5	6	7	8
9	10	11	12	13	14	15
16	17	18	19	20	21	22
23	24	25	26	27	28	29
30	31					

♈ March 23–29

I have standards I don't plan on lowering for anybody…
including myself.   ~ZENDAYA

Date	Qtr.	Sign	Activity
Mar. 24, 11:25 am– Mar. 26, 3:31 pm	4th	Aquarius	Cultivate. Destroy weeds and pests. Harvest fruits and root crops for food. Trim to retard growth.
Mar. 26, 3:31 pm– Mar. 28, 4:36 pm	4th	Pisces	Plant biennials, perennials, bulbs and roots. Prune. Irrigate. Fertilize (organic).
Mar. 28, 4:36 pm– Mar. 29, 6:58 am	4th	Aries	Cultivate. Destroy weeds and pests. Harvest fruits and root crops for food. Trim to retard growth.

Try a new, more creative arrangement in your garden by planting in concentric circles or spirals instead of rows. Put the tallest plants in the middle, with veggies, flowers, and herbs in descending order of height as you move away from the center. You will have a stunning garden.

March 29
6:58 am EDT

MARCH

S	M	T	W	T	F	S
						1
2	3	4	5	6	7	8
9	10	11	12	13	14	15
16	17	18	19	20	21	22
23	24	25	26	27	28	29
30	31					

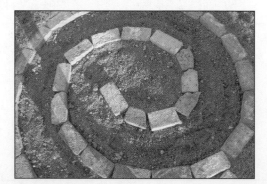

April ♈

March 30–April 5

No matter how chaotic it is, wildflowers will still spring up in the middle of nowhere.
                                                      ~SHERYL CROW

Date	Qtr.	Sign	Activity
Mar. 30, 4:16 pm–Apr. 1, 4:26 pm	1st	Taurus	Plant annuals for hardiness. Trim to increase growth.
Apr. 3, 6:50 pm–Apr. 4, 10:15 pm	1st	Cancer	Plant grains, leafy annuals. Fertilize (chemical). Graft or bud plants. Irrigate. Trim to increase growth.
Apr. 4, 10:15 pm–Apr. 6, 12:34 am	2nd	Cancer	Plant grains, leafy annuals. Fertilize (chemical). Graft or bud plants. Irrigate. Trim to increase growth.

If daily life is starting to weigh you down, consider a retreat weekend. Many are held all throughout the year in every corner of the country, each with a different focus. Want to meet some new friends? Improve your meditation practice? Go hiking in the desert? Or simply party the weekend away? Then a retreat might be right up your alley.

April 4
10:15 pm EDT

APRIL

S	M	T	W	T	F	S
		1	2	3	4	5
6	7	8	9	10	11	12
13	14	15	16	17	18	19
20	21	22	23	24	25	26
27	28	29	30			

♈ April 6–12

A garden is a grand teacher. It teaches patience and careful watchfulness; it teaches industry and thrift; above all, it teaches entire trust.   ∼GERTRUDE JEKYLL

Date	Qtr.	Sign	Activity
Apr. 10, 9:12 pm–Apr. 12, 8:22 pm	2nd	Libra	Plant annuals for fragrance and beauty. Trim to increase growth.

Native plants, or ones that are specific to your climate and soil type, can beautify your yard and help the environment in the process, since they generally require less watering and pesticides and are beneficial to local pollinators. Visit a nearby garden center or library to discover native plants you can grow. For instance, in the Midwest, milkweed is native, and monarch butterflies love it. Down south, plant a tree like the native live oak.

○
April 12
8:22 pm EDT

APRIL

S	M	T	W	T	F	S
		1	2	3	4	5
6	7	8	9	10	11	12
13	14	15	16	17	18	19
20	21	22	23	24	25	26
27	28	29	30			

April 13–19 ♈

*If we give our children sound self-love, they will be able to
deal with whatever life puts before them.* ～BELL HOOKS

Date	Qtr.	Sign	Activity
Apr. 13, 9:54 am– Apr. 15, 10:37 pm	3rd	Scorpio	Plant biennials, perennials, bulbs and roots. Prune. Irrigate. Fertilize (organic).
Apr. 15, 10:37 pm– Apr. 18, 10:12 am	3rd	Sagittarius	Cultivate. Destroy weeds and pests. Harvest fruits and root crops for food. Trim to retard growth.
Apr. 18, 10:12 am– Apr. 20, 7:22 pm	3rd	Capricorn	Plant potatoes and tubers. Trim to retard growth.

Need to give your dog a bath but can't afford it and don't want to do so in your bathtub? If it's a big dog, consider a shower outside using a hose hooked up to warm water from a utility sink. If it's a small dog, get an old-fashioned washtub from a farm-supply store and bathe your four-legged friend outside in the sunshine.

			April			
S	M	T	W	T	F	S
		1	2	3	4	5
6	7	8	9	10	11	12
13	14	15	16	17	18	19
20	21	22	23	24	25	26
27	28	29	30			

♉ April 20–26

I know who I am.   ~MIGUEL DE CERVANTES

Date	Qtr.	Sign	Activity
Apr. 20, 7:22 pm– Apr. 20, 9:36 pm	3rd	Aquarius	Cultivate. Destroy weeds and pests. Harvest fruits and root crops for food. Trim to retard growth.
Apr. 20, 9:36 pm– Apr. 23, 1:07 am	4th	Aquarius	Cultivate. Destroy weeds and pests. Harvest fruits and root crops for food. Trim to retard growth.
Apr. 23, 1:07 am– Apr. 25, 3:24 am	4th	Pisces	Plant biennials, perennials, bulbs and roots. Prune. Irrigate. Fertilize (organic).
Apr. 25, 3:24 am– Apr. 27, 3:17 am	4th	Aries	Cultivate. Destroy weeds and pests. Harvest fruits and root crops for food. Trim to retard growth.

For dry, dull hair that has no body, get a jar of cholesterol or other heavy-duty conditioner, then wash hair and apply the cholesterol liberally from the scalp to the ends. Cover hair with a plastic shower cap and leave on for the amount of time specified in the instructions. Rinse and style as usual. You will love the smooth, healthy look and feel of your hair and the way it holds its styling.

_____

_____

_____

_____

◗ *April 20*
9:36 pm EDT

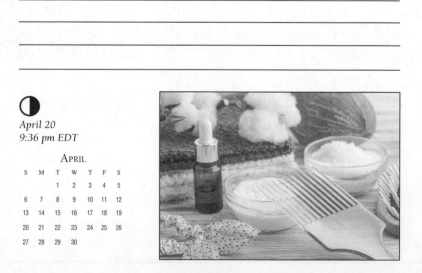

APRIL

S	M	T	W	T	F	S
		1	2	3	4	5
6	7	8	9	10	11	12
13	14	15	16	17	18	19
20	21	22	23	24	25	26
27	28	29	30			

May ♉

April 27–May 3

My garden is my most beautiful masterpiece.

~CLAUDE MONET

Date	Qtr.	Sign	Activity
Apr. 27, 3:17 am– Apr. 27, 3:31 pm	4th	Taurus	Plant potatoes and tubers. Trim to retard growth.
Apr. 27, 3:31 pm– Apr. 29, 2:34 am	1st	Taurus	Plant annuals for hardiness. Trim to increase growth.
May 1, 3:23 am– May 3, 7:29 am	1st	Cancer	Plant grains, leafy annuals. Fertilize (chemical). Graft or bud plants. Irrigate. Trim to increase growth.

Just because you leave a favorite hotel doesn't mean you can't take it with you! Take plenty of pictures while you're there and plan to style a room in your home that's inspired by its interiors. Pick up the color palette, emulate the artwork, or even buy a treasure or two from the hotel gift shop to display.

April 27
3:31 pm EDT

MAY

S	M	T	W	T	F	S
				1	2	3
4	5	6	7	8	9	10
11	12	13	14	15	16	17
18	19	20	21	22	23	24
25	26	27	28	29	30	31

May 4–10

*We with our lives are like islands in the sea, or like trees
in the forest.... The trees also commingle their roots in the
darkness underground, and the islands also hang together
through the ocean's bottom.*   ~WILLIAM JAMES

Date	Qtr.	Sign	Activity
May 8, 3:06 am– May 10, 3:58 pm	2nd	Libra	Plant annuals for fragrance and beauty. Trim to increase growth.
May 10, 3:58 pm– May 12, 12:56 pm	2nd	Scorpio	Plant grains, leafy annuals. Fertilize (chemical). Graft or bud plants. Irrigate. Trim to increase growth.

In recent years, medical professionals have discovered that
being near water can improve one's mental health. To lift your
mood, decrease stress, or even ease symptoms of anxiety or
depression, head to any body of water. It can be as simple as
a nearby pond in your neighborhood or a bubbling creek that
soothes your soul. If you really want to go big, plan a trip to the
ocean and maximize the mental health benefits.

May 4
9:52 am EDT

MAY

S	M	T	W	T	F	S
				1	2	3
4	5	6	7	8	9	10
11	12	13	14	15	16	17
18	19	20	21	22	23	24
25	26	27	28	29	30	31

May 11–17 ♉

I'll tell you, there is nothing better in life than being a late bloomer. I believe that success can happen at any time and at any age.   ~SALMA HAYEK

Date	Qtr.	Sign	Activity
May 12, 12:56 pm– May 13, 4:35 am	3rd	Scorpio	Plant biennials, perennials, bulbs and roots. Prune. Irrigate. Fertilize (organic).
May 13, 4:35 am– May 15, 3:58 pm	3rd	Sagittarius	Cultivate. Destroy weeds and pests. Harvest fruits and root crops for food. Trim to retard growth.
May 15, 3:58 pm– May 18, 1:29 am	3rd	Capricorn	Plant potatoes and tubers. Trim to retard growth.

Got a childhood hobby or interest you wish you could revisit as an adult? It's not immature, but a great way to boost your mental health with something fun and low-pressure. You may have to respect your adult body's limitations with demanding activities like sports, and your time and finances may be limited, but do what you can. Recapturing that childhood joy and curiosity may be just what you need to lighten up your life!

○
May 12
12:56 pm EDT

MAY

S	M	T	W	T	F	S
				1	2	3
4	5	6	7	8	9	10
11	12	13	14	15	16	17
18	19	20	21	22	23	24
25	26	27	28	29	30	31

May 18–24

Everything that slows us down and forces patience, everything that sets us back into the slow circles of nature, is a help. Gardening is an instrument of grace.   ~MAY SARTON

Date	Qtr.	Sign	Activity
May 18, 1:29 am– May 20, 7:59 am	3rd	Aquarius	Cultivate. Destroy weeds and pests. Harvest fruits and root crops for food. Trim to retard growth.
May 20, 7:59 am– May 20, 8:28 am	4th	Aquarius	Cultivate. Destroy weeds and pests. Harvest fruits and root crops for food. Trim to retard growth.
May 20, 8:28 am– May 22, 12:26 pm	4th	Pisces	Plant biennials, perennials, bulbs and roots. Prune. Irrigate. Fertilize (organic).
May 22, 12:26 pm– May 24, 1:38 pm	4th	Aries	Cultivate. Destroy weeds and pests. Harvest fruits and root crops for food. Trim to retard growth.
May 24, 1:38 pm– May 26, 1:21 pm	4th	Taurus	Plant potatoes and tubers. Trim to retard growth.

Get up on a spring morning, make a cup of tea or coffee, and sit outside to drink it. Enjoy the absence of bugs and mosquitos and the budding presence of leaves on trees, spring flowers, and the music of whatever birds come to nest in your region.

_____

_____

_____

_____

May 20
7:59 am EDT

MAY

S	M	T	W	T	F	S
				1	2	3
4	5	6	7	8	9	10
11	12	13	14	15	16	17
18	19	20	21	22	23	24
25	26	27	28	29	30	31

May 25–31 ♊

If you stand on the shoulders of others, you have a reciprocal responsibility to live your life so that others may stand on your shoulders. ∼VERNON JORDAN

Date	Qtr.	Sign	Activity
May 26, 1:21 pm– May 26, 11:02 pm	4th	Gemini	Cultivate. Destroy weeds and pests. Harvest fruits and root crops for food. Trim to retard growth.
May 28, 1:33 pm– May 30, 4:17 pm	1st	Cancer	Plant grains, leafy annuals. Fertilize (chemical). Graft or bud plants. Irrigate. Trim to increase growth.

To make your walls look truly one of a kind, purchase art from local art fairs. It's a great way to support artists in the area, and your home will look a lot more distinctive than if you simply decorated with pieces from big-box stores. Look for unique paintings in head-turning hues, professional photographs, and handmade sculptures.

_____

_____

_____

_____

●

May 26
11:02 pm EDT

MAY

S	M	T	W	T	F	S
				1	2	3
4	5	6	7	8	9	10
11	12	13	14	15	16	17
18	19	20	21	22	23	24
25	26	27	28	29	30	31

♊ June

June 1–7

The hum of bees is the voice of the garden.

~Elizabeth Lawrence

Date	Qtr.	Sign	Activity
Jun. 4, 9.38 am–Jun. 6, 10:23 pm	2nd	Libra	Plant annuals for fragrance and beauty. Trim to increase growth.
Jun. 6, 10:23 pm–Jun. 9, 10:56 am	2nd	Scorpio	Plant grains, leafy annuals. Fertilize (chemical). Graft or bud plants. Irrigate. Trim to increase growth.

Humans eat 365 days a year, yet many of us live in areas with a very short growing season and work at sedentary jobs. A greenhouse is a season extender, and raised beds are back savers for those who are mostly used to sitting at computers all day.

_____

_____

_____

_____

◑

June 2
11:41 pm EDT

JUNE

S	M	T	W	T	F	S
1	2	3	4	5	6	7
8	9	10	11	12	13	14
15	16	17	18	19	20	21
22	23	24	25	26	27	28
29	30					

June 8–14 ♊

Love does not consist in gazing at each other but in looking outward together in the same direction.

~ANTOINE DE SAINT-EXUPÉRY

Date	Qtr.	Sign	Activity
Jun. 11, 3:44 am–Jun. 11, 9:55 pm	3rd	Sagittarius	Cultivate. Destroy weeds and pests. Harvest fruits and root crops for food. Trim to retard growth.
Jun. 11, 9:55 pm–Jun. 14, 7:00 am	3rd	Capricorn	Plant potatoes and tubers. Trim to retard growth.
Jun. 14, 7:00 am–Jun. 16, 2:09 pm	3rd	Aquarius	Cultivate. Destroy weeds and pests. Harvest fruits and root crops for food. Trim to retard growth.

Nowadays, no matter where you live, you can count on an athletic event taking place in your area, often benefiting a worthy cause. Sign up for a 5K run or walk a few miles if you're feeling adventurous. You could also sign up to be a volunteer, handing out water and giving out medals.

○
June 11
3:44 am EDT

JUNE

S	M	T	W	T	F	S
1	2	3	4	5	6	7
8	9	10	11	12	13	14
15	16	17	18	19	20	21
22	23	24	25	26	27	28
29	30					

♊ June 15–21

It is through art that we will prevail and we will endure. It lives on after us and defines us as people.

~RITA MORENO

Date	Qtr.	Sign	Activity
Jun. 16, 2:09 pm– Jun. 18, 3:19 pm	3rd	Pisces	Plant biennials, perennials, bulbs and roots. Prune. Irrigate. Fertilize (organic).
Jun. 18, 3:19 pm– Jun. 18, 7:08 pm	4th	Pisces	Plant biennials, perennials, bulbs and roots. Prune. Irrigate. Fertilize (organic).
Jun. 18, 7:08 pm– Jun. 20, 9:53 pm	4th	Aries	Cultivate. Destroy weeds and pests. Harvest fruits and root crops for food. Trim to retard growth.
Jun. 20, 9:53 pm– Jun. 22, 10:57 pm	4th	Taurus	Plant potatoes and tubers. Trim to retard growth.

Find a book about the local birds near you or visit your area's Audubon Society website to learn all about the feathered friends you might see in your backyard or in a park. Do some birdwatching by bringing along a pair of binoculars, watching quietly from a distance, and even snapping a photo or two.

◐
June 18
3:19 pm EDT

JUNE

S	M	T	W	T	F	S
1	2	3	4	5	6	7
8	9	10	11	12	13	14
15	16	17	18	19	20	21
22	23	24	25	26	27	28
29	30					

June 22–28 ♋

We weren't a rich family, but we were very rich in experiences.

~GUY FIERI

Date	Qtr.	Sign	Activity
Jun. 22, 10:57 pm– Jun. 24, 11:44 pm	4th	Gemini	Cultivate. Destroy weeds and pests. Harvest fruits and root crops for food. Trim to retard growth.
Jun. 24, 11:44 pm– Jun. 25, 6:32 am	4th	Cancer	Plant biennials, perennials, bulbs and roots. Prune. Irrigate. Fertilize (organic).
Jun. 25, 6:32 am– Jun. 27, 2:05 am	1st	Cancer	Plant grains, leafy annuals. Fertilize (chemical). Graft or bud plants. Irrigate. Trim to increase growth.

Flowers are lovely to us, but to insects and other pollinators they are crucial food sources. This is especially true of plants native to where you are. Cutting flowers and bringing them inside deprives these animals of important meals. Instead, try planting more flowers where you can easily see them through windows so that you can still enjoy their beauty inside, but they keep feeding wildlife outside.

●

June 25
6:32 am EDT

JUNE

S	M	T	W	T	F	S
1	2	3	4	5	6	7
8	9	10	11	12	13	14
15	16	17	18	19	20	21
22	23	24	25	26	27	28
29	30					

♋ July

June 29–July 5

*Being normal is being completely unique, because nobody's
the same.*
                                                    ~Jonathan Van Ness

Date	Qtr.	Sign	Activity
Jul. 1, 5:16 pm– Jul. 2, 3:30 pm	1st	Libra	Plant annuals for fragrance and beauty. Trim to increase growth.
Jul. 2, 3:30 pm– Jul. 4, 5:33 am	2nd	Libra	Plant annuals for fragrance and beauty. Trim to increase growth.
Jul. 4, 5:33 am– Jul. 6, 6:06 pm	2nd	Scorpio	Plant grains, leafy annuals. Fertilize (chemical). Graft or bud plants. Irrigate. Trim to increase growth.

If you don't have yard space for a flower garden, get a collection
of large pots and plant them full of flowers: tall and graceful,
short and spiky, long and draping. Pick colors you love and put
them where you will see them frequently. They are a joy to the
soul.

July 2
3:30 pm EDT

July

S	M	T	W	T	F	S
		1	2	3	4	5
6	7	8	9	10	11	12
13	14	15	16	17	18	19
20	21	22	23	24	25	26
27	28	29	30	31		

July 6–12

*I had found that taking risks, being true to myself, and
making decisions with good intentions can exceed even my
own expectations.*   ~Jennifer Lopez

Date	Qtr.	Sign	Activity
Jul. 9, 4:55 am– Jul. 10, 4:37 pm	2nd	Capricorn	Graft or bud plants. Trim to increase growth.
Jul. 10, 4:37 pm– Jul. 11, 1:21 pm	3rd	Capricorn	Plant potatoes and tubers. Trim to retard growth.
Jul. 11, 1:21 pm– Jul. 13, 7:45 pm	3rd	Aquarius	Cultivate. Destroy weeds and pests. Harvest fruits and root crops for food. Trim to retard growth.

If you have a dog, discover dog-friendly locales in your town so you can spend lots of time with your furry friend at your side. Sign up for a playgroup at a dog-friendly brewery, track down a dog park you haven't visited yet so your pup can experience new smells, or find out if there's a shopping mall that allows dogs and make a fun afternoon of it.

○
July 10
4:37 pm EDT

JULY

S	M	T	W	T	F	S
		1	2	3	4	5
6	7	8	9	10	11	12
13	14	15	16	17	18	19
20	21	22	23	24	25	26
27	28	29	30	31		

July 13–19

You are not lucky to be here. The world needs your
perspective. They are lucky to have you.

~Antonio Tijerino

Date	Qtr.	Sign	Activity
Jul. 13, 7:45 pm– Jul. 16, 12:32 am	3rd	Pisces	Plant biennials, perennials, bulbs and roots. Prune. Irrigate. Fertilize (organic).
Jul. 16, 12:32 am– Jul. 17, 8:38 pm	3rd	Aries	Cultivate. Destroy weeds and pests. Harvest fruits and root crops for food. Trim to retard growth.
Jul. 17, 8:38 pm– Jul. 18, 3:59 am	4th	Aries	Cultivate. Destroy weeds and pests. Harvest fruits and root crops for food. Trim to retard growth.
Jul. 18, 3:59 am– Jul. 20, 6:22 am	4th	Taurus	Plant potatoes and tubers. Trim to retard growth.

If it's a nice, warm day, plan to spend an afternoon at a local pool. Whether it's a public pool or a friend's, make it the ultimate relaxation experience, with pleasant-smelling sunscreen, a soft beach towel, your most glamourous pair of sunglasses, and a stack of magazines. Take a dip when you need to cool off!

July 17
8:38 pm EDT

JULY

S	M	T	W	T	F	S
		1	2	3	4	5
6	7	8	9	10	11	12
13	14	15	16	17	18	19
20	21	22	23	24	25	26
27	28	29	30	31		

July 20–26 ♋

A joyful life is made up of joyful moments gracefully strung
together by trust, gratitude, inspiration, and faith.

~BRENÉ BROWN

Date	Qtr.	Sign	Activity
Jul. 20, 6:22 am– Jul. 22, 8:26 am	4th	Gemini	Cultivate. Destroy weeds and pests. Harvest fruits and root crops for food. Trim to retard growth.
Jul. 22, 8:26 am– Jul. 24, 11:28 am	4th	Cancer	Plant biennials, perennials, bulbs and roots. Prune. Irrigate. Fertilize (organic).
Jul. 24, 11:28 am– Jul. 24, 3:11 pm	4th	Leo	Cultivate. Destroy weeds and pests. Harvest fruits and root crops for food. Trim to retard growth.

Is your home's exterior feeling a bit lackluster these days? Add some personality through colorful landscaping, shutters in a new hue, pretty pathway lights, and a decorated porch that changes with the seasons. Whether you're looking to sell or simply want to enjoy your home a bit more, freshening the exterior can feel good.

●

July 24
3:11 pm EDT

JULY

S	M	T	W	T	F	S
		1	2	3	4	5
6	7	8	9	10	11	12
13	14	15	16	17	18	19
20	21	22	23	24	25	26
27	28	29	30	31		

♌ August

July 27–August 2

So knowledge come, no matter how it comes! No matter whence the light falls, so it fall!   ~EDITH WHARTON

Date	Qtr.	Sign	Activity
Jul. 29, 1:43 am– Jul. 31, 1:25 pm	1st	Libra	Plant annuals for fragrance and beauty. Trim to increase growth.
Jul. 31, 1:25 pm– Aug. 1, 8:41 am	1st	Scorpio	Plant grains, leafy annuals. Fertilize (chemical). Graft or bud plants. Irrigate. Trim to increase growth.
Aug. 1, 8:41 am– Aug. 3, 2:00 am	2nd	Scorpio	Plant grains, leafy annuals. Fertilize (chemical). Graft or bud plants. Irrigate. Trim to increase growth.

Make a paste of water and clay, such as bentonite or montmorillonite, and put a glob of it on bee stings, flea bites, gnat bites, and other bug bites. The bite will heal much faster, and there will be little to no itching.

August 1
8:41 am EDT

AUGUST

S	M	T	W	T	F	S
					1	2
3	4	5	6	7	8	9
10	11	12	13	14	15	16
17	18	19	20	21	22	23
24	25	26	27	28	29	30
31						

August 3–9 ♋

We must be impatient for change. Let us remember that our
voice is a precious gift and we must use it.

~CLAUDIA FLORES

Date	Qtr.	Sign	Activity
Aug. 5, 1:04 pm– Aug. 7, 9:18 pm	2nd	Capricorn	Graft or bud plants. Trim to increase growth.
Aug. 9, 3:55 am– Aug. 10, 2:50 am	3rd	Aquarius	Cultivate. Destroy weeds and pests. Harvest fruits and root crops for food. Trim to retard growth.

When foraging for wild plants or mushrooms, remember that these beings have important roles to play in nature. Never take more than 25 percent of a given species in an area, which means don't pick every berry off a bush or pull up every mushroom in sight. You want to leave something for wildlife to eat and allow some seeds and mushroom spores to create the next generation of these species.

_____

_____

_____

_____

○
August 9
3:55 am EDT

AUGUST

S	M	T	W	T	F	S
					1	2
3	4	5	6	7	8	9
10	11	12	13	14	15	16
17	18	19	20	21	22	23
24	25	26	27	28	29	30
31						

♌ August 10–16

*It's hard to understand failure when you're going through it,
but in the grand scheme of things it's good to fall down.*

~ELLEN DeGENERES

Date	Qtr.	Sign	Activity
Aug. 10, 2:50 am–Aug. 12, 6:33 am	3rd	Pisces	Plant biennials, perennials, bulbs and roots. Prune. Irrigate. Fertilize (organic).
Aug. 12, 6:33 am–Aug. 14, 9:22 am	3rd	Aries	Cultivate. Destroy weeds and pests. Harvest fruits and root crops for food. Trim to retard growth.
Aug. 14, 9:22 am–Aug. 16, 1:12 am	3rd	Taurus	Plant potatoes and tubers. Trim to retard growth.
Aug. 16, 1:12 am–Aug. 16, 12:01 pm	4th	Taurus	Plant potatoes and tubers. Trim to retard growth.
Aug. 16, 12:01 pm–Aug. 18, 3:05 pm	4th	Gemini	Cultivate. Destroy weeds and pests. Harvest fruits and root crops for food. Trim to retard growth.

Spearmint is a potent herb for relieving summertime rashes and itching. Pour a pint of boiling water over 6 teabags to make strong tea. Then use it on a compress or put the entire pint of tea into your bathwater to soak away the burning or itching.

August 16
1:12 am EDT

AUGUST

S	M	T	W	T	F	S
					1	2
3	4	5	6	7	8	9
10	11	12	13	14	15	16
17	18	19	20	21	22	23
24	25	26	27	28	29	30
31						

August 17–23 ♌

*It has almost always been the creative, dedicated minority
that has made the world better.*

~MARTIN LUTHER KING JR.

Date	Qtr.	Sign	Activity
Aug. 18, 3:05 pm– Aug. 20, 7:17 pm	4th	Cancer	Plant biennials, perennials, bulbs and roots. Prune. Irrigate. Fertilize (organic).
Aug. 20, 7:17 pm– Aug. 23, 1:24 am	4th	Leo	Cultivate. Destroy weeds and pests. Harvest fruits and root crops for food. Trim to retard growth.
Aug. 23, 1:24 am– Aug. 23, 2:07 am	4th	Virgo	Cultivate, especially medicinal plants. Destroy weeds and pests. Trim to retard growth.

If you're looking to explore some new, local trails, consider hopping on a rail trail. A rail trail is a bygone train corridor that's been transformed into a biking, walking, or hiking trail. Often showcasing an easy, flat grade and old-fashioned trestle bridges, they're a great way to soak up nature or explore your region.

August 23
2:07 am EDT

AUGUST

S	M	T	W	T	F	S
					1	2
3	4	5	6	7	8	9
10	11	12	13	14	15	16
17	18	19	20	21	22	23
24	25	26	27	28	29	30
31						

♍ August 24–30

Inspiration comes during work, not before it.

~MADELEINE L'ENGLE

Date	Qtr.	Sign	Activity
Aug. 25, 10:08 am–Aug. 27, 9:27 pm	1st	Libra	Plant annuals for fragrance and beauty. Trim to increase growth.
Aug. 27, 9:27 pm–Aug. 30, 10:04 am	1st	Scorpio	Plant grains, leafy annuals. Fertilize (chemical). Graft or bud plants. Irrigate. Trim to increase growth.

Summer's heat can be tough on our wild neighbors! If you have wildlife visiting your yard, put out dishes of water for them. Larger animals may like bowls, but little critters like insects will need a shallow plate with rocks or sticks in the water to keep them from drowning. Keep a close eye, especially on shallower vessels, to make sure they don't dry out. Clean the vessels regularly to prevent disease transmission.

AUGUST

S	M	T	W	T	F	S
					1	2
3	4	5	6	7	8	9
10	11	12	13	14	15	16
17	18	19	20	21	22	23
24	25	26	27	28	29	30
31						

September ♍

August 31–September 6

Love is a passion full of anxiety and fear.   ~OVID

Date	Qtr.	Sign	Activity
Sep. 1, 9:45 pm– Sep. 4, 6:32 am	2nd	Capricorn	Graft or bud plants. Trim to increase growth.
Sep. 6, 11:54 am– Sep. 7, 2:09 pm	2nd	Pisces	Plant grains, leafy annuals. Fertilize (chemical). Graft or bud plants. Irrigate. Trim to increase growth.

If you love pies but hate to make them, make a cobbler instead. Make two or three times the amount of crumbled topping needed for your cobbler and store the extra in your refrigerator in a Mason jar with a tight-fitting lid. The next time you have some extra fruit, put it in a pie pan and sprinkle some of the topping from the jar on it, then bake. It's quick and delicious!

◑

August 31
2:25 am EDT

SEPTEMBER

S	M	T	W	T	F	S
	1	2	3	4	5	6
7	8	9	10	11	12	13
14	15	16	17	18	19	20
21	22	23	24	25	26	27
28	29	30				

♍ September 7–13

I'm in a place where I want everything in my life to mean something. For me, life is about being positive and hopeful, choosing to be joyful, choosing to be encouraging, choosing to be empowering.
                                             ~BILLY PORTER

Date	Qtr.	Sign	Activity
Sep. 7, 2:09 pm– Sep. 8, 2:37 pm	3rd	Pisces	Plant biennials, perennials, bulbs and roots. Prune. Irrigate. Fertilize (organic).
Sep. 8, 2:37 pm– Sep. 10, 4:03 pm	3rd	Aries	Cultivate. Destroy weeds and pests. Harvest fruits and root crops for food. Trim to retard growth.
Sep. 10, 4:03 pm– Sep. 12, 5:38 pm	3rd	Taurus	Plant potatoes and tubers. Trim to retard growth.
Sep. 12, 5:38 pm– Sep. 14, 6:33 am	3rd	Gemini	Cultivate. Destroy weeds and pests. Harvest fruits and root crops for food. Trim to retard growth.

If you have an old dog or cat and are facing the end of that beloved relationship, decide on a place to bury him or her and plant perennial flowers or a small flowering tree over the final resting place. It will be a gentle reminder of the love shared.

○
September 7
2:09 pm EDT

SEPTEMBER

S	M	T	W	T	F	S
		1	2	3	4	5	6
7	8	9	10	11	12	13
14	15	16	17	18	19	20
21	22	23	24	25	26	27
28	29	30				

September 14–20

There is a great deal of unmapped country within us which
would have to be taken into account in an explanation of our
gusts and storms.   ～GEORGE ELIOT

Date	Qtr.	Sign	Activity
Sep. 14, 6:33 am– Sep. 14, 8:30 pm	4th	Gemini	Cultivate. Destroy weeds and pests. Harvest fruits and root crops for food. Trim to retard growth.
Sep. 14, 8:30 pm– Sep. 17, 1:20 am	4th	Cancer	Plant biennials, perennials, bulbs and roots. Prune. Irrigate. Fertilize (organic).
Sep. 17, 1:20 am– Sep. 19, 8:23 am	4th	Leo	Cultivate. Destroy weeds and pests. Harvest fruits and root crops for food. Trim to retard growth.
Sep. 19, 8:23 am– Sep. 21, 3:54 pm	4th	Virgo	Cultivate, especially medicinal plants. Destroy weeds and pests. Trim to retard growth.

Make some home-baked muffins and real lemonade using lemons and honey, and put some carrot sticks and other veggies in a small plastic baggie. Then go outside on a warm, sunny day, spread a blanket on the ground, and enjoy a private picnic, letting the sunlight relax you deeply.

September 14
6:33 am EDT

SEPTEMBER

S	M	T	W	T	F	S
	1	2	3	4	5	6
7	8	9	10	11	12	13
14	15	16	17	18	19	20
21	22	23	24	25	26	27
28	29	30				

♍ September 21–27

Have an adventure. Most of everything in human history was barely planned and probably a mistake anyways.

~BLYTHE ROBERSON

Date	Qtr.	Sign	Activity
Sep. 21, 5:41 pm– Sep. 24, 5:00 am	1st	Libra	Plant annuals for fragrance and beauty. Trim to increase growth.
Sep. 24, 5:00 am– Sep. 26, 5:37 pm	1st	Scorpio	Plant grains, leafy annuals. Fertilize (chemical). Graft or bud plants. Irrigate. Trim to increase growth.

When doing fall yard work, consider leaving some dead plant material right where it is. Piles of leaves create important winter habitat for many beneficial insects and other animals. The stiff, hollow stems of some flowers and other plants also give shelter to bees and other invertebrates. And wait until spring temperatures are warm enough for insects to be active before cleaning everything up and putting it into a compost pile.

September 21
3:54 pm EDT

SEPTEMBER

S	M	T	W	T	F	S
	1	2	3	4	5	6
7	8	9	10	11	12	13
14	15	16	17	18	19	20
21	22	23	24	25	26	27
28	29	30				

October ♎

September 28–October 4

I always did something I was a little not ready to do. I think
that's how you grow.   ~MARISSA MAYER

Date	Qtr.	Sign	Activity
Sep. 29, 5:55 am– Sep. 29, 7:54 pm	1st	Capricorn	Graft or bud plants. Trim to increase growth.
Sep. 29, 7:54 pm– Oct. 1, 3:52 pm	2nd	Capricorn	Graft or bud plants. Trim to increase growth.
Oct. 3, 10:07 pm– Oct. 6, 12:48 am	2nd	Pisces	Plant grains, leafy annuals. Fertilize (chemical). Graft or bud plants. Irrigate. Trim to increase growth.

Good face-care routines include a cleanser, a toner, and a moisturizer. Experiment with various organic or natural skin care systems, using the products every morning and evening. You'll be surprised at how lovely your skin can be, even at advanced ages.

September 29
7:54 pm EDT

OCTOBER

S	M	T	W	T	F	S
			1	2	3	4
5	6	7	8	9	10	11
12	13	14	15	16	17	18
19	20	21	22	23	24	25
26	27	28	29	30	31	

♎ October 5–11

I believe that love is the most powerful force for change in the world. I often compare great campaigns to great love affairs because they're an incredible container for transformation.

~AI-JEN POO

Date	Qtr.	Sign	Activity
Oct. 6, 11:48 pm– Oct. 8, 1:12 am	3rd	Aries	Cultivate. Destroy weeds and pests. Harvest fruits and root crops for food. Trim to retard growth.
Oct. 8, 1:12 am– Oct. 10, 1:12 am	3rd	Taurus	Plant potatoes and tubers. Trim to retard growth.
Oct. 10, 1:12 am– Oct. 12, 2:37 am	3rd	Gemini	Cultivate. Destroy weeds and pests. Harvest fruits and root crops for food. Trim to retard growth.

Removable wallpaper is a great, noncommittal way to add interest without ruining anything in your home, something that's particularly important if you're renting. Find a beautiful pattern online and see what areas you can update. Removable wallpaper can go on the walls, any furniture with a smooth finish, and even your kitchen island and refrigerator.

○
October 6
11:48 pm EDT

OCTOBER

S	M	T	W	T	F	S
			1	2	3	4
5	6	7	8	9	10	11
12	13	14	15	16	17	18
19	20	21	22	23	24	25
26	27	28	29	30	31	

October 12–18 ♎

Life is not easy for any of us. But what of that? We must have perseverance and above all confidence in ourselves.

*—*Marie Curie

Date	Qtr.	Sign	Activity
Oct. 12, 2:37 am– Oct. 13, 2:13 pm	3rd	Cancer	Plant biennials, perennials, bulbs and roots. Prune. Irrigate. Fertilize (organic).
Oct. 13, 2:13 pm– Oct. 14, 6:47 am	4th	Cancer	Plant biennials, perennials, bulbs and roots. Prune. Irrigate. Fertilize (organic).
Oct. 14, 6:47 am– Oct. 16, 2:06 pm	4th	Leo	Cultivate. Destroy weeds and pests. Harvest fruits and root crops for food. Trim to retard growth.
Oct. 16, 2:06 pm– Oct. 19, 12:01 am	4th	Virgo	Cultivate, especially medicinal plants. Destroy weeds and pests. Trim to retard growth.

If your closet has a collection of turtleneck shirts that you are tired of but the shirts are still good, dress them up with a pretty scarf, a new piece of jewelry, or a hand-crocheted vest.

October 13
2:13 pm EDT

October

S	M	T	W	T	F	S
			1	2	3	4
5	6	7	8	9	10	11
12	13	14	15	16	17	18
19	20	21	22	23	24	25
26	27	28	29	30	31	

♎ October 19–25

When we're talking about diversity, it's not a box to check. It is a reality that should be deeply felt and held and valued by all of us.   ~AVA DUVERNAY

Date	Qtr.	Sign	Activity
Oct. 21, 8:25 am–Oct. 21, 11:42 am	1st	Libra	Plant annuals for fragrance and beauty. Trim to increase growth.
Oct. 21, 11:42 am–Oct. 24, 12:19 am	1st	Scorpio	Plant grains, leafy annuals. Fertilize (chemical). Graft or bud plants. Irrigate. Trim to increase growth.

Have you ever seen a gorgeous vintage lamp at a flea market but passed it over because of its ragged wiring? You can absolutely take it home if you follow instructions on how to rewire a lamp. (You can find them online—just be sure to turn to a reputable source.) Or you can take it to the pros by going to an electrician or lamp repair shop.

October 21
8:25 am EDT

OCTOBER

S	M	T	W	T	F	S
			1	2	3	4
5	6	7	8	9	10	11
12	13	14	15	16	17	18
19	20	21	22	23	24	25
26	27	28	29	30	31	

November ♏

October 26–November 1

We study history not to know the future but to widen our horizons, to understand that our present situation is neither natural nor inevitable.   ~YUVAL NOAH HARARI

Date	Qtr.	Sign	Activity
Oct. 26, 12:53 pm– Oct. 28, 11:55 pm	1st	Capricorn	Graft or bud plants. Trim to increase growth.
Oct. 31, 7:46 am– Nov. 2, 10:39 am	2nd	Pisces	Plant grains, leafy annuals. Fertilize (chemical). Graft or bud plants. Irrigate. Trim to increase growth.

A s part of your effort to maintain good health, survey your kitchen to make sure you have the tools to prepare nutritious and tasty meals. Then make a list of the tools you need to put together excellent meals with the greatest of ease. Give the list to those who ask you what you want for Christmas or your birthday.

◐

October 29
12:21 pm EDT

NOVEMBER

S	M	T	W	T	F	S
						1
2	3	4	5	6	7	8
9	10	11	12	13	14	15
16	17	18	19	20	21	22
23	24	25	26	27	28	29
30						

♏ November 2–8

*I cannot endure to waste anything so precious as autumnal
sunshine by staying in the house. So I have spent almost all
the daylight hours in the open air.*

~NATHANIEL HAWTHORNE

Date	Qtr.	Sign	Activity
Nov. 4, 11:16 am – Nov. 5, 8:19 am	2nd	Taurus	Plant annuals for hardiness. Trim to increase growth.
Nov. 5, 8:19 am – Nov. 6, 10:20 am	3rd	Taurus	Plant potatoes and tubers. Trim to retard growth.
Nov. 6, 10:20 am – Nov. 8, 10:06 am	3rd	Gemini	Cultivate. Destroy weeds and pests. Harvest fruits and root crops for food. Trim to retard growth.
Nov. 8, 10:06 am – Nov. 10, 12:34 pm	3rd	Cancer	Plant biennials, perennials, bulbs and roots. Prune. Irrigate. Fertilize (organic).

Do you ever hear a quote and think, "I need to hold onto that one"? In that case, keep a journal (often called a commonplace book) of your favorites. Add a thought-provoking quote whenever you hear one, or head to Pinterest to pick up some new ones. Soon, you'll have pages and pages filled with inspiration.

---

*Daylight Saving Time
ends November 2, 2:00 am*

○

*November 5
8:19 am EST*

NOVEMBER

S	M	T	W	T	F	S
						1
2	3	4	5	6	7	8
9	10	11	12	13	14	15
16	17	18	19	20	21	22
23	24	25	26	27	28	29
30						

November 9–15 ♏

*Have patience with all things, but chiefly have patience
with yourself: do not lose courage in considering your own
imperfections, but instantly set about remedying them; —
every day begin the task anew.* ~St. Francis de Sales

Date	Qtr.	Sign	Activity
Nov. 10, 12:34 pm–Nov. 12, 12:28 am	3rd	Leo	Cultivate. Destroy weeds and pests. Harvest fruits and root crops for food. Trim to retard growth.
Nov. 12, 12:28 am–Nov. 12, 6:52 pm	4th	Leo	Cultivate. Destroy weeds and pests. Harvest fruits and root crops for food. Trim to retard growth.
Nov. 12, 6:52 pm–Nov. 15, 4:44 am	4th	Virgo	Cultivate, especially medicinal plants. Destroy weeds and pests. Trim to retard growth.

Brainstorm the absolute coziest spots in your hometown and make a day of it, especially if it's chilly outside. Make a list of coffeehouses, cafés, restaurants, bookshops, and more. Wear your warmest sweater, and be sure to settle in next to a fireplace with something hot to drink. Curl up with a good book too!

*November 12
12:28 am EST*

November

S	M	T	W	T	F	S
						1
2	3	4	5	6	7	8
9	10	11	12	13	14	15
16	17	18	19	20	21	22
23	24	25	26	27	28	29
30						

♏ November 16–22

Love does not dominate; it cultivates.

~JOHANN WOLFGANG VON GOETHE

Date	Qtr.	Sign	Activity
Nov. 17, 4:44 pm– Nov. 20, 1:47 am	4th	Scorpio	Plant biennials, perennials, bulbs and roots. Prune. Irrigate. Fertilize (organic).
Nov. 20, 1:47 am– Nov. 20, 5:26 am	1st	Scorpio	Plant grains, leafy annuals. Fertilize (chemical). Graft or bud plants. Irrigate. Trim to increase growth.
Nov. 22, 5:53 pm– Nov. 25, 5:16 am	1st	Capricorn	Graft or bud plants. Trim to increase growth.

Many spiders that are commonly found living in houses, such as cellar spiders, are adapted to indoor settings. Putting them outside may seem kinder than killing them outright, but they may die of exposure, especially if it's cold out there. Instead, consider relocating spiders to a less busy part of your home, such as a basement, attic, or garage. Most spiders are harmless to humans and can be left right where they are too.

●

November 20
1:47 am EST

NOVEMBER						
S	M	T	W	T	F	S
						1
2	3	4	5	6	7	8
9	10	11	12	13	14	15
16	17	18	19	20	21	22
23	24	25	26	27	28	29
30						

November 23–29

At the end of the day, the reality is: we're all losers and we're all uncoordinated. We're the worst of all of the animals on earth and there's something quite endearing about that.

~Taika Waititi

Date	Qtr.	Sign	Activity
Nov. 27, 2:24 pm– Nov. 28, 1:59 am	1st	Pisces	Plant grains, leafy annuals. Fertilize (chemical). Graft or bud plants. Irrigate. Trim to increase growth.
Nov. 28, 1:59 am– Nov. 29, 8:07 pm	2nd	Pisces	Plant grains, leafy annuals. Fertilize (chemical). Graft or bud plants. Irrigate. Trim to increase growth.

Redoing your bathroom? Consider an extra-deep tub as a commitment to your own healing. There is nothing as wonderful as sinking into a warm bath. Add a few drops of lavender oil or perhaps geranium oil mixed with carrier oil—both heavenly additions. Or add 1 cup of Epsom salts and 1 cup of baking soda for a deeply healing and alkalinizing experience.

November 28
1:59 am EST

NOVEMBER

S	M	T	W	T	F	S
						1
2	3	4	5	6	7	8
9	10	11	12	13	14	15
16	17	18	19	20	21	22
23	24	25	26	27	28	29
30						

⚐ December

November 30–December 6

The love that comes from friendship is the underlying facet of a happy life.
~CHELSEA HANDLER

Date	Qtr.	Sign	Activity
Dec. 1, 10:13 pm–Dec. 3, 9:48 pm	2nd	Taurus	Plant annuals for hardiness. Trim to increase growth.
Dec. 4, 6:14 pm–Dec. 5, 8:54 pm	3rd	Gemini	Cultivate. Destroy weeds and pests. Harvest fruits and root crops for food. Trim to retard growth.
Dec. 5, 8:54 pm–Dec. 7, 9:48 pm	3rd	Cancer	Plant biennials, perennials, bulbs and roots. Prune. Irrigate. Fertilize (organic).

Improve your skin, hair, and nails by taking B vitamins, lysine, and collagen. The B vitamins support all kinds of nutritional transactions in the body, while the lysine and collagen build sturdy connective tissues. Result: hair that stops falling out and skin with better resilience.

_____

_____

_____

_____

○

December 4
6:14 pm EST

DECEMBER

S	M	T	W	T	F	S
	1	2	3	4	5	6
7	8	9	10	11	12	13
14	15	16	17	18	19	20
21	22	23	24	25	26	27
28	29	30	31			

December 7–13 ⟋

Let us make our future now, and let us make our dreams
tomorrow's reality.   ~MALALA YOUSAFZAI

Date	Qtr.	Sign	Activity
Dec. 7, 9:48 pm– Dec. 10, 2:20 am	3rd	Leo	Cultivate. Destroy weeds and pests. Harvest fruits and root crops for food. Trim to retard growth.
Dec. 10, 2:20 am– Dec. 11, 3:52 pm	3rd	Virgo	Cultivate, especially medicinal plants. Destroy weeds and pests. Trim to retard growth.
Dec. 11, 3:52 pm– Dec. 12, 11:04 am	4th	Virgo	Cultivate, especially medicinal plants. Destroy weeds and pests. Trim to retard growth.

Having a good bedtime routine can help you sleep better. Make sure you go to bed at the same time each night (grown-ups can have bedtimes too!), plan on some self-care like a warm bath or facial mask, and do a relaxing activity that doesn't make your mind race, like reading a low-key book, doing a bit of yoga, or meditating. Keep the lights low along with your room temperature for optimal sleep.

◑
December 11
3:52 pm EST

DECEMBER

S	M	T	W	T	F	S
	1	2	3	4	5	6
7	8	9	10	11	12	13
14	15	16	17	18	19	20
21	22	23	24	25	26	27
28	29	30	31			

December 14–20

I find ecstasy in living—the mere sense of living is joy enough.

~EMILY DICKINSON

Date	Qtr.	Sign	Activity
Dec. 14, 10:51 pm–Dec. 17, 11:38 am	4th	Scorpio	Plant biennials, perennials, bulbs and roots. Prune. Irrigate. Fertilize (organic).
Dec. 17, 11:38 am–Dec. 19, 8:43 pm	4th	Sagittarius	Cultivate. Destroy weeds and pests. Harvest fruits and root crops for food. Trim to retard growth.
Dec. 19, 11:53 pm–Dec. 22, 10:52 am	1st	Capricorn	Graft or bud plants. Trim to increase growth.

Out of ideas for Christmas gifts? Buy gift cards from a local astrologer and give family and friends the gift of having their chart done.

_____

_____

_____

_____

●

December 19
8:43 pm EST

DECEMBER

S	M	T	W	T	F	S
		1	2	3	4	5	6
7	8	9	10	11	12	13
14	15	16	17	18	19	20
21	22	23	24	25	26	27
28	29	30	31			

December 21–27 ♑

Winter is a glorious spectacle of glittering fractals complete
with a soundscape and atmosphere entirely its own.

~Anders Swanson

Date	Qtr.	Sign	Activity
Dec. 24, 8:09 pm– Dec. 27, 3:02 am	1st	Pisces	Plant grains, leafy annuals. Fertilize (chemical). Graft or bud plants. Irrigate. Trim to increase growth.

If you aren't feeling good, whether physically or mentally, try some basic self-care. Drink some water to make sure you're hydrated, and eat some food if you can stomach it. (Remember that even "junk" food is better than no food at all!) Try to get a proper amount of sleep; if insomnia is a problem, remember that resting is still recuperative. These suggestions may not fix all your symptoms, but they might help you feel better.

◐

December 27
2:10 pm EST

DECEMBER

S	M	T	W	T	F	S
	1	2	3	4	5	6
7	8	9	10	11	12	13
14	15	16	17	18	19	20
21	22	23	24	25	26	27
28	29	30	31			

♑ December 28–January 3

No one changes the world who isn't obsessed.

~BILLIE JEAN KING

Date	Qtr.	Sign	Activity
Dec. 29, 6:57 am– Dec. 31, 8:13 am	2nd	Taurus	Plant annuals for hardiness. Trim to increase growth.
Jan. 3, 5:03 am– Jan. 4, 8:44 am	3rd	Cancer	Plant biennials, perennials, bulbs and roots. Prune. Irrigate. Fertilize (organic).

Remember, to refresh your home, you don't always need to tackle a giant project, like remodeling the kitchen or repainting the whole house. Instead, take on mini projects here and there, which can include things like painting your front door a new color, creating a built-in shelf for houseplants and decorative objects, or swapping out a faucet for an updated look.

○
January 3
5:03 am EST

DECEMBER

S	M	T	W	T	F	S
	1	2	3	4	5	6
7	8	9	10	11	12	13
14	15	16	17	18	19	20
21	22	23	24	25	26	27
28	29	30	31			

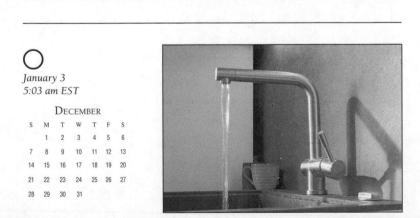

Gardening by the Moon

Welcome to the world of gardening by the Moon! Unlike most gardening advice, this article is not about how to garden, it's about when to garden. Timing is everything; if you know how to use the Moon, you'll not only be in sync with nature but you can sit back and watch your garden grow beyond your wildest dreams.

Gardening by the Moon is nothing new. It's been around since ancient times when people used both the Sun and the Moon to predict the tides, as well as fertility and growth cycles for plants and animals.

Lunar gardening is simple and the results are immediate. It doesn't matter whether you're a beginner gardener with a single pot or an old hand with years of master gardening experience—your garden will grow bigger and better if you follow the cycles of the Moon and match up the right time with the right garden activity. When the temperature has dropped and the sun is low on the horizon, you can apply what you've learned to your indoor plants as well.

The sky is a celestial clock, with the Sun and the Moon as the "hands" that tell the time. The Sun tells the season, and the light and location of the Moon tell the best times for birth, growth, and death in the garden. The Moon doesn't generate any light by itself, but as it circles the Earth it reflects the light of the Sun, which makes the Moon look like it's getting bigger and smaller. The cyclical increases and decreases in the light of the Moon are phases and tell times of growth.

Moon Phases

The theory behind gardening by the Moon is "as the Moon goes, so goes the garden." The Earth circles around the Sun once a year, but the Moon has a much shorter "life span" of twenty-eight to thirty days. Every month, as the light of the Moon increases and decreases, it mirrors the cycle of birth, growth, and death in the garden. After adjusting your garden activities to the light of the Moon, you'll be amazed to see how well your garden grows.

The **waxing phase** is the growth cycle in the garden. It begins with the New Moon and lasts for two weeks. Each month the Moon is "born" at the New Moon (day one) and grows bigger and brighter until it reaches maturity at the Full Moon (day fourteen). When the light of the Moon is increasing, it's the best time of the month to sow seeds, plant leafy annuals, and cut back or prune plants to encourage bigger growth.

The **waning phase** is the declining cycle in the garden. It begins with the Full Moon (day fourteen) and lasts for two weeks. The Moon grows older after the Full Moon as the light begins to decrease, until it disappears or "dies" at day twenty-eight. The decreasing light of the Moon is the time to plant bulbs, root vegetables, and perennials that store their energy underground. The waning Moon phase is also a good time for garden maintenance, including weeding, raking, deadheading, mowing, working the soil, destroying insects, and burning brush.

How can you tell if the Moon is waxing or waning?

Cup your right hand into a C shape and look up into the sky. If the crescent Moon fits into the closed part of your right hand, it's a waxing Moon.

Cup your left hand into a C shape and look up into the sky. If the crescent Moon fits into the closed part of your left hand, it's a waning Moon.

New Moon and Full Moon

Every month, the Moon takes one day off. This time-out between waning and waxing is called the New Moon. The time-out between waxing and waning is called the Full Moon. When the Moon reaches either of these stopping points, it's time for you to follow its example and take a one-day break from the garden.

Moon Signs

Once you know the Moon phases, the next step is to locate where the Moon is in the zodiac. The Moon hangs out in each of the zodiac signs for two to three days per month.

There's no such thing as a "bad" time in the garden, but there are Moon signs that are better for growth and others that are better for digging and weeding. Growth times alternate every two to three days with maintenance times. The trick is knowing which one is which.

The grow signs are Taurus, Cancer, Libra, Scorpio, Capricorn, and Pisces. When the Moon is in these signs, it's time to seed and plant.

The no-grow/maintenance signs are Aries, Gemini, Leo, Virgo, Sagittarius, and Aquarius. When the Moon is in these signs, it's time for digging, weeding, mowing, and pruning.

Remember: It's always a good time to garden something!

Putting It All Together

In order to get started, you'll need three tools: a calendar with New and Full Moons, the Moon tables (page 136), and the Moon phases and signs below.

Then follow these simple steps:

1. Mark your calendar with your time frame for gardening.
2. Figure out when the Moon is waxing (1st and 2nd quarters) and waning (3rd and 4th quarters). Use the tables in the Weekly Almanac section.
3. Locate the Moon by zodiac sign.
4. Check out the gardening advice below, which takes into account the Moon's phase and sign.

Moon Phases and Signs

Note: Can be applied to any calendar year.

Waxing Aries Moon (October–April)

Aries is one of the three fire signs that is hot and barren. Seeds planted under a waxing Aries Moon tend to be bitter or bolt quickly, but if you're feeling lucky, you could try your hand at hot and spicy peppers or herbs that thrive in dry heat.

Waning Aries Moon (April–October)

The decreasing light of the waning Aries Moon makes these two to three days a good time to focus on harvesting, cutting back, mowing the lawn, and getting rid of pests.

Waxing Taurus Moon (November–May)

Taurus is one of the three semi-fruitful earth signs. These days are perfect ones to establish your garden by planting or fertilizing annuals. Annuals with outside seeds like lettuces, cabbage, corn, and broccoli grow faster when planted under a waxing Taurus Moon that is one to seven days old. Vegetables with inside seeds like cucumbers, melons, squash, tomatoes, and beans should be planted when the Moon is seven to twelve days old. Annual flowers can be planted any time during this two-week phase.

Waning Taurus Moon (May–November)

The decreasing light of this semi-fruitful waning Taurus Moon gives you a perfect two- or three-day window for planting perennials or digging in root vegetables and flower bulbs.

Waxing Gemini Moon (December–June)

Gemini is one of the three dry and barren signs. But with the light of the Moon increasing, you can use these two to three days to prune or cut back plants you want to flourish and grow bigger.

Waning Gemini Moon (June–December)

Gemini can be all over the place, so use these couple of dry and barren days when the light is decreasing to weed invasive plants that are out of control.

Waxing Cancer Moon (January–July)

Cancer is one of the three wet and fruitful signs, so when the Moon is waxing in Cancer it's the perfect time to plant seeds or set out seedlings and annual flowers that live for only one season. Annuals with outside seeds grow faster when planted under a Moon that is one to seven days old. Vegetables with inside seeds should be planted when the Moon is seven to twelve days old. Annual flowers can be planted any time during these two weeks.

Waning Cancer Moon (July–January)

Plant perennials, root vegetables, and bulbs to your heart's content under the decreasing light of this fruitful Moon.

Waxing Leo Moon (February–August)

The light of the Moon is increasing, but Leo is one of the three hot and barren fire signs. Use the two or three days of this waxing Leo Moon to cut and prune the plants and shrubs you want to be the king or queen of your garden.

Waning Leo Moon (August–February)

With the light of the Moon decreasing, this Leo Moon is a good period to dig the soil, destroy pests and insects, and burn brush.

Waxing Virgo Moon (March–September)

Virgo is a semi-barren sign, which is good for fertilizing (Virgo is a "greenie" type that loves organics) and for planting woody vines and hardy herbs.

Waning Virgo Moon (September–March)

With the light of this semi-barren Moon decreasing for a couple of days, plan to hoe those rows and get rid of your weeds. Harvest Moon in September.

Waxing Libra Moon (October–April)

Libra is a semi-fruitful sign focused on beauty. Because the Moon is growing brighter in Libra, these two to three days are a great time to give your flower garden some heavy-duty TLC.

Waning Libra Moon (April–October)

If you want to encourage re-blooming, try deadheading your vegetables and flowers under the light of this decreasing Libra Moon. Harvest your flowers.

Waxing Scorpio Moon (November–May)

Scorpio is one of the three wet and fruitful signs. When the Moon is waxing in Scorpio, it's the perfect time for planting annuals that have a bite, like arugula and hot peppers. Annuals with outside seeds grow faster when planted under a Moon that is one to seven days old. Vegetables with inside seeds should be planted when the Moon is seven to twelve days old. Annual flowers can be planted anytime during this two-week phase.

Waning Scorpio Moon (May–November)

With the light of the Moon decreasing in Scorpio, a sign that likes strong and intense flavors, this is the perfect period to plant hardy perennials, garlic bulbs, and onion sets.

Waxing Sagittarius Moon (June–December)

Sagittarius is one of the three hot and barren signs. Because Sagittarius prefers roaming to staying still, this waxing Moon is not a good time for planting. But you can encourage growth during the two or three days when the light is increasing by cutting back, mowing, and pruning.

Waning Sagittarius Moon (December–June)

It's time to discourage growth during the days when the light of the Moon is decreasing in Sagittarius. Cut back, mow the lawn, prune, and destroy pests and insects you never want to darken your garden again.

Waxing Capricorn Moon (July–January)

Capricorn is a semi-fruitful earth sign. The couple of days when the light of the Moon is increasing in Capricorn are good for getting the garden into shape, setting out plants and transplants, and fertilizing.

Waning Capricorn Moon (January–July)

The decreasing light of this fruitful Capricorn Moon is the perfect window for digging and dividing bulbs and pinching back suckers to encourage bigger blooms on your flowers and vegetables.

Waxing Aquarius Moon (August–February)

Aquarius is a dry and barren sign. However, the increasing light of the Aquarian Moon makes this a good opportunity to experiment by pruning or cutting back plants you want to flourish.

Waning Aquarius Moon (February–August)

The light of the Moon is decreasing. Use this time to harvest or to weed, cut back, and prune the shrubs and plants that you want to banish forever from your garden. Harvest vegetables.

Waxing Pisces Moon (September–March)

When the Moon is increasing in fruitful Pisces, it's a perfect period for planting seeds and annuals. Annuals with outside seeds grow faster when planted under a Moon that is one to seven days old.

Vegetables with inside seeds should be planted when the Moon is seven to twelve days old. Annual flowers can be planted any time during these two weeks.

Waning Pisces Moon (March–September)
With the light of the Moon decreasing, it's time to plant all perennials, bulbs, and root vegetables except potatoes. Garden lore has it that potatoes planted under a Pisces Moon tend to grow bumps or "toes" because Pisces is associated with the feet.

Here's hoping that this has inspired you to give gardening by the Moon a try. Not only is it the secret ingredient that will make your garden more abundant, but you can use it as long as the Sun is in the sky and the Moon circles the Earth!

A Guide to Planting

Plant	Quarter	Sign
Annuals	1st or 2nd	
Apple tree	2nd or 3rd	Cancer, Pisces, Virgo
Artichoke	1st	Cancer, Pisces
Asparagus	1st	Cancer, Scorpio, Pisces
Aster	1st or 2nd	Virgo, Libra
Barley	1st or 2nd	Cancer, Pisces, Libra, Capricorn, Virgo
Beans (bush & pole)	2nd	Cancer, Taurus, Pisces, Libra
Beans (kidney, white & navy)	1st or 2nd	Cancer, Pisces
Beech tree	2nd or 3rd	Virgo, Taurus
Beets	3rd	Cancer, Capricorn, Pisces, Libra
Biennials	3rd or 4th	
Broccoli	1st	Cancer, Scorpio, Pisces, Libra
Brussels sprouts	1st	Cancer, Scorpio, Pisces, Libra
Buckwheat	1st or 2nd	Capricorn
Bulbs	3rd	Cancer, Scorpio, Pisces
Bulbs for seed	2nd or 3rd	
Cabbage	1st	Cancer, Scorpio, Pisces, Taurus, Libra
Canes (raspberry, blackberry & gooseberry)	2nd	Cancer, Scorpio, Pisces
Cantaloupe	1st or 2nd	Cancer, Scorpio, Pisces, Taurus, Libra
Carrots	3rd	Cancer, Scorpio, Pisces, Taurus, Libra
Cauliflower	1st	Cancer, Scorpio, Pisces, Libra
Celeriac	3rd	Cancer, Scorpio, Pisces
Celery	1st	Cancer, Scorpio, Pisces
Cereals	1st or 2nd	Cancer, Scorpio, Pisces, Libra
Chard	1st or 2nd	Cancer, Scorpio, Pisces
Chicory	2nd or 3rd	Cancer, Scorpio, Pisces
Chrysanthemum	1st or 2nd	Virgo
Clover	1st or 2nd	Cancer, Scorpio, Pisces

Plant	Quarter	Sign
Coreopsis	2nd or 3rd	Libra
Corn	1st	Cancer, Scorpio, Pisces
Corn for fodder	1st or 2nd	Libra
Cosmos	2nd or 3rd	Libra
Cress	1st	Cancer, Scorpio, Pisces
Crocus	1st or 2nd	Virgo
Cucumber	1st	Cancer, Scorpio, Pisces
Daffodil	1st or 2nd	Libra, Virgo
Dahlia	1st or 2nd	Libra, Virgo
Deciduous trees	2nd or 3rd	Cancer, Scorpio, Pisces, Virgo, Libra
Eggplant	2nd	Cancer, Scorpio, Pisces, Libra
Endive	1st	Cancer, Scorpio, Pisces, Libra
Flowers	1st	Cancer, Scorpio, Pisces, Libra, Taurus, Virgo
Garlic	3rd	Libra, Taurus, Pisces
Gladiola	1st or 2nd	Libra, Virgo
Gourds	1st or 2nd	Cancer, Scorpio, Pisces, Libra
Grapes	2nd or 3rd	Cancer, Scorpio, Pisces, Virgo
Hay	1st or 2nd	Cancer, Scorpio, Pisces, Libra, Taurus
Herbs	1st or 2nd	Cancer, Scorpio, Pisces
Honeysuckle	1st or 2nd	Scorpio, Virgo
Hops	1st or 2nd	Scorpio, Libra
Horseradish	1st or 2nd	Cancer, Scorpio, Pisces
Houseplants	1st	Cancer, Scorpio, Pisces, Libra
Hyacinth	3rd	Cancer, Scorpio, Pisces
Iris	1st or 2nd	Cancer, Virgo
Kohlrabi	1st or 2nd	Cancer, Scorpio, Pisces, Libra
Leek	2nd or 3rd	Sagittarius
Lettuce	1st	Cancer, Scorpio, Pisces, Libra, Taurus
Lily	1st or 2nd	Cancer, Scorpio, Pisces
Maple tree	2nd or 3rd	Taurus, Virgo, Cancer, Pisces
Melon	2nd	Cancer, Scorpio, Pisces
Moon vine	1st or 2nd	Virgo

Plant	Quarter	Sign
Morning glory	1st or 2nd	Cancer, Scorpio, Pisces, Virgo
Oak tree	2nd or 3rd	Taurus, Virgo, Cancer, Pisces
Oats	1st or 2nd	Cancer, Scorpio, Pisces, Libra
Okra	1st or 2nd	Cancer, Scorpio, Pisces, Libra
Onion seed	2nd	Cancer, Scorpio, Sagittarius
Onion set	3rd or 4th	Cancer, Pisces, Taurus, Libra
Pansies	1st or 2nd	Cancer, Scorpio, Pisces
Parsley	1st	Cancer, Scorpio, Pisces, Libra
Parsnip	3rd	Cancer, Scorpio, Taurus, Capricorn
Peach tree	2nd or 3rd	Cancer, Taurus, Virgo, Libra
Peanuts	3rd	Cancer, Scorpio, Pisces
Pear tree	2nd or 3rd	Cancer, Scorpio, Pisces, Libra
Peas	2nd	Cancer, Scorpio, Pisces, Libra
Peony	1st or 2nd	Virgo
Peppers	2nd	Cancer, Scorpio, Pisces
Perennials	3rd	
Petunia	1st or 2nd	Libra, Virgo
Plum tree	2nd or 3rd	Cancer, Pisces, Taurus, Virgo
Poppies	1st or 2nd	Virgo
Portulaca	1st or 2nd	Virgo
Potatoes	3rd	Cancer, Scorpio, Libra, Taurus, Capricorn
Privet	1st or 2nd	Taurus, Libra
Pumpkin	2nd	Cancer, Scorpio, Pisces, Libra
Quince	1st or 2nd	Capricorn
Radishes	3rd	Cancer, Scorpio, Pisces, Libra, Capricorn
Rhubarb	3rd	Cancer, Pisces
Rice	1st or 2nd	Scorpio
Roses	1st or 2nd	Cancer, Virgo
Rutabaga	3rd	Cancer, Scorpio, Pisces, Taurus
Saffron	1st or 2nd	Cancer, Scorpio, Pisces
Sage	3rd	Cancer, Scorpio, Pisces

Plant	Quarter	Sign
Salsify	1st	Cancer, Scorpio, Pisces
Shallot	2nd	Scorpio
Spinach	1st	Cancer, Scorpio, Pisces
Squash	2nd	Cancer, Scorpio, Pisces, Libra
Strawberries	3rd	Cancer, Scorpio, Pisces
String beans	1st or 2nd	Taurus
Sunflowers	1st or 2nd	Libra, Cancer
Sweet peas	1st or 2nd	Any
Tomatoes	2nd	Cancer, Scorpio, Pisces, Capricorn
Trees, shade	3rd	Taurus, Capricorn
Trees, ornamental	2nd	Libra, Taurus
Trumpet vine	1st or 2nd	Cancer, Scorpio, Pisces
Tubers for seed	3rd	Cancer, Scorpio, Pisces, Libra
Tulips	1st or 2nd	Libra, Virgo
Turnips	3rd	Cancer, Scorpio, Pisces, Taurus, Capricorn, Libra
Valerian	1st or 2nd	Virgo, Gemini
Watermelon	1st or 2nd	Cancer, Scorpio, Pisces, Libra
Wheat	1st or 2nd	Cancer, Scorpio, Pisces, Libra

Companion Planting Guide

Plant	Companions	Hindered by
Asparagus	Tomatoes, parsley, basil	None known
Beans	Tomatoes, carrots, cucumbers, garlic, cabbage, beets, corn	Onions, gladiolas
Beets	Onions, cabbage, lettuce, mint, catnip	Pole beans
Broccoli	Beans, celery, potatoes, onions	Tomatoes
Cabbage	Peppermint, sage, thyme, tomatoes	Strawberries, grapes
Carrots	Peas, lettuce, chives, radishes, leeks, onions, sage	Dill, anise
Citrus trees	Guava, live oak, rubber trees, peppers	None known
Corn	Potatoes, beans, peas, melon, squash, pumpkin, sunflowers, soybeans	Quack grass, wheat, straw, mulch
Cucumbers	Beans, cabbage, radishes, sunflowers, lettuce, broccoli, squash	Aromatic herbs
Eggplant	Green beans, lettuce, kale	None known
Grapes	Peas, beans, blackberries	Cabbage, radishes
Melons	Corn, peas	Potatoes, gourds
Onions, leeks	Beets, chamomile, carrots, lettuce	Peas, beans, sage
Parsnip	Peas	None known
Peas	Radishes, carrots, corn, cucumbers, beans, tomatoes, spinach, turnips	Onion, garlic
Potatoes	Beans, corn, peas, cabbage, hemp, cucumbers, eggplant, catnip	Raspberries, pumpkins, tomatoes, sunflowers
Radishes	Peas, lettuce, nasturtiums, cucumbers	Hyssop
Spinach	Strawberries	None known
Squash/ Pumpkin	Nasturtiums, corn, mint, catnip	Potatoes
Tomatoes	Asparagus, parsley, chives, onions, carrots, marigolds, nasturtiums, dill	Black walnut roots, fennel, potatoes
Turnips	Peas, beans, brussels sprouts	Potatoes

Plant	Companions	Uses
Anise	Coriander	Flavor candy, pastry, cheeses, cookies
Basil	Tomatoes	Dislikes rue; repels flies and mosquitoes
Borage	Tomatoes, squash	Use in teas
Buttercup	Clover	Hinders delphinium, peonies, monkshood, columbine
Catnip		Repels flea beetles
Chamomile	Peppermint, wheat, onions, cabbage	Roman chamomile may control damping-off disease, use in herbal sprays
Chervil	Radishes	Good in soups and other dishes
Chives	Carrots	Use in spray to deter black spot on roses
Coriander	Plant anywhere	Hinders seed formation in fennel
Cosmos		Repels corn earworms
Dill	Cabbage	Hinders carrots and tomatoes
Fennel	Plant in borders	Disliked by all garden plants
Horseradish		Repels potato bugs
Horsetail		Makes fungicide spray
Hyssop		Attracts cabbage flies; harmful to radishes
Lavender	Plant anywhere	Use in spray to control insects on cotton, repels clothes moths
Lovage		Lures horn worms away from tomatoes
Marigolds		Pest repellent; use against Mexican bean beetles and nematodes
Mint	Cabbage, tomatoes	Repels ants, flea beetles, cabbage worm butterflies
Morning glory	Corn	Helps melon germination
Nasturtium	Cabbage, cucumbers	Deters aphids, squash bugs, pumpkin beetles
Okra	Eggplant	Attracts leafhopper (lure insects from other plants)
Parsley	Tomatoes, asparagus	Freeze chopped-up leaves to flavor foods
Purslane		Good ground cover
Rosemary		Repels cabbage moths, bean beetles, carrot flies
Savory		Plant with onions for added sweetness
Tansy		Deters Japanese beetles, striped cucumber beetles, squash bugs
Thyme		Repels cabbage worms
Yarrow		Increases essential oils of neighbors

Moon Void-of-Course

Kim Rogers-Gallagher

The Moon circles the Earth in about twenty-eight days, moving through each zodiac sign in two and a half days. As she passes through the thirty degrees of each sign, she "visits" with the planets in numerical order, forming aspects with them. Because she moves one degree in just two to two and a half hours, her influence on each planet lasts only a few hours. She eventually reaches the planet that's in the highest degree of any sign and forms what will be her final aspect before leaving the sign. From this point until she enters the next sign, she is referred to as void-of-course.

Think of it this way: the Moon is the emotional "tone" of the day, carrying feelings with her particular to the sign she's "wearing" at the moment. After she has contacted each of the planets, she symbolically "rests" before changing her costume, so her instinct is temporarily on hold. It's during this time that many people feel "fuzzy" or "vague." Plans or decisions made now often do not pan out. Without the instinctual "knowing" the Moon provides as she touches each planet, we tend to be unrealistic or exercise poor judgment. The traditional definition of the void Moon is that "nothing will come of this." Actions initiated under a void Moon are often wasted, irrelevant, or incorrect—usually because information is hidden, missing, or has been overlooked.

Although it's not a good time to initiate plans, routine tasks seem to go along just fine. This period is ideal for reflection. On the lighter side, remember there are good uses for the void Moon. It is the period when the universe seems to be most open to loopholes. It's a great time to make plans you don't want to fulfill or schedule things you don't want to do. See the tables on pages 76–81 for a schedule of the Moon's void-of-course times.

Last Aspect   **Moon Enters New Sign**

		January		
1	1:02 am	1	Aquarius	5:50 am
2	11:13 pm	3	Pisces	10:21 am
5	9:30 am	5	Aries	2:01 pm
7	4:16 pm	7	Taurus	5:11 pm
9	5:50 pm	9	Gemini	8:07 pm
11	7:03 pm	11	Cancer	11:24 pm
13	11:46 pm	14	Leo	4:12 am
15	11:10 pm	16	Virgo	11:46 am
18	9:01 pm	18	Libra	10:33 pm
20	11:34 pm	21	Scorpio	11:20 am
23	7:03 pm	23	Sagittarius	11:29 pm
26	4:40 am	26	Capricorn	8:43 am
28	10:48 am	28	Aquarius	2:31 pm
30	6:29 am	30	Pisces	5:52 pm
		February		
1	5:06 pm	1	Aries	8:10 pm
3	5:19 am	3	Taurus	10:33 pm
5	10:29 pm	6	Gemini	1:44 am
8	2:52 am	8	Cancer	6:04 am
10	8:49 am	10	Leo	12:01 pm
12	2:12 pm	12	Virgo	8:07 pm
15	3:36 am	15	Libra	6:45 am
17	6:24 pm	17	Scorpio	7:19 pm
20	5:06 am	20	Sagittarius	7:55 am
22	3:38 pm	22	Capricorn	6:09 pm
24	10:28 pm	25	Aquarius	12:40 am
26	5:04 pm	27	Pisces	3:46 am

Last Aspect   **Moon Enters New Sign**

			March		
1	3:05 am	1	Aries	4:52 am
2	8:52 am	3	Taurus	5:37 am
5	5:53 am	5	Gemini	7:29 am
7	9:57 am	7	Cancer	11:29 am
9	5:32 pm	9	Leo	6:59 pm
11	4:16 pm	12	Virgo	3:56 am
14	1:47 pm	14	Libra	2:59 pm
16	5:53 am	17	Scorpio	3:30 am
19	3:28 pm	19	Sagittarius	4:17 pm
22	2:53 am	22	Capricorn	3:29 am
24	11:01 am	24	Aquarius	11:25 am
26	6:15 am	26	Pisces	3:31 pm
28	4:30 pm	28	Aries	4:36 pm
30	5:18 am	30	Taurus	4:16 pm
			April		
1	1:43 pm	1	Gemini	4:26 pm
3	2:26 pm	3	Cancer	6:50 pm
5	6:54 pm	6	Leo	12:34 am
8	12:08 am	8	Virgo	9:40 am
10	3:49 pm	10	Libra	9:12 pm
13	6:01 am	13	Scorpio	9:54 am
15	10:24 pm	15	Sagittarius	10:37 pm
18	7:38 am	18	Capricorn	10:12 am
20	1:21 pm	20	Aquarius	7:22 pm
22	5:55 pm	23	Pisces	1:07 am
24	10:57 pm	25	Aries	3:24 am
26	12:18 pm	27	Taurus	3:17 am
29	1:18 am	29	Gemini	2:34 am
30	11:49 pm	1	Cancer	3:23 am

Last Aspect   Moon Enters New Sign

		May		
3	4:02 am	3	Leo	7:29 am
5	9:03 am	5	Virgo	3:40 pm
8	12:11 am	8	Libra	3:06 am
10	2:17 am	10	Scorpio	3:58 pm
13	2:37 am	13	Sagittarius	4:35 am
15	2:29 pm	15	Capricorn	3:58 pm
18	12:27 am	18	Aquarius	1:29 am
20	7:59 am	20	Pisces	8:28 am
22	12:06 pm	22	Aries	12:26 pm
24	7:44 am	24	Taurus	1:38 pm
26	9:52 am	26	Gemini	1:21 pm
28	9:01 am	28	Cancer	1:33 pm
30	12:50 pm	30	Leo	4:17 pm
		June		
1	7:38 pm	1	Virgo	11:00 pm
4	7:11 am	4	Libra	9:38 am
6	9:04 pm	6	Scorpio	10:23 pm
9	8:06 am	9	Sagittarius	10:56 am
11	3:58 pm	11	Capricorn	9:55 pm
14	4:52 am	14	Aquarius	7:00 am
16	1:31 pm	16	Pisces	2:09 pm
18	5:34 pm	18	Aries	7:08 pm
20	9:49 pm	20	Taurus	9:53 pm
22	9:50 pm	22	Gemini	10:57 pm
23	4:26 am	24	Cancer	11:44 pm
27	1:16 am	27	Leo	2:05 am
29	7:03 am	29	Virgo	7:44 am

Last Aspect — Moon Enters New Sign

		July		
1	4:47 pm	1	Libra	5:16 pm
2	3:30 pm	4	Scorpio	5:33 am
6	6:04 pm	6	Sagittarius	6:06 pm
7	5:29 pm	9	Capricorn	4:55 am
10	4:37 pm	11	Aquarius	1:21 pm
12	3:45 pm	13	Pisces	7:45 pm
15	1:10 pm	16	Aries	12:32 am
17	8:38 pm	18	Taurus	3:59 am
20	2:43 am	20	Gemini	6:22 am
21	3:52 pm	22	Cancer	8:26 am
23	8:42 pm	24	Leo	11:28 am
26	7:02 am	26	Virgo	4:55 pm
28	8:57 pm	29	Libra	1:43 am
29	11:59 pm	31	Scorpio	1:25 pm
		August		
2	9:07 pm	3	Sagittarius	2:00 am
5	11:29 am	5	Capricorn	1:04 pm
6	1:40 pm	7	Aquarius	9:18 pm
9	3:55 am	10	Pisces	2:50 am
11	2:55 am	12	Aries	6:33 am
13	6:54 pm	14	Taurus	9:22 am
16	1:12 am	16	Gemini	12:01 pm
18	7:53 am	18	Cancer	3:05 pm
20	8:27 am	20	Leo	7:17 pm
21	2:13 pm	23	Virgo	1:24 am
25	9:53 am	25	Libra	10:08 am
26	10:06 pm	27	Scorpio	9:27 pm
29	8:47 pm	30	Sagittarius	10:04 am

Last Aspect   **Moon Enters New Sign**

		September		
1	9:39 pm	1	Capricorn	9:45 pm
4	6:08 am	4	Aquarius	6:32 am
5	4:51 pm	6	Pisces	11:54 am
8	1:44 pm	8	Aries	2:37 pm
10	2:54 am	10	Taurus	4:03 pm
12	4:14 pm	12	Gemini	5:38 pm
14	6:46 pm	14	Cancer	8:30 pm
16	11:14 pm	17	Leo	1:20 am
19	8:21 am	19	Virgo	8:23 am
21	3:54 pm	21	Libra	5:41 pm
23	12:02 pm	24	Scorpio	5:00 am
26	1:44 pm	26	Sagittarius	5:37 pm
29	1:44 am	29	Capricorn	5:55 am
		October		
1	11:33 am	1	Aquarius	3:52 pm
3	2:15 pm	3	Pisces	10:07 pm
5	8:30 pm	6	Aries	12:48 am
7	2:24 pm	8	Taurus	1:12 am
9	8:31 pm	10	Gemini	1:12 am
11	10:56 pm	12	Cancer	2:37 am
14	1:05 am	14	Leo	6:47 am
16	1:06 am	16	Virgo	2:06 pm
18	5:10 pm	19	Libra	12:01 am
21	8:25 am	21	Scorpio	11:42 am
24	12:14 am	24	Sagittarius	12:19 am
26	12:42 pm	26	Capricorn	12:53 pm
28	11:38 pm	28	Aquarius	11:55 pm
31	2:15 am	31	Pisces	7:46 am

Last Aspect **Moon Enters New Sign**

		November		
2	10:15 am	2	Aries	10:39 am
4	6:21 am	4	Taurus	11:16 am
6	9:51 am	6	Gemini	10:20 am
8	9:32 am	8	Cancer	10:06 am
10	12:23 pm	10	Leo	12:34 pm
12	6:29 pm	12	Virgo	6:52 pm
15	4:08 am	15	Libra	4:44 am
17	6:51 am	17	Scorpio	4:44 pm
20	4:24 am	20	Sagittarius	5:26 am
22	4:48 pm	22	Capricorn	5:53 pm
25	4:10 am	25	Aquarius	5:16 am
27	12:53 pm	27	Pisces	2:24 pm
29	7:05 pm	29	Aries	8:07 pm
		December		
1	1:14 pm	1	Taurus	10:13 pm
3	8:50 pm	3	Gemini	9:48 pm
5	7:55 pm	5	Cancer	8:54 pm
7	8:45 pm	7	Leo	9:48 pm
9	11:56 pm	10	Virgo	2:20 am
12	9:51 am	12	Libra	11:04 am
14	10:36 pm	14	Scorpio	10:51 pm
17	10:24 am	17	Sagittarius	11:38 am
19	10:41 pm	19	Capricorn	11:53 pm
22	9:44 am	22	Aquarius	10:52 am
24	4:42 pm	24	Pisces	8:09 pm
27	2:03 am	27	Aries	3:02 am
28	9:13 pm	29	Taurus	6:57 am
31	7:25 am	31	Gemini	8:13 am

The Moon's Rhythm

The Moon journeys around Earth in an elliptical orbit that takes about 27.33 days, which is known as a sidereal month (period of revolution of one body about another). She can move up to 15 degrees or as few as 11 degrees in a day, with the fastest motion occurring when the Moon is at perigee (closest approach to Earth). The Moon is never retrograde, but when her motion is slow, the effect is similar to a retrograde period.

Astrologers have observed that people born on a day when the Moon is fast will process information differently from those who are born when the Moon is slow in motion. People born when the Moon is fast process information quickly and tend to react quickly, while those born during a slow Moon will be more deliberate.

The time from New Moon to New Moon is called the synodic month (involving a conjunction), and the average time span between this Sun-Moon alignment is 29.53 days. Since 29.53 won't divide into 365 evenly, we can have a month with two Full Moons or two New Moons.

Moon Aspects

The aspects the Moon will make during the times you are considering are also important. A trine or sextile, and sometimes a conjunction, are considered favorable aspects. A trine or sextile between the Sun and Moon is an excellent foundation for success. Whether or not a conjunction is considered favorable depends upon the planet the Moon is making a conjunction to. If it's joining the Sun, Venus, Mercury, Jupiter, or even Saturn, the aspect is favorable. If the Moon joins Pluto or Mars, however, that would not be considered favorable. There may be exceptions, but it would depend on what you are electing to do. For example, a trine to Pluto might hasten the end of a relationship you want to be free of.

It is important to avoid times when the Moon makes an aspect to or is conjoining any retrograde planet, unless, of course, you want the thing started to end in failure.

After the Moon has completed an aspect to a planet, that planetary energy has passed. For example, if the Moon squares Saturn at 10:00 am, you can disregard Saturn's influence on your activity if it will occur after that time. You should always look ahead at aspects the Moon will make on the day in question, though, because if the Moon opposes Mars at 11:30 pm on that day, you can expect events that stretch into the evening to be affected by the Moon-Mars aspect. A testy conversation might lead to an argument, or more.

Moon Signs

Much agricultural work is ruled by earth signs—Virgo, Capricorn, and Taurus. The air signs—Gemini, Aquarius, and Libra—rule flying and intellectual pursuits.

Each planet has one or two signs in which its characteristics are enhanced or "dignified," and the planet is said to "rule" that sign. The Sun rules Leo and the Moon rules Cancer, for example. The ruling planet for each sign is listed below. These should not be considered complete lists. We recommend that you purchase a book of planetary rulerships for more complete information.

Aries Moon

The energy of an Aries Moon is masculine, dry, barren, and fiery. Aries provides great start-up energy, but things started at this time may be the result of impulsive action that lacks research or necessary support. Aries lacks staying power.

Use this assertive, outgoing Moon sign to initiate change, but have a plan in place for someone to pick up the reins when you're impatient to move on to the next thing. Work that requires skillful but not necessarily patient use of tools—cutting down trees, hammering, etc.—is appropriate in Aries. Expect things to occur rapidly but to also quickly pass. If you are prone to injury or accidents, exercise caution and good judgment in Aries-related activities.

RULER: Mars

IMPULSE: Action

RULES: Head and face

Taurus Moon

A Taurus Moon's energy is feminine, semi-fruitful, and earthy. The Moon is exalted—very strong—in Taurus. Taurus is known as the farmer's sign because of its associations with farmland and precipitation that is the typical day-long "soaker" variety. Taurus energy is good to incorporate into your plans when patience, practicality, and perseverance are needed. Be aware, though, that you may also experience stubbornness in this sign.

Things started in Taurus tend to be long lasting and to increase in value. This can be very supportive energy in a marriage election. On the downside, the fixed energy of this sign resists change or the letting go of even the most difficult situations. A divorce following a marriage that occurred during a Taurus Moon may be difficult and costly to end. Things begun now tend to become habitual and hard to alter. If you want to make changes in something you started, it would be better to wait for Gemini. This is a good time to get a loan, but expect the people in charge of money to be cautious and slow to make decisions.

RULER: Venus

IMPULSE: Stability

RULES: Neck, throat, and voice

Gemini Moon

A Gemini Moon's energy is masculine, dry, barren, and airy. People are more changeable than usual and may prefer to follow intellectual pursuits and play mental games rather than apply themselves to practical concerns.

This sign is not favored for agricultural matters, but it is an excellent time to prepare for activities, to run errands, and write letters. Plan to use a Gemini Moon to exchange ideas, meet people, go on vacations that include walking or biking, or be in situations that require versatility and quick thinking on your feet.

RULER: Mercury

IMPULSE: Versatility

RULES: Shoulders, hands, arms, lungs, and nervous system

Cancer Moon

A Cancer Moon's energy is feminine, fruitful, moist, and very strong. Use this sign when you want to grow things—flowers, fruits, vegetables, commodities, stocks, or collections—for example. This sensitive sign stimulates rapport between people. Considered the most fertile of the signs, it is often associated with mothering. You can use this moontime to build personal friendships that support mutual growth.

Cancer is associated with emotions and feelings. Prominent Cancer energy promotes growth, but it can also turn people pouty and prone to withdrawing into their shells.

RULER: The Moon

IMPULSE: Tenacity

RULES: Chest area, breasts, and stomach

Leo Moon

A Leo Moon's energy is masculine, hot, dry, fiery, and barren. Use it whenever you need to put on a show, make a presentation, or entertain colleagues or guests. This is a proud yet playful energy that exudes self-confidence and is often associated with romance.

This is an excellent time for fundraisers and ceremonies or to be straightforward, frank, and honest about something. It is advisable not to put yourself in a position of needing public approval or where you might have to cope with underhandedness, as trouble in these areas can bring out the worst Leo traits. There is a tendency in this sign to become arrogant or self-centered.

RULER: The Sun

IMPULSE: I am

RULES: Heart and upper back

Virgo Moon

A Virgo Moon is feminine, dry, barren, earthy energy. It is favorable for anything that needs painstaking attention—especially those things where exactness rather than innovation is preferred.

Use this sign for activities when you must analyze information or when you must determine the value of something. Virgo is the sign of bargain hunting. It's friendly toward agricultural matters with an emphasis on animals and harvesting vegetables. It is an excellent time to care for animals, especially training them and veterinary work.

This sign is most beneficial when decisions have already been made and now need to be carried out. The inclination here is to see details rather than the bigger picture.

There is a tendency in this sign to overdo. Precautions should be taken to avoid becoming too dull from all work and no play. Build relaxation and pleasure into your routine from the beginning.

RULER: Mercury

IMPULSE: Discriminating

RULES: Abdomen and intestines

Libra Moon

A Libra Moon's energy is masculine, semi-fruitful, and airy. This energy will benefit any attempt to bring beauty to a place or thing. Libra is considered good energy for starting things of an intellectual nature. Libra is the sign of partnership and unions, which makes it an excellent time to form partnerships of any kind, to make agreements, and to negotiate. Even though this sign is good for initiating things, it is crucial to work with a partner who will provide incentive and encouragement. A Libra Moon accentuates teamwork (particularly teams of two) and artistic work (especially work that involves color). Make use of this sign when you are decorating your home or shopping for better-quality clothing.

RULER: Venus

IMPULSE: Balance

RULES: Lower back, kidneys, and buttocks

Scorpio Moon

The Scorpio Moon is feminine, fruitful, cold, and moist. It is useful when intensity (that sometimes borders on obsession) is needed. Scorpio is considered a very psychic sign. Use this Moon sign when you must back up something you strongly believe in, such as union or employer relations. There is strong group loyalty here, but a Scorpio Moon is also a good time to end connections thoroughly. This is also a good time to conduct research.

The desire nature is so strong here that there is a tendency to manipulate situations to get what one wants or to not see one's responsibility in an act.

RULER: Pluto, Mars (traditional)

IMPULSE: Transformation

RULES: Reproductive organs, genitals, groin, and pelvis

Sagittarius Moon

The Moon's energy is masculine, dry, barren, and fiery in Sagittarius, encouraging flights of imagination and confidence in the flow of life. Sagittarius is the most philosophical sign. Candor and honesty are enhanced when the Moon is here. This is an excellent time to "get things off your chest" and to deal with institutions of higher learning, publishing companies, and the law. It's also a good time for sport and adventure.

Sagittarians are the crusaders of this world. This is a good time to tackle things that need improvement, but don't try to be the diplomat while influenced by this energy. Opinions can run strong, and the tendency to proselytize is increased.

RULER: Jupiter

IMPULSE: Expansion

RULES: Thighs and hips

Capricorn Moon

In Capricorn the Moon's energy is feminine, semi-fruitful, and earthy. Because Cancer and Capricorn are polar opposites, the Moon's energy is thought to be weakened here. This energy encourages the need for structure, discipline, and organization. This is a good time to set goals and plan for the future, tend to family business, and to take care of details requiring patience or a businesslike manner. Institutional activities are favored. This sign should be avoided if you're seeking favors, as those in authority can be insensitive under this influence.

RULER: Saturn

IMPULSE: Ambitious

RULES: Bones, skin, and knees

Aquarius Moon

An Aquarius Moon's energy is masculine, barren, dry, and airy. Activities that are unique, individualistic, concerned with humanitarian issues, society as a whole, and making improvements are favored under this Moon. It is this quality of making improvements that has caused this sign to be associated with inventors and new inventions.

An Aquarius Moon promotes the gathering of social groups for friendly exchanges. People tend to react and speak from an intellectual rather than emotional viewpoint when the Moon is in this sign.

RULER: Uranus and Saturn

IMPULSE: Reformer

RULES: Calves and ankles

Pisces Moon

A Pisces Moon is feminine, fruitful, cool, and moist. This is an excellent time to retreat, meditate, sleep, pray, or make that dreamed-of escape into a fantasy vacation. However, things are not always what they seem to be with the Moon in Pisces. Personal boundaries tend to be fuzzy, and you may not be seeing things clearly. People tend to be idealistic under this sign, which can prevent them from seeing reality.

There is a live-and-let-live philosophy attached to this sign, which in the idealistic world may work well enough, but chaos is frequently the result. That's why this sign is also associated with alcohol and drug abuse, drug trafficking, and counterfeiting. On the lighter side, many musicians and artists are ruled by Pisces. It's only when they move too far away from reality that the dark side of substance abuse, suicide, or crime takes away life.

RULER: Jupiter and Neptune

IMPULSE: Empathetic

RULES: Feet

More about Zodiac Signs

Element (Triplicity)

Each of the zodiac signs is classified as belonging to an element; these are the four basic elements:

Fire Signs

Aries, Sagittarius, and Leo are action-oriented, outgoing, energetic, and spontaneous.

Earth Signs

Taurus, Capricorn, and Virgo are stable, conservative, practical, and oriented to the physical and material realm.

Air Signs

Gemini, Aquarius, and Libra are sociable and critical, and they tend to represent intellectual responses rather than feelings.

Water Signs

Cancer, Scorpio, and Pisces are emotional, receptive, intuitive, and can be very sensitive.

Quality (Quadruplicity)

Each zodiac sign is further classified as being cardinal, mutable, or fixed. There are four signs in each quadruplicity, one sign from each element.

Cardinal Signs

Aries, Cancer, Libra, and Capricorn represent beginnings and newly initiated action. They initiate each new season in the cycle of the year.

Fixed Signs

Taurus, Leo, Scorpio, and Aquarius want to maintain the status quo through stubbornness and persistence; they represent that "between" time. For example, Leo is the month when summer really feels like summer.

Mutable Signs

Pisces, Gemini, Virgo, and Sagittarius adapt to change and tolerate situations. They represent the last month of each season, when things are changing in preparation for the coming season.

Nature and Fertility

In addition to a sign's element and quality, each sign is further classified as either fruitful, semi-fruitful, or barren. This classification is the most important for readers who use the gardening information in the *Moon Sign Book* because the timing of most events depends on the fertility of the sign occupied by the Moon. The water signs of Cancer, Scorpio, and Pisces are the most fruitful. The semi-fruitful signs are the earth signs Taurus and Capricorn, and the air sign Libra. The barren signs correspond to fire signs Aries, Leo, and Sagittarius; air signs Gemini and Aquarius; and earth sign Virgo.

Good Timing

Sharon Leah

Electional astrology is the art of electing times to begin any undertaking. Say, for example, you want to start a business. That business will experience ups and downs, as well as reach its potential, according to the promise held in the universe at the time the business was started—its birth time. The horoscope (birth chart) set for the date, time, and place that a business starts would indicate the outcome—its potential to succeed.

So, you might ask yourself the question: If the horoscope for a business start can show success or failure, why not begin at a time that is more favorable to the venture? Well, you can.

While no time is perfect, there are better times and better days to undertake specific activities. There are thousands of examples that prove electional astrology is not only practical, but that it can make a difference in our lives. There are rules for electing times to begin various activities—even shopping. You'll find detailed instructions about how to make elections beginning on page 107.

Personalizing Elections

The election rules in this almanac are based upon the planetary positions at the time for which the election is made. They do not depend on any type of birth chart. However, a birth chart based upon the time, date, and birthplace of an event has advantages. No election is effective for every person. For example, you may leave home to begin a trip at the same time as a friend, but each of you will have a different experience according to whether or not your birth chart favors the trip.

Not all elections require a birth chart, but the timing of very important events—business starts, marriages, etc.—would benefit from the additional accuracy a birth chart provides. To order a birth chart for yourself or a planned event, visit our website at www.llewellyn.com.

Some Things to Consider

You've probably experienced good timing in your life. Maybe you were at the right place at the right time to meet a friend whom you hadn't seen in years. Frequently, when something like that happens, it is the result of following an intuitive impulse—that "gut instinct." Consider for a moment that you were actually responding to planetary energies. Electional astrology is a tool that can help you to align with energies, present and future, that are available to us through planetary placements.

Significators

Decide upon the important significators (planet, sign, and house ruling the matter) for which the election is being made. The Moon is the most important significator in any election, so the Moon should always be fortified (strong by sign and making favorable aspects to other planets).

The Moon's aspects to other planets are more important than the sign the Moon is in.

Other important considerations are the significators of the Ascendant and Midheaven—the house ruling the election matter and the ruler of the sign on that house cusp. Finally, any planet or sign that has a general rulership over the matter in question should be taken into consideration.

Nature and Fertility

Determine the general nature of the sign that is appropriate for your election. For example, much agricultural work is ruled by the earth signs of Virgo, Capricorn, and Taurus; while the air signs—Gemini, Aquarius, and Libra—rule intellectual pursuits.

One Final Comment

Use common sense. If you must do something, like plant your garden or take an airplane trip on a day that doesn't have the best aspects, proceed anyway, but try to minimize problems. For example, leave early for the airport to avoid being left behind due to delays in the security lanes. When you have no other choice, do the best that you can under the circumstances at the time.

If you want to personalize your elections, please turn to page 107 for more information. If you want a quick and easy answer, you can refer to Llewellyn's Astro Almanac on the following pages.

Llewellyn's Astro Almanac

The Astro Almanac tables, beginning on the next page, can help you find the dates best suited to particular activities. The dates provided are determined from the Moon's sign, phase, and aspects to other planets. Please note that the Astro Almanac does not take personal factors, such as your Sun and Moon sign, into account. The dates are general, and they will apply for everyone. Some activities will not have ideal dates during a particular month.

Activity	January
Animals (Neuter or spay)	24–26, 28
Animals (Sell or buy)	2, 8, 12
Automobile (Buy)	17, 18, 27, 28
Brewing	22, 23
Build (Start foundation)	no ideal dates
Business (Conducting for self and others)	4, 9, 18, 24
Business (Start new)	8
Can Fruits and Vegetables	22, 23
Can Preserves	22, 23
Concrete (Pour)	15
Construction (Begin new)	2, 6, 9, 15, 18, 19, 24, 29
Consultants (Begin work with)	2, 6, 7, 10, 15, 17, 19, 23, 28, 29
Contracts (Bid on)	2, 6, 7, 10
Cultivate	no ideal dates
Decorating	1, 2, 9, 10, 11, 29, 30
Demolition	14, 15, 24, 25
Electronics (Buy)	2, 28
Entertain Guests	8, 12
Floor Covering (Laying new)	14–21, 28
Habits (Break)	26, 28
Hair (Cut to increase growth)	4, 7–10, 31
Hair (Cut to decrease growth)	14, 24–27
Harvest (Grain for storage)	14–16
Harvest (Root crops)	14, 15, 24, 25, 28
Investments (New)	9, 18
Loan (Ask for)	7–9
Massage (Relaxing)	8, 12
Mow Lawn (Decrease growth)	14–28
Mow Lawn (Increase growth)	1–12, 30, 31
Mushrooms (Pick)	12–14
Negotiate (Business for the elderly)	8, 22, 27
Prune for Better Fruit	21–25
Prune to Promote Healing	26–28
Wean Children	1, 2, 24–30
Wood Floors (Installing)	26–28
Write Letters or Contracts	13, 18, 28

Activity	February
Animals (Neuter or spay)	20–23
Animals (Sell or buy)	2, 6, 11
Automobile (Buy)	7, 14, 24
Brewing	18, 19
Build (Start foundation)	no ideal dates
Business (Conducting for self and others)	2, 7, 17, 23
Business (Start new)	5
Can Fruits and Vegetables	18, 19, 27
Can Preserves	18, 19
Concrete (Pour)	25, 26
Construction (Begin new)	2, 7, 11, 16, 17, 23, 25
Consultants (Begin work with)	2, 6, 7, 11, 16, 18, 24, 25, 28
Contracts (Bid on)	2, 3, 6, 7, 11, 28
Cultivate	25, 26
Decorating	6–8
Demolition	20, 21
Electronics (Buy)	7
Entertain Guests	6, 10
Floor Covering (Laying new)	13–17, 25, 26
Habits (Break)	23, 25, 26
Hair (Cut to increase growth)	3–7, 10, 28
Hair (Cut to decrease growth)	20–24
Harvest (Grain for storage)	20
Harvest (Root crops)	12, 20, 21, 22, 25, 26
Investments (New)	7, 17
Loan (Ask for)	3–5, 10, 11
Massage (Relaxing)	10, 25
Mow Lawn (Decrease growth)	13–26
Mow Lawn (Increase growth)	1–11, 28
Mushrooms (Pick)	11–13
Negotiate (Business for the elderly)	9, 19
Prune for Better Fruit	18–22
Prune to Promote Healing	23, 24
Wean Children	20–26
Wood Floors (Installing)	23, 24
Write Letters or Contracts	1, 9, 14, 24, 28

Activity	March
Animals (Neuter or spay)	20, 21, 22, 27
Animals (Sell or buy)	10
Automobile (Buy)	5, 14, 23, 24
Brewing	17–19, 27, 28
Build (Start foundation)	4
Business (Conducting for self and others)	4, 8, 19, 24
Business (Start new)	4, 13
Can Fruits and Vegetables	17–19, 27, 28
Can Preserves	17–19
Concrete (Pour)	25, 26
Construction (Begin new)	2, 4, 8, 10, 15, 24, 25, 29
Consultants (Begin work with)	2, 5, 6, 10, 15, 20, 24, 25, 28, 29
Contracts (Bid on)	2, 5, 6, 10
Cultivate	20, 21, 25, 26
Decorating	5–7
Demolition	19–22, 28
Electronics (Buy)	5, 24
Entertain Guests	6, 10
Floor Covering (Laying new)	14–17, 24–26
Habits (Break)	24–26, 28
Hair (Cut to increase growth)	3–6, 9, 30, 31
Hair (Cut to decrease growth)	19–23, 27
Harvest (Grain for storage)	19–21
Harvest (Root crops)	19–21, 24–26, 28
Investments (New)	8, 19
Loan (Ask for)	3–5, 9–12, 30, 31
Massage (Relaxing)	10, 24
Mow Lawn (Decrease growth)	15–28
Mow Lawn (Increase growth)	1–12, 30, 31
Mushrooms (Pick)	13–15
Negotiate (Business for the elderly)	4, 23
Prune for Better Fruit	17–21
Prune to Promote Healing	22–24
Wean Children	20–26
Wood Floors (Installing)	22–24
Write Letters or Contracts	9, 14, 24, 28

Activity	April
Animals (Neuter or spay)	16–20, 23, 24
Animals (Sell or buy)	1, 7, 29
Automobile (Buy)	10, 20, 30
Brewing	14, 15, 23, 24
Build (Start foundation)	1, 28
Business (Conducting for self and others)	2, 7, 18, 23
Business (Start new)	1, 9, 28
Can Fruits and Vegetables	14, 15, 23, 24
Can Preserves	14, 15, 27
Concrete (Pour)	21
Construction (Begin new)	2, 7, 12, 18, 22, 26
Consultants (Begin work with)	1, 2, 5, 7, 12, 15, 21, 22, 25, 26, 30
Contracts (Bid on)	1, 2, 5, 7, 12, 30
Cultivate	16, 17, 21, 22, 25, 26
Decorating	1–3, 10–12, 29, 30
Demolition	15–17, 25, 26
Electronics (Buy)	21, 30
Entertain Guests	1, 5, 29
Floor Covering (Laying new)	13, 20–22, 27
Habits (Break)	21, 22, 25, 26
Hair (Cut to increase growth)	1, 2, 28, 29, 30
Hair (Cut to decrease growth)	15–19, 23, 24, 27
Harvest (Grain for storage)	15–18, 20
Harvest (Root crops)	15–17, 20–22, 25, 26
Investments (New)	7, 18
Loan (Ask for)	1, 6–8, 28, 29
Massage (Relaxing)	1, 5, 29
Mow Lawn (Decrease growth)	13–26
Mow Lawn (Increase growth)	1–11, 28–30
Mushrooms (Pick)	11–13
Negotiate (Business for the elderly)	5, 15, 20, 28
Prune for Better Fruit	13–17
Prune to Promote Healing	18–20
Wean Children	16–22
Wood Floors (Installing)	18–20
Write Letters or Contracts	5, 10, 20, 24, 25

Activity	May
Animals (Neuter or spay)	13–17, 20–22
Animals (Sell or buy)	5, 10, 27
Automobile (Buy)	7, 16–18, 26
Brewing	21, 22
Build (Start foundation)	3
Business (Conducting for self and others)	1, 7, 17, 22, 31
Business (Start new)	7
Can Fruits and Vegetables	21
Can Preserves	25
Concrete (Pour)	18, 19, 25
Construction (Begin new)	1, 5, 7, 10, 17, 20, 22, 24, 31
Consultants (Begin work with)	4, 5, 10, 16, 20, 21, 24, 26, 28, 31
Contracts (Bid on)	4, 5, 10, 28, 31
Cultivate	13–15, 23, 24
Decorating	8–10, 26–28
Demolition	13, 14, 22, 23
Electronics (Buy)	26
Entertain Guests	3, 27
Floor Covering (Laying new)	18, 19, 25, 26
Habits (Break)	23, 24
Hair (Cut to increase growth)	3, 27, 30
Hair (Cut to decrease growth)	13–18, 21, 24–26
Harvest (Grain for storage)	13–15, 18, 19
Harvest (Root crops)	13–15, 18, 19, 22–24
Investments (New)	7, 17
Loan (Ask for)	3–5, 30, 31
Massage (Relaxing)	3, 19
Mow Lawn (Decrease growth)	13–25
Mow Lawn (Increase growth)	1–11, 27, 28, 30, 31
Mushrooms (Pick)	11–13
Negotiate (Business for the elderly)	26, 30
Prune for Better Fruit	12, 13, 15
Prune to Promote Healing	16–18
Wean Children	13–20
Wood Floors (Installing)	15–18
Write Letters or Contracts	3, 7, 17, 22, 26, 30

Activity	June
Animals (Neuter or spay)	12, 13, 17, 18
Animals (Sell or buy)	6, 26
Automobile (Buy)	4, 14, 23
Brewing	17, 18
Build (Start foundation)	27
Business (Conducting for self and others)	5, 16, 20, 29
Business (Start new)	4, 29
Can Fruits and Vegetables	17, 18, 25
Can Preserves	21, 22, 25
Concrete (Pour)	15, 21, 22
Construction (Begin new)	1, 5, 6, 16, 20, 21, 29
Consultants (Begin work with)	1, 6, 16, 17, 21, 22, 25, 27, 29
Contracts (Bid on)	1, 6, 8, 27, 29
Cultivate	11, 19, 20, 23, 24
Decorating	4–6
Demolition	18, 19
Electronics (Buy)	6
Entertain Guests	1, 22, 26
Floor Covering (Laying new)	14–16, 21–24
Habits (Break)	19, 20, 24
Hair (Cut to increase growth)	9, 10
Hair (Cut to decrease growth)	12, 13, 17, 20–23
Harvest (Grain for storage)	14, 15, 18
Harvest (Root crops)	11, 14–16, 18–20, 23, 24
Investments (New)	5, 16
Loan (Ask for)	1, 27–29
Massage (Relaxing)	1, 22, 26
Mow Lawn (Decrease growth)	12–24
Mow Lawn (Increase growth)	1–10, 26–30
Mushrooms (Pick)	10–12
Negotiate (Business for the elderly)	9, 14
Prune for Better Fruit	11
Prune to Promote Healing	12–14
Wean Children	10–16
Wood Floors (Installing)	11–14
Write Letters or Contracts	4, 14, 18, 27

Activity	July
Animals (Neuter or spay)	11, 14
Animals (Sell or buy)	1, 4, 26, 27, 31
Automobile (Buy)	1, 20, 21
Brewing	14, 23
Build (Start foundation)	no ideal dates
Business (Conducting for self and others)	5, 15, 20, 29
Business (Start new)	9, 27
Can Fruits and Vegetables	14, 23
Can Preserves	18, 19, 23
Concrete (Pour)	12, 13, 18, 19
Construction (Begin new)	18, 20, 27, 29
Consultants (Begin work with)	2, 4, 7, 14, 17, 18, 21, 23, 25, 27, 29
Contracts (Bid on)	2, 4, 7, 25, 27, 29
Cultivate	20, 21
Decorating	1–4, 29–31
Demolition	16, 17, 24
Electronics (Buy)	2, 11, 20, 21, 29
Entertain Guests	26, 31
Floor Covering (Laying new)	11–13, 18–20, 21, 24
Habits (Break)	20, 22
Hair (Cut to increase growth)	6–10
Hair (Cut to decrease growth)	14, 15, 18–21, 24
Harvest (Grain for storage)	11–13, 16, 17
Harvest (Root crops)	11–13, 16, 17, 20, 21
Investments (New)	5, 15
Loan (Ask for)	25, 26
Massage (Relaxing)	12, 26
Mow Lawn (Decrease growth)	11–23
Mow Lawn (Increase growth)	1–9, 25–31
Mushrooms (Pick)	9–11
Negotiate (Business for the elderly)	6, 11, 20, 24
Prune for Better Fruit	no ideal dates
Prune to Promote Healing	10, 11
Wean Children	7–13
Wood Floors (Installing)	10, 11
Write Letters or Contracts	1, 11, 16, 24, 25, 29

Activity	August
Animals (Neuter or spay)	10, 11
Animals (Sell or buy)	24, 25, 29, 30
Automobile (Buy)	16
Brewing	10, 11, 19, 20
Build (Start foundation)	no ideal dates
Business (Conducting for self and others)	4, 13, 18, 28
Business (Start new)	6, 24
Can Fruits and Vegetables	10, 11, 19, 20
Can Preserves	15, 19, 20
Concrete (Pour)	15, 21
Construction (Begin new)	4, 13, 15, 18, 24
Consultants (Begin work with)	1, 3, 11, 12, 15, 16, 19, 21, 24, 26, 29
Contracts (Bid on)	1, 3, 24, 26, 29
Cultivate	17, 18, 21, 22
Decorating	7–9, 25–27
Demolition	12, 13, 20–22
Electronics (Buy)	7, 16, 25, 26
Entertain Guests	15, 20, 25
Floor Covering (Laying new)	14–18, 21, 22
Habits (Break)	16–18, 20, 21
Hair (Cut to increase growth)	3–6, 30, 31
Hair (Cut to decrease growth)	11, 14–17, 20
Harvest (Grain for storage)	12, 13
Harvest (Root crops)	9, 12, 13, 16–18, 20, 21
Investments (New)	4, 13
Loan (Ask for)	no ideal dates
Massage (Relaxing)	15, 20
Mow Lawn (Decrease growth)	10–21
Mow Lawn (Increase growth)	1–8, 24–31
Mushrooms (Pick)	8–10
Negotiate (Business for the elderly)	7, 16, 20, 30
Prune for Better Fruit	no ideal dates
Prune to Promote Healing	no ideal dates
Wean Children	3–10, 31
Wood Floors (Installing)	no ideal dates
Write Letters or Contracts	7, 12, 20, 21, 25

Activity	September
Animals (Neuter or spay)	8
Animals (Sell or buy)	26, 30
Automobile (Buy)	4, 12
Brewing	8, 15
Build (Start foundation)	26
Business (Conducting for self and others)	2, 12, 16, 27
Business (Start new)	3, 4
Can Fruits and Vegetables	15
Can Preserves	11, 12, 15
Concrete (Pour)	11, 12, 17, 18
Construction (Begin new)	2, 12, 16, 21, 27
Consultants (Begin work with)	1, 7, 11, 12, 16, 21, 22, 26, 28
Contracts (Bid on)	1, 7, 22, 26, 28
Cultivate	14, 17, 18, 20, 21
Decorating	4–6, 21–24
Demolition	8, 9, 17, 18
Electronics (Buy)	4, 12, 21, 22
Entertain Guests	14
Floor Covering (Laying new)	11–14, 17–21
Habits (Break)	17–19
Hair (Cut to increase growth)	1, 2, 3, 7, 26–30
Hair (Cut to decrease growth)	10–13
Harvest (Grain for storage)	8–10, 12, 13
Harvest (Root crops)	8–10, 12–14, 17, 18
Investments (New)	2, 12
Loan (Ask for)	no ideal dates
Massage (Relaxing)	19
Mow Lawn (Decrease growth)	8–20
Mow Lawn (Increase growth)	1–6, 22–30
Mushrooms (Pick)	6–8
Negotiate (Business for the elderly)	12, 16, 26
Prune for Better Fruit	no ideal dates
Prune to Promote Healing	no ideal dates
Wean Children	1–6, 27–30
Wood Floors (Installing)	no ideal dates
Write Letters or Contracts	4, 8, 17, 21, 22

Activity	October
Animals (Neuter or spay)	no ideal dates
Animals (Sell or buy)	5, 25, 30
Automobile (Buy)	1, 10, 17, 28
Brewing	12, 13
Build (Start foundation)	23
Business (Conducting for self and others)	2, 11, 16, 26, 31
Business (Start new)	1, 28
Can Fruits and Vegetables	12, 13
Can Preserves	8, 12, 13
Concrete (Pour)	8, 15
Construction (Begin new)	2, 9, 11, 16, 18, 26
Consultants (Begin work with)	3, 5, 9, 12, 13, 17, 18, 23, 28
Contracts (Bid on)	3, 5, 23, 24, 28
Cultivate	14–18
Decorating	1–3, 21, 29–31
Demolition	6, 7, 14, 15
Electronics (Buy)	1, 3, 10, 19, 29
Entertain Guests	9, 14
Floor Covering (Laying new)	8–11, 14–21
Habits (Break)	14, 16
Hair (Cut to increase growth)	4, 5, 24–27
Hair (Cut to decrease growth)	8–12, 14
Harvest (Grain for storage)	10
Harvest (Root crops)	7, 10, 11, 14–16
Investments (New)	2, 11, 31
Loan (Ask for)	no ideal dates
Massage (Relaxing)	9, 14, 19, 30
Mow Lawn (Decrease growth)	7–20
Mow Lawn (Increase growth)	1–5, 22–31
Mushrooms (Pick)	5–7
Negotiate (Business for the elderly)	1, 9, 23, 28
Prune for Better Fruit	no ideal dates
Prune to Promote Healing	no ideal dates
Wean Children	1–3, 24–31
Wood Floors (Installing)	no ideal dates
Write Letters or Contracts	1, 6, 14, 19, 23, 29

Activity	November
Animals (Neuter or spay)	no ideal dates
Animals (Sell or buy)	2, 24, 29
Automobile (Buy)	6, 15, 24, 25
Brewing	9, 10, 18
Build (Start foundation)	no ideal dates
Business (Conducting for self and others)	9, 14, 25, 30
Business (Start new)	24
Can Fruits and Vegetables	9, 18, 19
Can Preserves	9, 18, 19
Concrete (Pour)	11, 12
Construction (Begin new)	6, 9, 14, 25, 30
Consultants (Begin work with)	2, 6, 10, 11, 14, 15, 19, 20, 24, 29
Contracts (Bid on)	2, 22, 24, 29
Cultivate	12–14
Decorating	25–27
Demolition	10, 11
Electronics (Buy)	6, 15
Entertain Guests	8
Floor Covering (Laying new)	6, 7, 11–17
Habits (Break)	12
Hair (Cut to increase growth)	1, 4, 20–24, 28
Hair (Cut to decrease growth)	6, 7, 10
Harvest (Grain for storage)	6, 7, 10, 11
Harvest (Root crops)	6, 7, 10–12
Investments (New)	9, 30
Loan (Ask for)	4
Massage (Relaxing)	8
Mow Lawn (Decrease growth)	6–18
Mow Lawn (Increase growth)	1–4, 21–30
Mushrooms (Pick)	4–6
Negotiate (Business for the elderly)	19, 24
Prune for Better Fruit	17–19
Prune to Promote Healing	no ideal dates
Wean Children	20–27
Wood Floors (Installing)	no ideal dates
Write Letters or Contracts	2, 10, 15, 20, 25, 29

Activity	December
Animals (Neuter or spay)	17–19
Animals (Sell or buy)	3, 24, 26, 29
Automobile (Buy)	12, 22
Brewing	6, 7, 15, 16
Build (Start foundation)	no ideal dates
Business (Conducting for self and others)	9, 14, 25, 29
Business (Start new)	3, 21, 22, 30, 31
Can Fruits and Vegetables	6, 7, 15, 16
Can Preserves	6, 7, 15, 16
Concrete (Pour)	8
Construction (Begin new)	3, 9, 11, 14, 29, 30
Consultants (Begin work with)	3, 7, 11, 12, 16, 18, 23, 26, 28, 30
Contracts (Bid on)	3, 23, 26, 28, 30
Cultivate	no ideal dates
Decorating	4, 22, 23, 24, 31
Demolition	8–10, 17, 18
Electronics (Buy)	12, 23
Entertain Guests	8, 13
Floor Covering (Laying new)	5, 8, 9, 10–14
Habits (Break)	no ideal dates
Hair (Cut to increase growth)	1–4, 20, 21, 25, 26, 29–31
Hair (Cut to decrease growth)	7, 17–19
Harvest (Grain for storage)	5, 7–10
Harvest (Root crops)	5, 8, 9, 17, 18
Investments (New)	9, 29
Loan (Ask for)	1–3, 29–31
Massage (Relaxing)	8, 13, 29
Mow Lawn (Decrease growth)	5–18
Mow Lawn (Increase growth)	1–3, 20–31
Mushrooms (Pick)	3–5
Negotiate (Business for the elderly)	3, 7
Prune for Better Fruit	15–17, 19
Prune to Promote Healing	no ideal dates
Wean Children	18–24
Wood Floors (Installing)	no ideal dates
Write Letters or Contracts	7, 12, 18, 22

Choose the Best Time for Your Activities

When rules or elections refer to "favorable" and "unfavorable" aspects to your Sun or other planets, please refer to the Favorable and Unfavorable Days Tables and Lunar Aspectarian for more information. You'll find instructions beginning on page 129 and the tables beginning on page 136.

The material in this section came from several sources including: *The New A to Z Horoscope Maker and Delineator* by Llewellyn George (Llewellyn, 1999), *Moon Sign Book* (Llewellyn, 1945), and *Electional Astrology* by Vivian Robson (Slingshot Publishing, 2000). Robson's book was originally published in 1937.

Advertise (Internet)

The Moon should be conjunct, sextile, or trine Mercury or Uranus and in the sign of Gemini, Capricorn, or Aquarius.

Advertise (Print)

Write ads on a day favorable to your Sun. The Moon should be conjunct, sextile, or trine Mercury or Venus. Avoid hard aspects to Mars and Saturn. Ad campaigns produce the best results when the Moon is well aspected in Gemini (to enhance communication) or Capricorn (to build business).

Animals

Take home new pets when the day is favorable to your Sun, or when the Moon is trine, sextile, or conjunct Mercury, Jupiter or Venus, or in the sign of Virgo or Pisces. However, avoid days when the Moon is either square or opposing the Sun, Mars, Saturn, Uranus, Neptune, or Pluto. When selecting a pet, have the Moon well aspected by the planet that rules the animal. Cats are ruled by the Sun, dogs by Mercury, birds by Venus, horses by Jupiter, and fish by Neptune. Buy large animals when the Moon is in Sagittarius or Pisces and making favorable aspects to Jupiter or Mercury. Buy animals smaller than sheep when the Moon is in Virgo with favorable aspects to Mercury or Venus.

Animals (Breed)

Animals are easiest to handle when the Moon is in Taurus, Cancer, Libra, or Pisces, but try to avoid the Full Moon. To encourage healthy births, animals should be mated so births occur when the Moon is increasing in Taurus, Cancer, Pisces, or Libra. Those born during a semi-fruitful sign (Taurus and Capricorn) will produce leaner meat. Libra yields beautiful animals for showing and racing.

Animals (Neuter or Spay)

Have livestock and pets neutered or spayed when the Moon is in Sagittarius, Capricorn, or Pisces, after it has passed through Scorpio, the sign that rules reproductive organs. Avoid the week before and after the Full Moon.

Animals (Sell or Buy)

In either buying or selling, it is important to keep the Moon and Mercury free from any aspect to Mars. Aspects to Mars will create discord and increase the likelihood of wrangling over price and quality. The Moon should be passing from the first quarter to full and sextile or trine Venus or Jupiter. When buying racehorses, let the Moon be in an air sign. The Moon should be in air signs when you buy birds. If the birds are to be pets, let the Moon be in good aspect to Venus.

Animals (Train)

Train pets when the Moon is in Virgo or trine to Mercury.

Animals (Train Dogs to Hunt)

Let the Moon be in Aries in conjunction with Mars, which makes them courageous and quick to learn. But let Jupiter also be in aspect to preserve them from danger in hunting.

Automobiles

When buying an automobile, select a time when the Moon is conjunct, sextile, or trine to Mercury, Saturn, or Uranus and in the sign of Gemini or Capricorn. Avoid times when Mercury is in retrograde motion.

Baking Cakes

Your cakes will have a lighter texture if you see that the Moon is in Gemini, Libra, or Aquarius and in good aspect to Venus or Mercury. If you are decorating a cake or confections are being made, have the Moon placed in Libra.

Beauty Treatments (Massage, etc.)

See that the Moon is in Taurus, Cancer, Leo, Libra, or Aquarius and in favorable aspect to Venus. In the case of plastic surgery, aspects to Mars should be avoided, and the Moon should not be in the sign ruling the part to be operated on.

Borrow (Money or Goods)

See that the Moon is not placed between 15 degrees Libra and 15 degrees Scorpio. Let the Moon be waning and in Leo, Scorpio (16 to 30 degrees), Sagittarius, or Pisces. Venus should be in good aspect to the Moon, and the Moon should not be square, opposing, or conjunct either Saturn or Mars.

Brewing

Start brewing during the third or fourth quarter, when the Moon is in Cancer, Scorpio, or Pisces.

Build (Start Foundation)

Turning the first sod for the foundation marks the beginning of the building. For best results, excavate the site when the Moon is in the first quarter of a fixed sign and making favorable aspects to Saturn.

Business (Start New)

When starting a business, have the Moon be in Taurus, Virgo, or Capricorn and increasing. The Moon should be sextile or trine Jupiter or Saturn, but avoid oppositions or squares. The planet ruling the business should be well aspected too.

Buy Goods

Buy during the third quarter, when the Moon is in Taurus for quality or in a mutable sign (Gemini, Sagittarius, Virgo, or Pisces) for savings. Good aspects to Venus or the Sun are desirable. If you are buying for yourself, it is good if the day is favorable for your Sun sign. You may also apply rules for buying specific items.

Canning

Can fruits and vegetables when the Moon is in either the third or fourth quarter and in the water sign Cancer or Pisces. Preserves and jellies use the same quarters and the signs Cancer, Pisces, or Taurus.

Clothing

Buy clothing on a day that is favorable for your Sun sign and when Venus or Mercury is well aspected. Avoid aspects to Mars and Saturn. Buy your clothing when the Moon is in Taurus if you want to remain satisfied. Do not buy clothing or jewelry when the Moon is in Scorpio or Aries. See·that the Moon is sextile or trine the Sun during the first or second quarters.

Collections

Try to make collections on days when your natal Sun is well aspected. Avoid days when the Moon is opposing or square Mars or Saturn. If possible, the Moon should be in a cardinal sign (Aries, Cancer, Libra, or Capricorn). It is more difficult to collect when the Moon is in Taurus or Scorpio.

Concrete

Pour concrete when the Moon is in the third quarter of the fixed sign Taurus, Leo, or Aquarius.

Construction (Begin New)

The Moon should be sextile or trine Jupiter. According to Hermes, no building should be begun when the Moon is in Scorpio or Pisces. The best time to begin building is when the Moon is in Aquarius.

Consultants (Work with)

The Moon should be conjunct, sextile, or trine Mercury or Jupiter.

Contracts (Bid On)

The Moon should be in Gemini or Capricorn and either the Moon or Mercury should be conjunct, sextile, or trine Jupiter.

Copyrights/Patents

The Moon should be conjunct, trine, or sextile either Mercury or Jupiter.

Coronations and Installations

Let the Moon be in Leo and in favorable aspect to Venus, Jupiter, or Mercury. The Moon should be applying to these planets.

Cultivate

Cultivate when the Moon is in a barren sign and waning, ideally the fourth quarter in Aries, Gemini, Leo, Virgo, or Aquarius. The third quarter in the sign of Sagittarius will also work.

Cut Timber

Timber cut during the waning Moon does not become worm-eaten; it will season well and not warp, decay, or snap during burning. Cut when the Moon is in Taurus, Gemini, Virgo, or Capricorn—especially in August. Avoid the water signs. Look for favorable aspects to Mars.

Decorating or Home Repairs

Have the Moon waxing and in the sign of Libra, Gemini, or Aquarius. Avoid squares or oppositions to either Mars or Saturn. Venus in good aspect to Mars or Saturn is beneficial.

Demolition

Let the waning Moon be in Leo, Sagittarius, or Aries.

Dental and Dentists

Visit the dentist when the Moon is in Virgo, or pick a day marked favorable for your Sun sign. Mars should be marked sextile, conjunct, or trine; avoid squares or oppositions to Saturn, Uranus, or Jupiter.

Teeth are best removed when the Moon is in Gemini, Virgo, Sagittarius, or Pisces and during the first or second quarter. Avoid the Full Moon! The day should be favorable for your lunar cycle, and Mars and Saturn should be marked conjunct, trine, or sextile. Fillings should be done in the third or fourth quarters in the sign of Taurus, Leo, Scorpio, or Pisces. The same applies for dentures.

Dressmaking

William Lilly wrote in 1676: "Make no new clothes, or first put them on when the Moon is in Scorpio or afflicted by Mars, for they will be apt to be torn and quickly worn out." Design, repair, and sew clothes in the first and second quarters of Taurus, Leo, or Libra on a day marked favorable for your Sun sign. Venus, Jupiter, and Mercury should be favorably aspected, but avoid hard aspects to Mars or Saturn.

Egg-Setting (see p. 161)

Eggs should be set so chicks will hatch during fruitful signs. To set eggs, subtract the number of days given for incubation or gestation from the fruitful dates. Chickens incubate in twenty-one days, turkeys and geese in twenty-eight days.

A freshly laid egg loses quality rapidly if it is not handled properly. Use plenty of clean litter in the nests to reduce the number of dirty or cracked eggs. Gather eggs daily in mild weather and at least two times daily in hot or cold weather. The eggs should be placed in a cooler immediately after gathering and stored at 50 to 55°F. Do not store eggs with foods or products that give off pungent odors since eggs may absorb the odors.

Eggs saved for hatching purposes should not be washed. Only clean and slightly soiled eggs should be saved for hatching. Dirty eggs should not be incubated. Eggs should be stored in a cool place with the large ends up. It is not advisable to store the eggs longer than one week before setting them in an incubator.

Electricity and Gas (Install)

The Moon should be in a fire sign, and there should be no squares, oppositions, or conjunctions with Uranus (ruler of electricity), Neptune (ruler of gas), Saturn, or Mars. Hard aspects to Mars can cause fires.

Electronics (Buying)

Choose a day when the Moon is in an air sign (Gemini, Libra, Aquarius) and well aspected by Mercury and/or Uranus when buying electronics.

Electronics (Repair)

The Moon should be sextile or trine Mars or Uranus and in a fixed sign (Taurus, Leo, Scorpio, Aquarius).

Entertain Friends

Let the Moon be in Leo or Libra and making good aspects to Venus. Avoid squares or oppositions to either Mars or Saturn by the Moon or Venus.

Eyes and Eyeglasses

Have your eyes tested and glasses fitted on a day marked favorable for your Sun sign, and on a day that falls during your favorable lunar cycle. Mars should not be in aspect with the Moon.

The same applies for any treatment of the eyes, which should also be started during the Moon's first or second quarter.

Fence Posts

Set posts when the Moon is in the third or fourth quarter of the fixed sign Taurus or Leo.

Fertilize and Compost

Fertilize when the Moon is in a fruitful sign (Cancer, Scorpio, Pisces). Organic fertilizers are best when the Moon is waning. Use chemical fertilizers when the Moon is waxing. Start compost when the Moon is in the fourth quarter in a water sign.

Find Hidden Treasure

Let the Moon be in good aspect to Jupiter or Venus. If you erect a horoscope for this election, place the Moon in the Fourth House.

Find Lost Articles

Search for lost articles during the first quarter and when your Sun sign is marked favorable. Also check to see that the planet ruling the lost item is trine, sextile, or conjunct the Moon. The Moon rules household utensils; Mercury rules letters and books; and Venus rules clothing, jewelry, and money.

Fishing

During the summer months, the best time of the day to fish is from sunrise to three hours after and from two hours before sunset until one hour after. Fish do not bite in cooler months until the air is warm, from noon to three pm. Warm, cloudy days are good. The most favorable winds are from the south and southwest. Easterly winds are unfavorable. The best days of the month for fishing are when the Moon changes quarters, especially if the change occurs on a day when the Moon is in a water sign (Cancer, Scorpio, Pisces). The best period in any month is the day after the Full Moon.

Friendship

The need for friendship is greater when the Moon is in Aquarius or when Uranus aspects the Moon. Friendship prospers when Venus or Uranus is trine, sextile, or conjunct the Moon. The Moon in Gemini facilitates the chance meeting of acquaintances and friends.

Grafting or Budding

Grafting is the process of introducing new varieties of fruit on less desirable trees. For this process you should use the increasing phase of the Moon in fruitful signs such as Cancer, Scorpio, or Pisces. Capricorn may be used, too. Cut your grafts while trees are dormant, from December to March. Keep them in a cool, dark place, not too dry or too damp. Do the grafting before the sap starts to flow and while the Moon is waxing, preferably while it is in Cancer, Scorpio, or Pisces. The type of plant should determine both cutting and planting times.

Habit (Breaking)

To end an undesirable habit, and this applies to ending everything from a bad relationship to smoking, start on a day when the Moon is in the fourth quarter and in the barren sign of Gemini, Leo, or Aquarius. Aries, Virgo, and Capricorn may be suitable as well, depending on the habit you want to be rid of. Make sure that your lunar cycle is favorable. Avoid lunar aspects to Mars or Jupiter. However, favorable aspects to Pluto are helpful.

Haircuts

Cut hair when the Moon is in Gemini, Sagittarius, Pisces, Taurus, or Capricorn, but not in Virgo. Look for favorable aspects to Venus. For faster growth, cut hair when the Moon is increasing in Cancer or Pisces. To make hair grow thicker, cut when the Moon is full in the signs of Taurus, Cancer, or Leo. If you want your hair to grow more slowly, have the Moon be decreasing in Aries, Gemini, or Virgo, and have the Moon square or opposing Saturn.

Permanents, straightening, and hair coloring will take well if the Moon is in Taurus or Leo and trine or sextile Venus. Avoid hair treatments if Mars is marked as square or in opposition, especially if heat is to be used. For permanents, a trine to Jupiter is helpful. The Moon also should be in the first quarter. Check the lunar cycle for a favorable day in relation to your Sun sign.

Harvest Crops

Harvest root crops when the Moon is in a dry sign (Aries, Leo, Sagittarius, Gemini, Aquarius) and waning. Harvest grain for storage just after the Full Moon, avoiding Cancer, Scorpio, or Pisces. Harvest in the third and fourth quarters in dry signs. Dry crops in the third quarter in fire signs.

Health

A diagnosis is more likely to be successful when the Moon is in Aries, Cancer, Libra, or Capricorn and less so when in Gemini, Sagittarius, Pisces, or Virgo. Begin a recuperation program or enter a hospital when the Moon is in a cardinal or fixed sign and the day is favorable to your Sun sign. For surgery, see "Surgical Procedures." Buy medicines when the Moon is in Virgo or Scorpio.

Home (Buy New)

If you desire a permanent home, buy when the New Moon is in a fixed sign—Taurus or Leo, for example. Each sign will affect your decision in a different way. A house bought when the Moon is in Taurus is likely to be more practical and have a country look—right down to the split-rail fence. A house purchased when the Moon is in Leo will more likely be a real showplace.

If you're buying for speculation and a quick turnover, be certain that the Moon is in a cardinal sign (Aries, Cancer, Libra, Capricorn). Avoid buying when the Moon is in a fixed sign (Leo, Scorpio, Aquarius, Taurus).

Home (Make Repairs)

In all repairs, avoid squares, oppositions, or conjunctions to the planet ruling the place or thing to be repaired. For example, bathrooms are ruled by Scorpio and Cancer. You would not want to start a project in those rooms when the Moon or Pluto is receiving hard aspects. The front entrance, hall, dining room, and porch are ruled by the Sun So you would want to avoid times when Saturn or Mars are square, opposing, or conjunct the Sun. Also, let the Moon be waxing.

Home (Sell)

Make a strong effort to list your property for sale when the Sun is marked favorable in your sign and in good aspect to Jupiter. Avoid adverse aspects to as many planets as possible.

Home Furnishings (Buy New)

Saturn days (Saturday) are good for buying, and Jupiter days (Thursday) are good for selling. Items bought on days when Saturn is well aspected tend to wear longer and purchases tend to be more conservative.

Job (Start New)

Jupiter and Venus should be sextile, trine, or conjunct the Moon. A day when your Sun is receiving favorable aspects is preferred.

Legal Matters

Good Moon-Jupiter aspects improve the outcome in legal decisions. To gain damages through a lawsuit, begin the process during the increasing Moon. To avoid paying damages, a court date during the decreasing Moon is desirable. Good Moon-Sun aspects strengthen your chance of success. A well-aspected Moon in Cancer or Leo, making good aspects to the Sun, brings the best results in custody cases. In divorce cases, a favorable Moon-Venus aspect is best.

Loan (Ask For)

A first and second quarter phase favors the lender, the third and fourth quarters favor the borrower. Good aspects of Jupiter and Venus to the Moon are favorable to both, as is having the Moon in Leo or Taurus.

Machinery, Appliances, or Tools (Buy)

Tools, machinery, and other implements should be bought on days when your lunar cycle is favorable and when Mars and Uranus are trine, sextile, or conjunct the Moon. Any quarter of the Moon is suitable. When buying gas or electrical appliances, the Moon should be in Aquarius.

Make a Will

Let the Moon be in a fixed sign (Taurus, Leo, Scorpio, or Aquarius) to ensure permanence. If the Moon is in a cardinal sign (Aries, Cancer, Libra, or Capricorn), the will could be altered. Let the Moon be waxing—increasing in light—and in good aspect to Saturn, Venus, or Mercury. In case the will is made in an emergency during illness and the Moon is slow in motion, void-of-course, combust, or under the Sun's beams, the testator will die and the will remain unaltered. There is some danger that it will be lost or stolen, however.

Marriage

The best time for marriage to take place is when the Moon is increasing, but not yet full. Good signs for the Moon to be in are Taurus, Cancer, Leo, or Libra.

The Moon in Taurus produces the most steadfast marriages, but if the partners later want to separate, they may have a difficult time. Make sure that the Moon is well aspected, especially to Venus or Jupiter. Avoid aspects to Mars, Uranus, or Pluto and the signs Aries, Gemini, Virgo, Scorpio, or Aquarius.

The values of the signs are as follows:

- Aries is not favored for marriage
- Taurus from 0 to 19 degrees is good, the remaining degrees are less favorable
- Cancer is unfavorable unless you are marrying a widow
- Leo is favored, but it may cause one party to deceive the other as to his or her money or possessions
- Virgo is not favored except when marrying a widow
- Libra is good for engagements but not for marriage
- Scorpio from 0 to 15 degrees is good, but the last 15 degrees are entirely unfortunate. The woman may be fickle, envious, and quarrelsome
- Sagittarius is neutral
- Capricorn, from 0 to 10 degrees, is difficult for marriage; however, the remaining degrees are favorable, especially when marrying a widow
- Aquarius is not favored
- Pisces is favored, although marriage under this sign can incline a woman to chatter a lot

These effects are strongest when the Moon is in the sign. If the Moon and Venus are in a cardinal sign, happiness between the couple may not continue long.

On no account should the Moon apply to Saturn or Mars, even by good aspect.

Medical Treatment for the Eyes

Let the Moon be increasing in light and motion and making favorable aspects to Venus or Jupiter and be unaspected by Mars. Keep the Moon out of Taurus, Capricorn, or Virgo. If an aspect between the Moon and Mars is unavoidable, let it be separating.

Medical Treatment for the Head

If possible, have Mars and Saturn free of hard aspects. Let the Moon be in Aries or Taurus, decreasing in light, in conjunction or aspect with Venus or Jupiter and free of hard aspects. The Sun should not be in any aspect to the Moon.

Medical Treatment for the Nose

Let the Moon be in Cancer, Leo, or Virgo and not aspecting Mars or Saturn and also not in conjunction with a retrograde or weak planet.

Mining

Saturn rules mining. Begin work when Saturn is marked conjunct, trine, or sextile. Mine for gold when the Sun is marked conjunct, trine, or sextile. Mercury rules quicksilver, Venus rules copper, Jupiter rules tin, Saturn rules lead and coal, Uranus rules radioactive elements, Neptune rules oil, the Moon rules water. Mine for these items when the ruling planet is marked conjunct, trine, or sextile.

Move to New Home

If you have a choice, and sometimes you don't, make sure that Mars is not aspecting the Moon. Move on a day favorable to your Sun sign or when the Moon is conjunct, sextile, or trine the Sun.

Mow Lawn

Mow in the first and second quarters (waxing phase) to increase growth and lushness, and in the third and fourth quarters (waning phase) to decrease growth.

Negotiate

When you are choosing a time to negotiate, consider what the meeting is about and what you want to have happen. If it is agreement or compromise between two parties that you desire, have the Moon be in the sign of Libra. When you are making contracts, it is best to have the Moon in the same element. For example, if your concern is communication, then elect a time when the Moon is in an air sign. If, on the other hand, your concern is about possessions, an earth sign would be more appropriate. Fixed signs are unfavorable, with the exception of Leo; so are cardinal signs, except for Capricorn. If you are negotiating the end of something, use the rules that apply to ending habits.

Occupational Training

When you begin training, see that your lunar cycle is favorable that day and that the planet ruling your occupation is marked conjunct or trine.

Paint

Paint buildings during the waning Libra or Aquarius Moon. If the weather is hot, paint when the Moon is in Taurus. If the weather is cold, paint when the Moon is in Leo. Schedule the painting to start in the fourth quarter as the wood is drier and paint will penetrate wood better. Avoid painting around the New Moon, though, as the wood is likely to be damp, making the paint subject to scalding when hot weather hits it. If the temperature is below 70°F, it is not advisable to paint while the Moon is in Cancer, Scorpio, or Pisces as the paint is apt to creep, check, or run.

Party (Host or Attend)

A party timed so the Moon is in Gemini, Leo, Libra, or Sagittarius, with good aspects to Venus and Jupiter, will be fun and well attended. There should be no aspects between the Moon and Mars or Saturn.

Pawn

Do not pawn any article when Jupiter is receiving a square or opposition from Saturn or Mars or when Jupiter is within 17 degrees of the Sun, for you will have little chance to redeem the items.

Pick Mushrooms

Mushrooms, one of the most promising traditional medicines in the world, should be gathered at the Full Moon.

Plant

Root crops, like carrots and potatoes, are best if planted in the sign Taurus or Capricorn. Beans, peas, tomatoes, peppers, and other fruit-bearing plants are best if planted in a sign that supports seed growth. Leaf plants, like lettuce, broccoli, or cauliflower, are best planted when the Moon is in a water sign.

It is recommended that you transplant during a decreasing Moon, when forces are streaming into the lower part of the plant. This helps root growth.

Promotion (Ask For)

Choose a day favorable to your Sun sign. Mercury should be marked conjunct, trine, or sextile. Avoid days when Mars or Saturn is aspected.

Prune

Prune during the third and fourth quarter of a Scorpio Moon to retard growth and to promote better fruit. Prune when the Moon is in cardinal Capricorn to promote healing.

Reconcile with People

If the reconciliation is with a woman, let Venus be strong and well aspected. If elders or superiors are involved, see that Saturn is receiving good aspects; if the reconciliation is between young people or between an older and younger person, see that Mercury is well aspected.

Romance

There is less control of when a romance starts, but romances begun under an increasing Moon are more likely to be permanent or satisfying, while those begun during the decreasing Moon tend to transform the participants. The tone of the relationship can be guessed from the sign the Moon is in. Romances begun with the Moon in Aries may be impulsive. Those begun in Capricorn will take greater effort to bring to a desirable conclusion, but they may be very rewarding. Good aspects between the Moon and Venus will have a positive influence on the relationship. Avoid unfavorable aspects to Mars, Uranus, and Pluto. A decreasing Moon, particularly the fourth quarter, facilitates ending a relationship and causes the least pain.

Roof a Building

Begin roofing a building during the third or fourth quarter, when the Moon is in Aries or Aquarius. Shingles laid during the New Moon have a tendency to curl at the edges.

Sauerkraut

The best-tasting sauerkraut is made just after the Full Moon in the fruitful signs of Cancer, Scorpio, or Pisces.

Select a Child's Sex

Count from the last day of menstruation to the first day of the next cycle and divide the interval between the two dates in half. Pregnancy in the first half produces females, but copulation should take place with the Moon in a feminine sign. Pregnancy in the latter half, up to three days before the beginning of menstruation, produces males, but copulation should take place with the Moon in a masculine sign. The three-day period before the next period again produces females.

Sell or Canvass

Begin these activities during a day favorable to your Sun sign. Otherwise, sell on days when Jupiter, Mercury, or Mars is trine, sextile, or conjunct the Moon. Avoid days when Saturn is square or opposing the Moon, for that always hinders business and causes discord. If the Moon is passing from the first quarter to full, it is best to have the Moon swift in motion and in good aspect with Venus and/or Jupiter.

Sign Papers

Sign contracts or agreements when the Moon is increasing in a fruitful sign and on a day when the Moon is making favorable aspects to Mercury. Avoid days when Mars, Saturn, or Neptune are square or opposite the Moon.

Spray and Weed

Spray pests and weeds during the fourth quarter when the Moon is in the barren sign Leo or Aquarius and making favorable aspects to Pluto. Weed during a waning Moon in a barren sign.

Staff (Fire)

Have the Moon in the third or fourth quarter, but not full. The Moon should not be square any planets.

Staff (Hire)

The Moon should be in the first or second quarter, and preferably in the sign of Gemini or Virgo. The Moon should be conjunct, trine, or sextile Mercury or Jupiter.

Stocks (Buy)

The Moon should be in Taurus or Capricorn, and there should be a sextile or trine to Jupiter or Saturn.

Surgical Procedures

Blood flow, like ocean tides, appears to be related to Moon phases. To reduce hemorrhage after a surgery, schedule it within one week before or after a New Moon. Schedule surgery to occur during the increase of the Moon if possible, as wounds heal better and vitality is greater than during the decrease of the Moon. Avoid surgery within one week before or after the Full Moon. Select a date when the Moon is past the sign governing the part of the body involved in the operation. For example, abdominal operations should be done when the Moon is in Sagittarius, Capricorn, or Aquarius. The further removed the Moon sign is from the sign ruling the afflicted part of the body, the better.

For successful operations, avoid times when the Moon is applying to any aspect of Mars. (This tends to promote inflammation and complications.) See the Lunar Aspectarian on odd pages 137–159 to find days with negative Mars aspects and positive

Venus and Jupiter aspects. Never operate with the Moon in the same sign as a person's Sun sign or Ascendant. Let the Moon be in a fixed sign and avoid square or opposing aspects. The Moon should not be void-of-course. Cosmetic surgery should be done in the increase of the Moon, when the Moon is not square or in opposition to Mars. Avoid days when the Moon is square or opposing Saturn or the Sun.

Travel (Air)

Start long trips when the Moon is making favorable aspects to the Sun For enjoyment, aspects to Jupiter are preferable; for visiting, look for favorable aspects to Mercury. To prevent accidents, avoid squares or oppositions to Mars, Saturn, Uranus, or Pluto. Choose a day when the Moon is in Sagittarius or Gemini and well aspected to Mercury, Jupiter, or Uranus. Avoid adverse aspects of Mars, Saturn, or Uranus.

Visit

On setting out to visit a person, let the Moon be in aspect with any retrograde planet, for this ensures that the person you're visiting will be at home. If you desire to stay a long time in a place, let the Moon be in good aspect to Saturn. If you desire to leave the place quickly, let the Moon be in a cardinal sign.

Wean Children

To wean a child successfully, do so when the Moon is in Sagittarius, Capricorn, Aquarius, or Pisces—signs that do not rule vital human organs. By observing this astrological rule, much trouble for parents and child may be avoided.

Weight (Reduce)

If you want to lose weight, the best time to get started is when the Moon is in the third or fourth quarter and in the barren sign of Virgo. Review the section on How to Use the Moon Tables and

Lunar Aspectarian beginning on page 136 to help you select a date that is favorable to begin your weight-loss program.

Wine and Drink Other Than Beer

Start brewing when the Moon is in Pisces or Taurus. Sextiles or trines to Venus are favorable, but avoid aspects to Mars or Saturn.

Write

Write for pleasure or publication when the Moon is in Gemini. Mercury should be making favorable aspects to Uranus and Neptune.

How to Use the Moon Tables and Lunar Aspectarian

Timing activities is one of the most important things you can do to ensure success. In many Eastern countries, timing by the planets is so important that practically no event takes place without first setting up a chart for it. Weddings have occurred in the middle of the night because the influences were at the best then. You may not want to take it that far, but you can still make use of the influences of the Moon whenever possible. It's easy and it works!

Llewellyn's Moon Sign Book has information to help you plan just about any activity: weddings, fishing, making purchases, cutting your hair, traveling, and more. We provide the guidelines you need to pick the best day out of the several from which you have to choose. The Moon Tables are the *Moon Sign Book's* primary method for choosing dates. Following are instructions, examples, and directions on how to read the Moon Tables. More advanced information on using the tables containing the Lunar Aspectarian and favorable and unfavorable days (found on odd-numbered pages opposite the Moon Tables), Moon void-of-course and retrograde information to choose the dates best for you is also included.

The Five Basic Steps

Step 1: Directions for Choosing Dates

Look up the directions for choosing dates for the activity that you wish to begin, then go to step 2.

Step 2: Check the Moon Tables

You'll find two tables for each month of the year beginning on page 136. The Moon Tables (on the left-hand pages) include the day, date, and sign the Moon is in; the element and nature of the sign; the Moon's phase; and when it changes sign or phase. If there is a time listed after a date, that time is the time when the Moon moves into that zodiac sign. Until then, the Moon is considered to be in the sign for the previous day.

The abbreviation Full signifies Full Moon and New signifies New Moon. The times listed with dates indicate when the Moon changes sign. The times listed after the phase indicate when the Moon changes phase.

Turn to the month you would like to begin your activity. You will be using the Moon's sign and phase information most often when you begin choosing your own dates. Remember to convert the time to your own time zone.

When you find dates that meet the criteria for the correct Moon phase and sign for your activity, you may have completed the process. For certain simple activities, such as getting a haircut, the phase and sign information is all that is needed. If the directions for your activity include information on certain lunar aspects, however, you should consult the Lunar Aspectarian. An example of this would be if the directions told you not to perform a certain activity when the Moon is square (Q) Jupiter.

Step 3: Check the Lunar Aspectarian

On the pages opposite the Moon Tables you will find tables containing the Lunar Aspectarian and Favorable and Unfavorable Days. The Lunar Aspectarian gives the aspects (or angles) of the Moon to other planets. Some aspects are favorable, while others are not. To use the Lunar Aspectarian, find the planet that the directions list as favorable for your activity, and run down the column to the date desired. For example, you should avoid aspects to Mars if you are planning surgery. So you would look for Mars across the top and then run down that column looking for days where there are no aspects to Mars (as signified by empty boxes). If you want to find a **favorable** aspect (sextile (X) or trine (T)) to Mercury, run your finger down the column under Mercury until you find an X or T. **Adverse** aspects to planets are squares (Q) or oppositions (O). A conjunction (C) is sometimes beneficial, sometimes not, depending on the activity or planets involved.

Step 4: Favorable and Unfavorable Days

The tables listing favorable and unfavorable days are helpful when you want to choose your personal best dates because your Sun sign is taken into consideration. The twelve Sun signs are listed on the right side of the tables. Once you have determined which days meet your criteria for phase, sign, and aspects, you can determine whether or not those days are positive for you by checking the favorable and unfavorable days for your Sun sign.

To find out if a day is positive for you, find your Sun sign and then look down the column. If it is marked F, it is very favorable. The Moon is in the same sign as your Sun on a favorable day. If it is marked f, it is slightly favorable; U is very unfavorable; and u means slightly unfavorable. A day marked very unfavorable (U) indicates that the Moon is in the sign opposing your Sun

Once you have selected good dates for the activity you are about to begin, you can go straight to "Using What You've Learned," beginning on the next page. To learn how to fine-tune your selections even further, read on.

Step 5: Void-of-Course Moon and Retrogrades

This last step is perhaps the most advanced portion of the procedure. It is generally considered poor timing to make decisions, sign important papers, or start special activities during a Moon void-of-course period or during a Mercury retrograde. Once you have chosen the best date for your activity based on steps one through four, you can check the Void-of-Course tables, beginning on page 76, to find out if any of the dates you have chosen have void periods.

The Moon is said to be void-of-course after it has made its last aspect to a planet within a particular sign, but before it has moved into the next sign. Put simply, the Moon is "resting" during the void-of-course period, so activities initiated at this time generally don't come to fruition. You will notice that there are many void periods during the year, and it is nearly impossible to avoid all of them. Some people choose to ignore these altogether and do not take them into consideration when planning activities.

Next, you can check the Retrograde Planets tables on page 160 to see what planets are retrograde during your chosen date(s).

A planet is said to be retrograde when it appears to move backward in the sky as viewed from Earth. Generally, the farther a planet is away from the Sun, the longer it can stay retrograde. Some planets will retrograde for several months at a time. Avoiding retrogrades is not as important in lunar planning as avoiding the Moon void-of-course, with the exception of the planet Mercury.

Mercury rules thought and communication, so it is advisable not to sign important papers, initiate important business or legal work, or make crucial decisions during these times. As with the Moon void-of-course, it is difficult to avoid all planetary retrogrades when beginning events, and you may choose to ignore this step of the process. Following are some examples using some or all of the steps outlined above.

Using What You've Learned

Let's say it's a new year and you want to have your hair cut. It's thin and you would like it to look fuller, so you find the directions for hair care and you see that for thicker hair you should cut hair while the Moon is Full and in the sign of Taurus, Cancer, or Leo. You should avoid the Moon in Aries, Gemini, or Virgo. Look at the January Moon Table on page 136. You see that the Full Moon is on January 13 at 5:27 pm. The Moon is in Cancer on January 25 and moves into Virgo on January 16 at 11:46 am, so January 13–15 meet both the phase and sign criteria.

Let's move on to a more difficult example using the sign and phase of the Moon. You want to buy a permanent home. After checking the instructions for purchasing a house: "Home (Buy New)" on page 118, you see that you should buy a home when the Moon is in Taurus, Cancer, or Leo. You need to get a loan, so you should also look under "Loan (Ask For)" on page 119. Here it says that the third and fourth quarters favor the borrower (you). You are going to buy the house in October, so go to page 154. The Moon is in the third quarter Oct 6–12 and fourth quarter Oct 13–20. The Moon is in Leo at 6:47 am on Oct 14 until Oct 16 at 2:06 pm; in Taurus from Oct 8 at 1:12 am until Oct 10 at 1:12 am; in Cancer from 2:37 am on Oct 12 to Oct 14 at 6:47 am. The best days for obtaining a loan would be October 8–9 and 12–15.

Just match up the best sign and phase (quarter) to come up with the best date. With all activities, be sure to check the favorable and unfavorable days for your Sun sign in the table adjoining the Lunar Aspectarian. If there is a choice between several dates, pick the one most favorable for you. Because buying a home is an important business decision, you may also wish to see if the Moon is void or if Mercury is retrograde during these dates.

Now let's look at an example that uses signs, phases, and aspects. Our example is starting new home construction. We will use the month of February. Look under "Build (Start Foundation)" on page 110 and you'll see that the Moon should be in the first quarter of a fixed sign—Leo, Taurus, Aquarius, or Scorpio. You should select a time when the Moon is making favorable aspects to Saturn. (Conjunctions are usually considered unfavorable if they are to Mars, Saturn, or Neptune.) Look in the February Moon Table on page 138. You will see that the Moon is in the first quarter Feb 1–4 and Feb 27–28 and in Taurus from 10:33 pm on Feb 3 until 1:44 am on Feb 6. Now, look to the February Lunar Aspectarian. We see that there are no favorable dates to Saturn the 1–4; therefore, February does not have any ideal dates to start a foundation.

A Note about Time and Time Zones

All tables in the Moon Sign Book use Eastern Time. You must calculate the difference between your time zone and the Eastern Time Zone. The sign the Moon is in at midnight is the sign shown in the Aspectarian and Favorable and Unfavorable Days tables.

How Does the Time Matter?

Due to the three-hour time difference between the East and West Coasts of the United States, those of you living on the East Coast may be, for example, under the influence of a Virgo Moon, while those of you living on the West Coast will still have a Leo Moon influence.

We follow a commonly held belief among astrologers: whatever sign the Moon is in at the start of a day—12:00 am Eastern Time— is considered the dominant influence of the day. That sign is indicated in the Moon Tables. If the date you select for an activity shows the Moon changing signs, you can decide how important the sign change may be for your specific election and adjust your election date and time accordingly.

Use Common Sense

Some activities depend on outside factors. Obviously, you can't go out and plant when there is a foot of snow on the ground. You should adjust to the conditions at hand. If the weather was bad during the first quarter, when it was best to plant crops, do it during the second quarter while the Moon is in a fruitful sign. If the Moon is not in a fruitful sign during the first or second quarter, choose a day when it is in a semi-fruitful sign. The best advice is to choose either the sign or phase that is most favorable, when the two don't coincide.

To Summarize

First, look up the activity under the proper heading, then look for the information given in the tables. Choose the best date considering the number of positive factors in effect. If most of the dates are favorable, there is no problem choosing the one that will fit your schedule. However, if there aren't any really good dates, pick the ones with the least number of negative influences. Please keep in mind that the information found here applies in the broadest sense to the events you want to plan or are considering. To be the most effective, when you use electional astrology, you should also consider your own birth chart in relation to a chart drawn for the time or times you have under consideration. The best advice we can offer you is: read the entire introduction to each section.

January Moon Table

Date	Sign	Element	Nature	Phase
1 Wed 5:50 am	Aquarius	Air	Barren	1st
2 Thu	Aquarius	Air	Barren	1st
3 Fri 10:21 am	Pisces	Water	Fruitful	1st
4 Sat	Pisces	Water	Fruitful	1st
5 Sun 2:01 pm	Aries	Fire	Barren	1st
6 Mon	Aries	Fire	Barren	2nd 6:56 pm
7 Tue 5:11 pm	Taurus	Earth	Semi-fruitful	2nd
8 Wed	Taurus	Earth	Semi-fruitful	2nd
9 Thu 8:07 pm	Gemini	Air	Barren	2nd
10 Fri	Gemini	Air	Barren	2nd
11 Sat 11:24 pm	Cancer	Water	Fruitful	2nd
12 Sun	Cancer	Water	Fruitful	2nd
13 Mon	Cancer	Water	Fruitful	Full 5:27 pm
14 Tue 4:12 am	Leo	Fire	Barren	3rd
15 Wed	Leo	Fire	Barren	3rd
16 Thu 11:46 am	Virgo	Earth	Barren	3rd
17 Fri	Virgo	Earth	Barren	3rd
18 Sat 10:33 pm	Libra	Air	Semi-fruitful	3rd
19 Sun	Libra	Air	Semi-fruitful	3rd
20 Mon	Libra	Air	Semi-fruitful	3rd
21 Tue 11:20 am	Scorpio	Water	Fruitful	4th 3:31 pm
22 Wed	Scorpio	Water	Fruitful	4th
23 Thu 11:29 pm	Sagittarius	Fire	Barren	4th
24 Fri	Sagittarius	Fire	Barren	4th
25 Sat	Sagittarius	Fire	Barren	4th
26 Sun 8:43 am	Capricorn	Earth	Semi-fruitful	4th
27 Mon	Capricorn	Earth	Semi-fruitful	4th
28 Tue 2:31 pm	Aquarius	Air	Barren	4th
29 Wed	Aquarius	Air	Barren	New 7:36 am
30 Thu 5:52 pm	Pisces	Water	Fruitful	1st
31 Fri	Pisces	Water	Fruitful	1st

January Aspectarian/Favorable & Unfavorable Days

Date	Sun	Mercury	Venus	Mars	Jupiter	Saturn	Uranus	Neptune	Pluto
1				O				X	C
2		X			T		Q		
3			C						
4	X				Q	C			
5		Q		T			X	C	X
6	Q				X				
7		T		Q					Q
8			X			X			
9	T			X			C	X	T
10			Q		C	Q			
11								Q	
12		O	T						
13	O			C		T	X	T	
14									O
15					X		Q		
16									
17		T	O		Q	O			
18	T			X			T	O	
19					T				T
20		Q		Q					
21	Q								Q
22						T			
23		X	T	T			O	T	
24	X				O				X
25			Q			Q			
26								Q	
27				O		X			
28		C	X				T	X	C
29	C				T				
30								Q	
31					Q	C			

Date	Aries	Taurus	Gemini	Cancer	Leo	Virgo	Libra	Scorpio	Sagittarius	Capricorn	Aquarius	Pisces
1	u	f		U		f	u	f		F		f
2	f	u	f		U		f	u	f		F	
3	f	u	f		U		f	u	f		F	
4		f	u	f		U		f	u	f		F
5		f	u	f		U		f	u	f		F
6	F		f	u	f		U		f	u	f	
7	F		f	u	f		U		f	u	f	
8		F		f	u	f		U		f	u	f
9		F		f	u	f		U		f	u	f
10	f		F		f	u	f		U		f	u
11	f		F		f	u	f		U		f	u
12	u	f		F		f	u	f		U		f
13	u	f		F		f	u	f		U		f
14	u	f		F		f	u	f		U		f
15	f	u	f		F		f	u	f		U	
16	f	u	f		F		f	u	f		U	
17		f	u	f		F		f	u	f		U
18		f	u	f		F		f	u	f		U
19	U		f	u	f		F		f	u	f	
20	U		f	u	f		F		f	u	f	
21	U		f	u	f		F		f	u	f	
22		U		f	u	f		F		f	u	f
23		U		f	u	f		F		f	u	f
24	f		U		f	u	f		F		f	u
25	f		U		f	u	f		F		f	u
26	f		U		f	u	f		F		f	u
27	u	f		U		f	u	f		F		f
28	u	f		U		f	u	f		F		f
29	f	u	f		U		f	u	f		F	
30	f	u	f		U		f	u	f		F	
31		f	u	f		U		f	u	f		F

February Moon Table

Date	Sign	Element	Nature	Phase
1 Sat 8:10 pm	Aries	Fire	Barren	1st
2 Sun	Aries	Fire	Barren	1st
3 Mon 10:33 pm	Taurus	Earth	Semi-fruitful	1st
4 Tue	Taurus	Earth	Semi-fruitful	1st
5 Wed	Taurus	Earth	Semi-fruitful	2nd 3:02 am
6 Thu 1:44 am	Gemini	Air	Barren	2nd
7 Fri	Gemini	Air	Barren	2nd
8 Sat 6:04 am	Cancer	Water	Fruitful	2nd
9 Sun	Cancer	Water	Fruitful	2nd
10 Mon 12:01 pm	Leo	Fire	Barren	2nd
11 Tue	Leo	Fire	Barren	2nd
12 Wed 8:07 pm	Virgo	Earth	Barren	Full 8:53 am
13 Thu	Virgo	Earth	Barren	3rd
14 Fri	Virgo	Earth	Barren	3rd
15 Sat 6:45 am	Libra	Air	Semi-fruitful	3rd
16 Sun	Libra	Air	Semi-fruitful	3rd
17 Mon 7:19 pm	Scorpio	Water	Fruitful	3rd
18 Tue	Scorpio	Water	Fruitful	3rd
19 Wed	Scorpio	Water	Fruitful	3rd
20 Thu 7:55 am	Sagittarius	Fire	Barren	4th 12:33 pm
21 Fri	Sagittarius	Fire	Barren	4th
22 Sat 6:09 pm	Capricorn	Earth	Semi-fruitful	4th
23 Sun	Capricorn	Earth	Semi-fruitful	4th
24 Mon	Capricorn	Earth	Semi-fruitful	4th
25 Tue 12:40 am	Aquarius	Air	Barren	4th
26 Wed	Aquarius	Air	Barren	4th
27 Thu 3:46 am	Pisces	Water	Fruitful	New 7:45 pm
28 Fri	Pisces	Water	Fruitful	1st

February Aspectarian/Favorable & Unfavorable Days

Date	Sun	Mercury	Venus	Mars	Jupiter	Saturn	Uranus	Neptune	Pluto
1			C	T			X	C	X
2	X	X			X				
3				Q					
4		Q							Q
5	Q			X		X	C	X	
6			X		C				T
7	T	T				Q			
8			Q					Q	
9			C		T	X			
10			T					T	O
11					X				
12	O	O					Q		
13					Q				
14				X		O	T		
15			O					O	T
16				Q	T				
17	T								
18		T							Q
19				T		T	O		
20	Q							T	X
21		Q	T		O	Q			
22								Q	
23	X		Q						
24		X		O		X	T	X	
25			X		T				C
26							Q		
27	C				Q				
28		C		T		C	X		

Date	Aries	Taurus	Gemini	Cancer	Leo	Virgo	Libra	Scorpio	Sagittarius	Capricorn	Aquarius	Pisces
1		f	u	f		U		f	u	f		F
2	F		f	u	f		U		f	u	f	
3	F		f	u	f		U		f	u	f	
4		F		f	u	f		U		f	u	f
5		F		f	u	f		U		f	u	f
6	f		F		f	u	f		U		f	u
7	f		F		f	u	f		U		f	u
8	f		F		f	u	f		U		f	u
9	u	f		F		f	u	f		U		f
10	u	f		F		f	u	f		U		f
11	f	u	f		F		f	u	f		U	
12	f	u	f		F		f	u	f		U	
13		f	u	f		F		f	u	f		U
14		f	u	f		F		f	u	f		U
15		f	u	f		F		f	u	f		U
16	U		f	u	f		F		f	u	f	
17	U		f	u	f		F		f	u	f	
18		U		f	u	f		F		f	u	f
19		U		f	u	f		F		f	u	f
20		U		f	u	f		F		f	u	f
21	f		U		f	u	f		F		f	u
22	f		U		f	u	f		F		f	u
23	u	f		U		f	u	f		F		f
24	u	f		U		f	u	f		F		f
25	f	u	f		U		f	u	f		F	
26	f	u	f		U		f	u	f		F	
27	f	u	f		U		f	u	f		F	
28		f	u	f		U		f	u	f		F

March Moon Table

Date	Sign	Element	Nature	Phase
1 Sat 4:52 am	Aries	Fire	Barren	1st
2 Sun	Aries	Fire	Barren	1st
3 Mon 5:37 am	Taurus	Earth	Semi-fruitful	1st
4 Tue	Taurus	Earth	Semi-fruitful	1st
5 Wed 7:29 am	Gemini	Air	Barren	1st
6 Thu	Gemini	Air	Barren	2nd 11:32 am
7 Fri 11:29 am	Cancer	Water	Fruitful	2nd
8 Sat	Cancer	Water	Fruitful	2nd
9 Sun 6:59 pm	Leo	Fire	Barren	2nd
10 Mon	Leo	Fire	Barren	2nd
11 Tue	Leo	Fire	Barren	2nd
12 Wed 3:56 am	Virgo	Earth	Barren	2nd
13 Thu	Virgo	Earth	Barren	2nd
14 Fri 2:59 pm	Libra	Air	Semi-fruitful	Full 2:55 am
15 Sat	Libra	Air	Semi-fruitful	3rd
16 Sun	Libra	Air	Semi-fruitful	3rd
17 Mon 3:30 am	Scorpio	Water	Fruitful	3rd
18 Tue	Scorpio	Water	Fruitful	3rd
19 Wed 4:17 pm	Sagittarius	Fire	Barren	3rd
20 Thu	Sagittarius	Fire	Barren	3rd
21 Fri	Sagittarius	Fire	Barren	3rd
22 Sat 3:29 am	Capricorn	Earth	Semi-fruitful	4th 7:29 am
23 Sun	Capricorn	Earth	Semi-fruitful	4th
24 Mon 11:25 am	Aquarius	Air	Barren	4th
25 Tue	Aquarius	Air	Barren	4th
26 Wed 3:31 pm	Pisces	Water	Fruitful	4th
27 Thu	Pisces	Water	Fruitful	4th
28 Fri 4:36 pm	Aries	Fire	Barren	4th
29 Sat	Aries	Fire	Barren	New 6:58 am
30 Sun 4:16 pm	Taurus	Earth	Semi-fruitful	1st
31 Mon	Taurus	Earth	Semi-fruitful	1st

March Aspectarian/Favorable & Unfavorable Days

Date	Sun	Mercury	Venus	Mars	Jupiter	Saturn	Uranus	Neptune	Pluto
1			C					C	X
2				Q	X				
3									Q
4	X			X		X	C		
5		X						X	T
6	Q		X		C	Q			
7		Q						Q	
8	T		Q	C					
9						T	X	T	
10		T	T		X				O
11							Q		
12									
13				X	Q	O			
14	O						T	O	T
15		O	O		T				
16				Q					
17									Q
18					T				
19	T					T	O	T	X
20		T	T		O				
21						Q			
22	Q	Q	Q					Q	
23				O		X			
24	X	X	X				T	X	C
25						T			
26							Q		
27					Q				
28		C	C	T		C	X	C	X
29	C				X				
30				Q					Q
31									

Date	Aries	Taurus	Gemini	Cancer	Leo	Virgo	Libra	Scorpio	Sagittarius	Capricorn	Aquarius	Pisces
1		f	u	f		U		f	u	f		F
2	F		f	u	f		U		f	u	f	
3	F		f	u	f		U		f	u	f	
4		F		f	u	f		U		f	u	f
5		F		f	u	f		U		f	u	f
6	f		F		f	u	f		U		f	u
7	f		F		f	u	f		U		f	u
8	u	f		F		f	u	f		U		f
9	u	f		F		f	u	f		U		f
10	f	u	f		F		f	u	f		U	
11	f	u	f		F		f	u	f		U	
12	f	u	f		F		f	u	f		U	
13		f	u	f		F		f	u	f		U
14		f	u	f		F		f	u	f		U
15	U		f	u	f		F		f	u	f	
16	U		f	u	f		F		f	u	f	
17	U		f	u	f		F		f	u	f	
18		U		f	u	f		F		f	u	f
19		U		f	u	f		F		f	u	f
20	f		U		f	u	f		F		f	u
21	f		U		f	u	f		F		f	u
22	f		U		f	u	f		F		f	u
23	u	f		U		f	u	f		F		f
24	u	f		U		f	u	f		F		f
25	f	u	f		U		f	u	f		F	
26	f	u	f		U		f	u	f		F	
27		f	u	f		U		f	u	f		F
28		f	u	f		U		f	u	f		F
29	F		f	u	f		U		f	u	f	
30	F		f	u	f		U		f	u	f	
31		F		f	u	f		U		f	u	f

April Moon Table

Date	Sign	Element	Nature	Phase
1 Tue 4:26 pm	Gemini	Air	Barren	1st
2 Wed	Gemini	Air	Barren	1st
3 Thu 6:50 pm	Cancer	Water	Fruitful	1st
4 Fri	Cancer	Water	Fruitful	2nd 10:15 pm
5 Sat	Cancer	Water	Fruitful	2nd
6 Sun 12:34 am	Leo	Fire	Barren	2nd
7 Mon	Leo	Fire	Barren	2nd
8 Tue 9:40 am	Virgo	Earth	Barren	2nd
9 Wed	Virgo	Earth	Barren	2nd
10 Thu 9:12 pm	Libra	Air	Semi-fruitful	2nd
11 Fri	Libra	Air	Semi-fruitful	2nd
12 Sat	Libra	Air	Semi-fruitful	Full 8:22 pm
13 Sun 9:54 am	Scorpio	Water	Fruitful	3rd
14 Mon	Scorpio	Water	Fruitful	3rd
15 Tue 10:37 pm	Sagittarius	Fire	Barren	3rd
16 Wed	Sagittarius	Fire	Barren	3rd
17 Thu	Sagittarius	Fire	Barren	3rd
18 Fri 10:12 am	Capricorn	Earth	Semi-fruitful	3rd
19 Sat	Capricorn	Earth	Semi-fruitful	3rd
20 Sun 7:22 pm	Aquarius	Air	Barren	4th 9:36 pm
21 Mon	Aquarius	Air	Barren	4th
22 Tue	Aquarius	Air	Barren	4th
23 Wed 1:07 am	Pisces	Water	Fruitful	4th
24 Thu	Pisces	Water	Fruitful	4th
25 Fri 3:24 am	Aries	Fire	Barren	4th
26 Sat	Aries	Fire	Barren	4th
27 Sun 3:17 am	Taurus	Earth	Semi-fruitful	New 3:31 pm
28 Mon	Taurus	Earth	Semi-fruitful	1st
29 Tue 2:34 am	Gemini	Air	Barren	1st
30 Wed	Gemini	Air	Barren	1st

April Aspectarian/Favorable & Unfavorable Days

Date	Sun	Mercury	Venus	Mars	Jupiter	Saturn	Uranus	Neptune	Pluto
1		X	X	X		X	C	X	T
2	X				C				
3		Q	Q			Q		Q	
4	Q								
5		T	T	C		T	X		
6								T	O
7	T				X				
8							Q		
9					Q				
10		O	O	X		O	T	O	
11									T
12	O				T				
13				Q					Q
14									
15		T	T	T		T	O	T	
16									X
17					O				
18	T	Q	Q			Q		Q	
19									
20	Q		X	O		X	T	X	
21		X							C
22					T		Q		
23	X								
24			C		Q	C	X		
25		C		T				C	X
26					X				
27	C			Q					Q
28						X	C		
29			X	X				X	T
30		X			C	Q			

Date	Aries	Taurus	Gemini	Cancer	Leo	Virgo	Libra	Scorpio	Sagittarius	Capricorn	Aquarius	Pisces
1		F		f	u	f		U		f	u	f
2	f		F		f	u	f		U		f	u
3	f		F		f	u	f		U		f	u
4	u	f		F		f	u	f		U		f
5	u	f		F		f	u	f		U		f
6	f	u	f		F		f	u	f		U	
7	f	u	f		F		f	u	f		U	
8	f	u	f		F		f	u	f		U	
9		f	u	f		F		f	u	f		U
10		f	u	f		F		f	u	f		U
11	U		f	u	f		F		f	u	f	
12	U		f	u	f		F		f	u	f	
13	U		f	u	f		F		f	u	f	
14		U		f	u	f		F		f	u	f
15		U		f	u	f		F		f	u	f
16	f		U		f	u	f		F		f	u
17	f		U		f	u	f		F		f	u
18	f		U		f	u	f		F		f	u
19	u	f		U		f	u	f		F		f
20	u	f		U		f	u	f		F		f
21	f	u	f		U		f	u	f		F	
22	f	u	f		U		f	u	f		F	
23		f	u	f		U		f	u	f		F
24		f	u	f		U		f	u	f		F
25		f	u	f		U		f	u	f		F
26	F		f	u	f		U		f	u	f	
27	F		f	u	f		U		f	u	f	
28		F		f	u	f		U		f	u	f
29	f		F		f	u	f		U		f	u
30	f		F		f	u	f		U		f	u

May Moon Table

Date	Sign	Element	Nature	Phase
1 Thu 3:23 am	Cancer	Water	Fruitful	1st
2 Fri	Cancer	Water	Fruitful	1st
3 Sat 7:29 am	Leo	Fire	Barren	1st
4 Sun	Leo	Fire	Barren	2nd 9:52 am
5 Mon 3:40 pm	Virgo	Earth	Barren	2nd
6 Tue	Virgo	Earth	Barren	2nd
7 Wed	Virgo	Earth	Barren	2nd
8 Thu 3:06 am	Libra	Air	Semi-fruitful	2nd
9 Fri	Libra	Air	Semi-fruitful	2nd
10 Sat 3:58 pm	Scorpio	Water	Fruitful	2nd
11 Sun	Scorpio	Water	Fruitful	2nd
12 Mon	Scorpio	Water	Fruitful	Full 12:56 pm
13 Tue 4:35 am	Sagittarius	Fire	Barren	3rd
14 Wed	Sagittarius	Fire	Barren	3rd
15 Thu 3:58 pm	Capricorn	Earth	Semi-fruitful	3rd
16 Fri	Capricorn	Earth	Semi-fruitful	3rd
17 Sat	Capricorn	Earth	Semi-fruitful	3rd
18 Sun 1:29 am	Aquarius	Air	Barren	3rd
19 Mon	Aquarius	Air	Barren	3rd
20 Tue 8:28 am	Pisces	Water	Fruitful	4th 7:59 am
21 Wed	Pisces	Water	Fruitful	4th
22 Thu 12:26 pm	Aries	Fire	Barren	4th
23 Fri	Aries	Fire	Barren	4th
24 Sat 1:38 pm	Taurus	Earth	Semi-fruitful	4th
25 Sun	Taurus	Earth	Semi-fruitful	4th
26 Mon 1:21 pm	Gemini	Air	Barren	New 11:02 pm
27 Tue	Gemini	Air	Barren	1st
28 Wed 1:33 pm	Cancer	Water	Fruitful	1st
29 Thu	Cancer	Water	Fruitful	1st
30 Fri 4:17 pm	Leo	Fire	Barren	1st
31 Sat	Leo	Fire	Barren	1st

May Aspectarian/Favorable & Unfavorable Days

Date	Sun	Mercury	Venus	Mars	Jupiter	Saturn	Uranus	Neptune	Pluto
1	X		Q					Q	
2		Q							
3			T	C		T	X	T	O
4	Q	T							
5					X		Q		
6									
7	T				Q		T		
8			O	X		O		O	T
9									
10		O			T				Q
11			Q						
12	O						O		
13			T			T		T	X
14			T						
15					O	Q		Q	
16		T	Q						
17	T							T	
18						X		X	C
19		Q	X	O					
20	Q				T		Q		
21		X							
22	X				Q	C	X	C	X
23			C	T					
24				X					Q
25				Q					
26	C	C				X	C	X	T
27			X	X					
28						C	Q		Q
29									
30			Q			T	X	T	O
31	X	X							

Date	Aries	Taurus	Gemini	Cancer	Leo	Virgo	Libra	Scorpio	Sagittarius	Capricorn	Aquarius	Pisces
1	f		F		f	u	f		U		f	u
2	u	f		F		f	u	f		U		f
3	u	f		F		f	u	f		U		f
4	f	u	f		F		f	u	f		U	
5	f	u	f		F		f	u	f		U	
6		f	u	f		F		f	u	f		U
7		f	u	f		F		f	u	f		U
8		f	u	f		F		f	u	f		U
9	U		f	u	f		F		f	u	f	
10	U		f	u	f		F		f	u	f	
11		U		f	u	f		F		f	u	f
12		U		f	u	f		F		f	u	f
13		U		f	u	f		F		f	u	f
14	f		U		f	u	f		F		f	u
15	f		U		f	u	f		F		f	u
16	u	f		U		f	u	f		F		f
17	u	f		U		f	u	f		F		f
18	f	u	f		U		f	u	f		F	
19	f	u	f		U		f	u	f		F	
20	f	u	f		U		f	u	f		F	
21		f	u	f		U		f	u	f		F
22		f	u	f		U		f	u	f		F
23	F		f	u	f		U		f	u	f	
24	F		f	u	f		U		f	u	f	
25		F		f	u	f		U		f	u	f
26		F		f	u	f		U		f	u	f
27	f		F		f	u	f		U		f	u
28	f		F		f	u	f		U		f	u
29	u	f		F		f	u	f		U		f
30	u	f		F		f	u	f		U		f
31	f	u	f		F		f	u	f		U	

June Moon Table

Date	Sign	Element	Nature	Phase
1 Sun 11:00 pm	Virgo	Earth	Barren	1st
2 Mon	Virgo	Earth	Barren	2nd 11:41 pm
3 Tue	Virgo	Earth	Barren	2nd
4 Wed 9:38 am	Libra	Air	Semi-fruitful	2nd
5 Thu	Libra	Air	Semi-fruitful	2nd
6 Fri 10:23 pm	Scorpio	Water	Fruitful	2nd
7 Sat	Scorpio	Water	Fruitful	2nd
8 Sun	Scorpio	Water	Fruitful	2nd
9 Mon 10:56 am	Sagittarius	Fire	Barren	2nd
10 Tue	Sagittarius	Fire	Barren	2nd
11 Wed 9:55 pm	Capricorn	Earth	Semi-fruitful	Full 3:44 am
12 Thu	Capricorn	Earth	Semi-fruitful	3rd
13 Fri	Capricorn	Earth	Semi-fruitful	3rd
14 Sat 7:00 am	Aquarius	Air	Barren	3rd
15 Sun	Aquarius	Air	Barren	3rd
16 Mon 2:09 pm	Pisces	Water	Fruitful	3rd
17 Tue	Pisces	Water	Fruitful	3rd
18 Wed 7:08 pm	Aries	Fire	Barren	4th 3:19 pm
19 Thu	Aries	Fire	Barren	4th
20 Fri 9:53 pm	Taurus	Earth	Semi-fruitful	4th
21 Sat	Taurus	Earth	Semi-fruitful	4th
22 Sun 10:57 pm	Gemini	Air	Barren	4th
23 Mon	Gemini	Air	Barren	4th
24 Tue 11:44 pm	Cancer	Water	Fruitful	4th
25 Wed	Cancer	Water	Fruitful	New 6:32 am
26 Thu	Cancer	Water	Fruitful	1st
27 Fri 2:05 am	Leo	Fire	Barren	1st
28 Sat	Leo	Fire	Barren	1st
29 Sun 7:44 am	Virgo	Earth	Barren	1st
30 Mon	Virgo	Earth	Barren	1st

June Aspectarian/Favorable & Unfavorable Days

Date	Sun	Mercury	Venus	Mars	Jupiter	Saturn	Uranus	Neptune	Pluto
1			T	C	X		Q		
2	Q								
3		Q							
4					Q	O	T	O	T
5	T								
6		T		X	T				
7			O						Q
8									
9				Q		T	O	T	X
10									
11	O			T	O				
12		O	T			Q		Q	
13									
14			Q			X	T	X	C
15									
16	T			O	T		Q		
17		T	X						
18	Q				Q	C	X	C	
19									X
20	X	Q							
21				T	X				Q
22		X	C				C		
23				Q	X		X		T
24									
25	C			X	C	Q		Q	
26			X						
27		C				T	X	T	O
28		Q							
29	X			C	X		Q		
30									

Date	Aries	Taurus	Gemini	Cancer	Leo	Virgo	Libra	Scorpio	Sagittarius	Capricorn	Aquarius	Pisces
1	f	u	f		F		f	u	f		U	
2		f	u	f		F		f	u	f		U
3		f	u	f		F		f	u	f		U
4		f	u	f		F		f	u	f		U
5	U		f	u	f		F		f	u	f	
6	U		f	u	f		F		f	u	f	
7		U		f	u	f		F		f	u	f
8		U		f	u	f		F		f	u	f
9		U		f	u	f		F		f	u	f
10	f		U		f	u	f		F		f	u
11	f		U		f	u	f		F		f	u
12	u	f		U		f	u	f		F		f
13	u	f		U		f	u	f		F		f
14	u	f		U		f	u	f		F		f
15	f	u	f		U		f	u	f		F	
16	f	u	f		U		f	u	f		F	
17		f	u	f		U		f	u	f		F
18		f	u	f		U		f	u	f		F
19	F		f	u	f		U		f	u	f	
20	F		f	u	f		U		f	u	f	
21		F		f	u	f		U		f	u	f
22		F		f	u	f		U		f	u	f
23	f		F		f	u	f		U		f	u
24	f		F		f	u	f		U		f	u
25	u	f		F		f	u	f		U		f
26	u	f		F		f	u	f		U		f
27	f	u	f		F		f	u	f		U	
28	f	u	f		F		f	u	f		U	
29	f	u	f		F		f	u	f		U	
30		f	u	f		F		f	u	f		U

July Moon Table

Date	Sign	Element	Nature	Phase
1 Tue 5:16 pm	Libra	Air	Semi-fruitful	1st
2 Wed	Libra	Air	Semi-fruitful	2nd 3:30 pm
3 Thu	Libra	Air	Semi-fruitful	2nd
4 Fri 5:33 am	Scorpio	Water	Fruitful	2nd
5 Sat	Scorpio	Water	Fruitful	2nd
6 Sun 6:06 pm	Sagittarius	Fire	Barren	2nd
7 Mon	Sagittarius	Fire	Barren	2nd
8 Tue	Sagittarius	Fire	Barren	2nd
9 Wed 4:55 am	Capricorn	Earth	Semi-fruitful	2nd
10 Thu	Capricorn	Earth	Semi-fruitful	Full 4:37 pm
11 Fri 1:21 pm	Aquarius	Air	Barren	3rd
12 Sat	Aquarius	Air	Barren	3rd
13 Sun 7:45 pm	Pisces	Water	Fruitful	3rd
14 Mon	Pisces	Water	Fruitful	3rd
15 Tue	Pisces	Water	Fruitful	3rd
16 Wed 12:32 am	Aries	Fire	Barren	3rd
17 Thu	Aries	Fire	Barren	4th 8:38 pm
18 Fri 3:59 am	Taurus	Earth	Semi-fruitful	4th
19 Sat	Taurus	Earth	Semi-fruitful	4th
20 Sun 6:22 am	Gemini	Air	Barren	4th
21 Mon	Gemini	Air	Barren	4th
22 Tue 8:26 am	Cancer	Water	Fruitful	4th
23 Wed	Cancer	Water	Fruitful	4th
24 Thu 11:28 am	Leo	Fire	Barren	New 3:11 pm
25 Fri	Leo	Fire	Barren	1st
26 Sat 4:55 pm	Virgo	Earth	Barren	1st
27 Sun	Virgo	Earth	Barren	1st
28 Mon	Virgo	Earth	Barren	1st
29 Tue 1:43 am	Libra	Air	Semi-fruitful	1st
30 Wed	Libra	Air	Semi-fruitful	1st
31 Thu 1:25 pm	Scorpio	Water	Fruitful	1st

July Aspectarian/Favorable & Unfavorable Days

Date	Sun	Mercury	Venus	Mars	Jupiter	Saturn	Uranus	Neptune	Pluto
1			T			O	T	O	T
2	Q	X			Q				
3									
4					T				Q
5	T	Q		X					
6			O			T	O	T	
7		T		Q					X
8									
9						O	Q	Q	
10	O			T					
11						X	T	X	C
12		O	T						
13							Q		
14			Q		T				
15	T			O					
16					Q	C	X	C	X
17	Q	T	X						
18				X					Q
19		Q		T					
20	X					X	C	X	T
21		X	C	Q					
22						Q		Q	
23				X	C				
24	C					T	X	T	O
25		C							
26			X				Q		
27					X				
28			Q	C					
29	X	X			Q	O	T	O	T
30									
31			T						Q

Date	Aries	Taurus	Gemini	Cancer	Leo	Virgo	Libra	Scorpio	Sagittarius	Capricorn	Aquarius	Pisces
1		f	u	f		F		f	u	f		U
2	U		f	u	f		F		f	u	f	
3	U		f	u	f		F		f	u	f	
4	U		f	u	f		F		f	u	f	
5		U		f	u	f		F		f	u	f
6		U		f	u	f		F		f	u	f
7	f		U		f	u	f		F		f	u
8	f		U		f	u	f		F		f	u
9	f		U		f	u	f		F		f	u
10	u	f		U		f	u	f		F		f
11	u	f		U		f	u	f		F		f
12	f	u	f		U		f	u	f		F	
13	f	u	f		U		f	u	f		F	
14		f	u	f		U		f	u	f		F
15		f	u	f		U		f	u	f		F
16	F		f	u	f		U		f	u	f	
17	F		f	u	f		U		f	u	f	
18	F		f	u	f		U		f	u	f	
19		F		f	u	f		U		f	u	f
20		F		f	u	f		U		f	u	f
21	f		F		f	u	f		U		f	u
22	f		F		f	u	f		U		f	u
23	u	f		F		f	u	f		U		f
24	u	f		F		f	u	f		U		f
25	f	u	f		F		f	u	f		U	
26	f	u	f		F		f	u	f		U	
27		f	u	f		F		f	u	f		U
28		f	u	f		F		f	u	f		U
29	U		f	u	f		F		f	u	f	
30	U		f	u	f		F		f	u	f	
31	U		f	u	f		F		f	u	f	

August Moon Table

Date	Sign	Element	Nature	Phase
1 Fri	Scorpio	Water	Fruitful	2nd 8:41 am
2 Sat	Scorpio	Water	Fruitful	2nd
3 Sun 2:00 am	Sagittarius	Fire	Barren	2nd
4 Mon	Sagittarius	Fire	Barren	2nd
5 Tue 1:04 pm	Capricorn	Earth	Semi-fruitful	2nd
6 Wed	Capricorn	Earth	Semi-fruitful	2nd
7 Thu 9:18 pm	Aquarius	Air	Barren	2nd
8 Fri	Aquarius	Air	Barren	2nd
9 Sat	Aquarius	Air	Barren	Full 3:55 am
10 Sun 2:50 am	Pisces	Water	Fruitful	3rd
11 Mon	Pisces	Water	Fruitful	3rd
12 Tue 6:33 am	Aries	Fire	Barren	3rd
13 Wed	Aries	Fire	Barren	3rd
14 Thu 9:22 am	Taurus	Earth	Semi-fruitful	3rd
15 Fri	Taurus	Earth	Semi-fruitful	3rd
16 Sat 12:01 pm	Gemini	Air	Barren	4th 1:12 am
17 Sun	Gemini	Air	Barren	4th
18 Mon 3:05 pm	Cancer	Water	Fruitful	4th
19 Tue	Cancer	Water	Fruitful	4th
20 Wed 7:17 pm	Leo	Fire	Barren	4th
21 Thu	Leo	Fire	Barren	4th
22 Fri	Leo	Fire	Barren	4th
23 Sat 1:24 am	Virgo	Earth	Barren	New 2:07 am
24 Sun	Virgo	Earth	Barren	1st
25 Mon 10:08 am	Libra	Air	Semi-fruitful	1st
26 Tue	Libra	Air	Semi-fruitful	1st
27 Wed 9:27 pm	Scorpio	Water	Fruitful	1st
28 Thu	Scorpio	Water	Fruitful	1st
29 Fri	Scorpio	Water	Fruitful	1st
30 Sat 10:04 am	Sagittarius	Fire	Barren	1st
31 Sun	Sagittarius	Fire	Barren	2nd 2:25 am

August Aspectarian/Favorable & Unfavorable Days

Date	Sun	Mercury	Venus	Mars	Jupiter	Saturn	Uranus	Neptune	Pluto
1	Q	Q			T				
2				X					
3		T				T	O	T	X
4	T								
5				Q		Q		Q	
6			O		O				
7				T		X	T		
8		O						X	C
9	O								
10							Q		
11			T		T				
12		T		O		C	X	C	X
13	T		Q		Q				
14		Q							Q
15			X		X				
16	Q	X		T		X	C	X	T
17									
18	X					Q		Q	
19				Q	C				
20			C			T	X	T	O
21		C		X					
22									
23	C						Q		
24					X				
25			X			O	T	O	T
26		X		C	Q				
27									
28	X		Q						Q
29		Q			T				
30			T			T	O	T	X
31	Q			X					

Date	Aries	Taurus	Gemini	Cancer	Leo	Virgo	Libra	Scorpio	Sagittarius	Capricorn	Aquarius	Pisces
1		U		f	u	f		F		f	u	f
2		U		f	u	f		F		f	u	f
3	f		U		f	u	f		F		f	u
4	f		U		f	u	f		F		f	u
5	f		U		f	u	f		F		f	u
6	u	f		U		f	u	f		F		f
7	u	f		U		f	u	f		F		f
8	f	u	f		U		f	u	f		F	
9	f	u	f		U		f	u	f		F	
10		f	u	f		U		f	u	f		F
11		f	u	f		U		f	u	f		F
12		f	u	f		U		f	u	f		F
13	F		f	u	f		U		f	u	f	
14	F		f	u	f		U		f	u	f	
15		F		f	u	f		U		f	u	f
16		F		f	u	f		U		f	u	f
17	f		F		f	u	f		U		f	u
18	f		F		f	u	f		U		f	u
19	u	f		F		f	u	f		U		f
20	u	f		F		f	u	f		U		f
21	f	u	f		F		f	u	f		U	
22	f	u	f		F		f	u	f		U	
23		f	u	f		F		f	u	f		U
24		f	u	f		F		f	u	f		U
25		f	u	f		F		f	u	f		U
26	U		f	u	f		F		f	u	f	
27	U		f	u	f		F		f	u	f	
28		U		f	u	f		F		f	u	f
29		U		f	u	f		F		f	u	f
30		U		f	u	f		F		f	u	f
31	f		U		f	u	f		F		f	u

September Moon Table

Date	Sign	Element	Nature	Phase
1 Mon 9:45 pm	Capricorn	Earth	Semi-fruitful	2nd
2 Tue	Capricorn	Earth	Semi-fruitful	2nd
3 Wed	Capricorn	Earth	Semi-fruitful	2nd
4 Thu 6:32 am	Aquarius	Air	Barren	2nd
5 Fri	Aquarius	Air	Barren	2nd
6 Sat 11:54 am	Pisces	Water	Fruitful	2nd
7 Sun	Pisces	Water	Fruitful	Full 2.09 pm
8 Mon 2:37 pm	Aries	Fire	Barren	3rd
9 Tue	Aries	Fire	Barren	3rd
10 Wed 4:03 pm	Taurus	Earth	Semi-fruitful	3rd
11 Thu	Taurus	Earth	Semi-fruitful	3rd
12 Fri 5:38 pm	Gemini	Air	Barren	3rd
13 Sat	Gemini	Air	Barren	3rd
14 Sun 8:30 pm	Cancer	Water	Fruitful	4th 6:33 am
15 Mon	Cancer	Water	Fruitful	4th
16 Tue	Cancer	Water	Fruitful	4th
17 Wed 1:20 am	Leo	Fire	Barren	4th
18 Thu	Leo	Fire	Barren	4th
19 Fri 8:23 am	Virgo	Earth	Barren	4th
20 Sat	Virgo	Earth	Barren	4th
21 Sun 5:41 pm	Libra	Air	Semi-fruitful	New 3:54 pm
22 Mon	Libra	Air	Semi-fruitful	1st
23 Tue	Libra	Air	Semi-fruitful	1st
24 Wed 5:00 am	Scorpio	Water	Fruitful	1st
25 Thu	Scorpio	Water	Fruitful	1st
26 Fri 5:37 pm	Sagittarius	Fire	Barren	1st
27 Sat	Sagittarius	Fire	Barren	1st
28 Sun	Sagittarius	Fire	Barren	1st
29 Mon 5:55 am	Capricorn	Earth	Semi-fruitful	2nd 7:54 pm
30 Tue	Capricorn	Earth	Semi-fruitful	2nd

September Aspectarian/Favorable & Unfavorable Days

Date	Sun	Mercury	Venus	Mars	Jupiter	Saturn	Uranus	Neptune	Pluto
1		T				Q			
2	T							Q	
3				Q	O				
4						X	T	X	C
5			O	T					
6						Q			
7	O	O			T				
8						C	X	C	X
9			T		Q				
10			O						Q
11		T							
12	T		Q		X	X	C	X	T
13									
14	Q	Q	X	T		Q		Q	
15									
16	X	X		Q	C	T			
17							X	T	O
18									
19			C	X				Q	
20									
21	C				X	O	T	O	T
22		C							
23					Q				
24			X	C					Q
25									
26					T	T	O	T	X
27	X		Q						
28		X	'						
29	Q			X		Q		Q	
30		Q	T						

Date	Aries	Taurus	Gemini	Cancer	Leo	Virgo	Libra	Scorpio	Sagittarius	Capricorn	Aquarius	Pisces
1	f		U		f	u	f		F		f	u
2	u	f		U		f	u	f		F		f
3	u	f		U		f	u	f		F		f
4	u	f		U		f	u	f		F		f
5	f	u	f		U		f	u	f		F	
6	f	u	f		U		f	u	f		F	
7		f	u	f		U		f	u	f		F
8		f	u	f		U		f	u	f		F
9	F		f	u	f		U		f	u	f	
10	F		f	u	f		U		f	u	f	
11		F		f	u	f		U		f	u	f
12		F		f	u	f		U		f	u	f
13	f		F		f	u	f		U		f	u
14	f		F		f	u	f		U		f	u
15	u	f		F		f	u	f		U		f
16	u	f		F		f	u	f		U		f
17	f	u	f		F		f	u	f		U	
18	f	u	f		F		f	u	f		U	
19	f	u	f		F		f	u	f		U	
20		f	u	f		F		f	u	f		U
21		f	u	f		F		f	u	f		U
22	U		f	u	f		F		f	u	f	
23	U		f	u	f		F		f	u	f	
24	U		f	u	f		F		f	u	f	
25		U		f	u	f		F		f	u	f
26		U		f	u	f		F		f	u	f
27	f		U		f	u	f		F		f	u
28	f		U		f	u	f		F		f	u
29	f		U		f	u	f		F		f	u
30	u	f		U		f	u	f		F		f

October Moon Table

Date	Sign	Element	Nature	Phase
1 Wed 3:52 pm	Aquarius	Air	Barren	2nd
2 Thu	Aquarius	Air	Barren	2nd
3 Fri 10:07 pm	Pisces	Water	Fruitful	2nd
4 Sat	Pisces	Water	Fruitful	2nd
5 Sun	Pisces	Water	Fruitful	2nd
6 Mon 12:48 am	Aries	Fire	Barren	Full 11:48 pm
7 Tue	Aries	Fire	Barren	3rd
8 Wed 1:12 am	Taurus	Earth	Semi-fruitful	3rd
9 Thu	Taurus	Earth	Semi-fruitful	3rd
10 Fri 1:12 am	Gemini	Air	Barren	3rd
11 Sat	Gemini	Air	Barren	3rd
12 Sun 2:37 am	Cancer	Water	Fruitful	3rd
13 Mon	Cancer	Water	Fruitful	4th 2:13 pm
14 Tue 6:47 am	Leo	Fire	Barren	4th
15 Wed	Leo	Fire	Barren	4th
16 Thu 2:06 pm	Virgo	Earth	Barren	4th
17 Fri	Virgo	Earth	Barren	4th
18 Sat	Virgo	Earth	Barren	4th
19 Sun 12:01 am	Libra	Air	Semi-fruitful	4th
20 Mon	Libra	Air	Semi-fruitful	4th
21 Tue 11:42 am	Scorpio	Water	Fruitful	New 8:25 am
22 Wed	Scorpio	Water	Fruitful	1st
23 Thu	Scorpio	Water	Fruitful	1st
24 Fri 12:19 am	Sagittarius	Fire	Barren	1st
25 Sat	Sagittarius	Fire	Barren	1st
26 Sun 12:53 pm	Capricorn	Earth	Semi-fruitful	1st
27 Mon	Capricorn	Earth	Semi-fruitful	1st
28 Tue 11:55 pm	Aquarius	Air	Barren	1st
29 Wed	Aquarius	Air	Barren	2nd 12:21 pm
30 Thu	Aquarius	Air	Barren	2nd
31 Fri 7:46 am	Pisces	Water	Fruitful	2nd

October Aspectarian/Favorable & Unfavorable Days

Date	Sun	Mercury	Venus	Mars	Jupiter	Saturn	Uranus	Neptune	Pluto
1					O	X	T	X	C
2	T			Q					
3		T							
4				T				Q	
5			O		T	C			
6	O						X	C	X
7					Q				
8		O		O					Q
9			T		X	X			
10							C	X	T
11	T		Q		Q				
12		T						Q	
13	Q			T	C				
14			X			T	X	T	O
15		Q		Q					
16	X							Q	
17		X							
18				X	X	O			
19			C				T	O	T
20									
21	C				Q				Q
22									
23		C		C	T	T			
24							O	T	X
25			X						
26	X					Q		Q	
27									
28		X	Q	X	O	X		X	
29	Q						T		C
30			T						
31	T	Q		Q				Q	

Date	Aries	Taurus	Gemini	Cancer	Leo	Virgo	Libra	Scorpio	Sagittarius	Capricorn	Aquarius	Pisces
1	u	f		U		f	u	f		F		f
2	f	u	f		U		f	u	f		F	
3	f	u	f		U		f	u	f		F	
4		f	u	f		U		f	u	f		F
5		f	u	f		U		f	u	f		F
6	F		f	u	f		U		f	u	f	
7	F		f	u	f		U		f	u	f	
8		F		f	u	f		U		f	u	f
9		F		f	u	f		U		f	u	f
10	t		F		f	u	f		U		f	u
11	f		F		f	u	f		U		f	u
12	u	f		F		f	u	f		U		f
13	u	f		F		f	u	f		U		f
14	u	f		F		f	u	f		U		f
15	f	u	f		F		f	u	f		U	
16	f	u	f		F		f	u	f		U	
17		f	u	f		F		f	u	f		U
18		f	u	f		F		f	u	f		U
19	U		f	u	f		F		f	u	f	
20	U		f	u	f		F		f	u	f	
21	U		f	u	f		F		f	u	f	
22		U		f	u	f		F		f	u	f
23		U		f	u	f		F		f	u	f
24	f		U		f	u	f		F		f	u
25	f		U		f	u	f		F		f	u
26	f		U		f	u	f		F		f	u
27	u	f		U		f	u	f		F		f
28	u	f		U		f	u	f		F		f
29	f	u	f		U		f	u	f		F	
30	f	u	f		U		f	u	f		F	
31	f	u	f		U		f	u	f		F	

November Moon Table

Date	Sign	Element	Nature	Phase
1 Sat	Pisces	Water	Fruitful	2nd
2 Sun 10:39 am	Aries	Fire	Barren	2nd
3 Mon	Aries	Fire	Barren	2nd
4 Tue 11:16 am	Taurus	Earth	Semi-fruitful	2nd
5 Wed	Taurus	Earth	Semi-fruitful	Full 8:19 am
6 Thu 10:20 am	Gemini	Air	Barren	3rd
7 Fri	Gemini	Air	Barren	3rd
8 Sat 10:06 am	Cancer	Water	Fruitful	3rd
9 Sun	Cancer	Water	Fruitful	3rd
10 Mon 12:34 pm	Leo	Fire	Barren	3rd
11 Tue	Leo	Fire	Barren	3rd
12 Wed 6:52 pm	Virgo	Earth	Barren	4th 12:28 am
13 Thu	Virgo	Earth	Barren	4th
14 Fri	Virgo	Earth	Barren	4th
15 Sat 4:44 am	Libra	Air	Semi-fruitful	4th
16 Sun	Libra	Air	Semi-fruitful	4th
17 Mon 4:44 pm	Scorpio	Water	Fruitful	4th
18 Tue	Scorpio	Water	Fruitful	4th
19 Wed	Scorpio	Water	Fruitful	4th
20 Thu 5:26 am	Sagittarius	Fire	Barren	New 1:47 am
21 Fri	Sagittarius	Fire	Barren	1st
22 Sat 5:53 pm	Capricorn	Earth	Semi-fruitful	1st
23 Sun	Capricorn	Earth	Semi-fruitful	1st
24 Mon	Capricorn	Earth	Semi-fruitful	1st
25 Tue 5:16 am	Aquarius	Air	Barren	1st
26 Wed	Aquarius	Air	Barren	1st
27 Thu 2:24 pm	Pisces	Water	Fruitful	1st
28 Fri	Pisces	Water	Fruitful	2nd 1:59 am
29 Sat 8:07 pm	Aries	Fire	Barren	2nd
30 Sun	Aries	Fire	Barren	2nd

November Aspectarian/Favorable & Unfavorable Days

Date	Sun	Mercury	Venus	Mars	Jupiter	Saturn	Uranus	Neptune	Pluto
1									
2		T		T	T	C	X	C	X
3									
4			O		Q				Q
5	O								
6		O		O	X	X	C	X	T
7									
8			T			Q		Q	
9	T								
10			Q	T	C	T	X	T	O
11		T							
12	Q						Q		
13		Q	X	Q					
14	X				X	O			
15		X		X			T	O	T
16									
17					Q				Q
18			C						
19					T	T			
20	C	C					O	T	X
21				C					
22						Q		Q	
23									
24		X	X		O	X			
25	X						T	X	C
26		Q		X					
27			Q				Q		
28	Q			Q					
29		T	T		T	C	X	C	X
30	T								

Date	Aries	Taurus	Gemini	Cancer	Leo	Virgo	Libra	Scorpio	Sagittarius	Capricorn	Aquarius	Pisces
1		f	u	f		U		f	u	f		F
2		f	u	f		U		f	u	f		F
3	F		f	u	f		U		f	u	f	
4	F		f	u	f		U		f	u	f	
5		F		f	u	f		U		f	u	f
6		F		f	u	f		U		f	u	f
7	f		F		f	u	f		U		f	u
8	f		F		f	u	f		U		f	u
9	u	f		F		f	u	f		U		f
10	u	f		F		f	u	f		U		f
11	f	u	f		F		f	u	f		U	
12	f	u	f		F		f	u	f		U	
13		f	u	f		F		f	u	f		U
14		f	u	f		F		f	u	f		U
15		f	u	f		F		f	u	f		U
16	U		f	u	f		F		f	u	f	
17	U		f	u	f		F		f	u	f	
18		U		f	u	f		F		f	u	f
19		U		f	u	f		F		f	u	f
20		U		f	u	f		F		f	u	f
21	f		U		f	u	f		F		f	u
22	f		U		f	u	f		F		f	u
23	u	f		U		f	u	f		F		f
24	u	f		U		f	u	f		F		f
25	u	f		U		f	u	f		F		f
26	f	u	f		U		f	u	f		F	
27	f	u	f		U		f	u	f		F	
28		f	u	f		U		f	u	f		F
29		f	u	f		U		f	u	f		F
30	F		f	u	f		U		f	u	f	

December Moon Table

Date	Sign	Element	Nature	Phase
1 Mon 10:13 pm	Taurus	Earth	Semi-fruitful	2nd
2 Tue	Taurus	Earth	Semi-fruitful	2nd
3 Wed 9:48 pm	Gemini	Air	Barren	2nd
4 Thu	Gemini	Air	Barren	Full 6:14 pm
5 Fri 8:54 pm	Cancer	Water	Fruitful	3rd
6 Sat	Cancer	Water	Fruitful	3rd
7 Sun 9:48 pm	Leo	Fire	Barren	3rd
8 Mon	Leo	Fire	Barren	3rd
9 Tue	Leo	Fire	Barren	3rd
10 Wed 2:20 am	Virgo	Earth	Barren	3rd
11 Thu	Virgo	Earth	Barren	4th 3:52 pm
12 Fri 11:04 am	Libra	Air	Semi-fruitful	4th
13 Sat	Libra	Air	Semi-fruitful	4th
14 Sun 10:51 pm	Scorpio	Water	Fruitful	4th
15 Mon	Scorpio	Water	Fruitful	4th
16 Tue	Scorpio	Water	Fruitful	4th
17 Wed 11:38 am	Sagittarius	Fire	Barren	4th
18 Thu	Sagittarius	Fire	Barren	4th
19 Fri 11:53 pm	Capricorn	Earth	Semi-fruitful	New 8:43 pm
20 Sat	Capricorn	Earth	Semi-fruitful	1st
21 Sun	Capricorn	Earth	Semi-fruitful	1st
22 Mon 10:52 am	Aquarius	Air	Barren	1st
23 Tue	Aquarius	Air	Barren	1st
24 Wed 8:09 pm	Pisces	Water	Fruitful	1st
25 Thu	Pisces	Water	Fruitful	1st
26 Fri	Pisces	Water	Fruitful	1st
27 Sat 3:02 am	Aries	Fire	Barren	2nd 2:10 pm
28 Sun	Aries	Fire	Barren	2nd
29 Mon 6:57 am	Taurus	Earth	Semi-fruitful	2nd
30 Tue	Taurus	Earth	Semi-fruitful	2nd
31 Wed 8:13 am	Gemini	Air	Barren	2nd

December Aspectarian/Favorable & Unfavorable Days

Date	Sun	Mercury	Venus	Mars	Jupiter	Saturn	Uranus	Neptune	Pluto
1				T	Q				
2									Q
3		O			X	X	C	X	
4	O		O						T
5				O		Q		Q	
6									
7		T				C	T	X	
8			T						O
9	T	Q		T				Q	
10									
11	Q		Q		X				
12		X		Q		O	T	O	T
13			X						
14	X			X	Q				
15									Q
16						T			
17						T	O	T	X
18		C							
19	C		C			Q		Q	
20			C						
21					O				
22						X	T	X	C
23		X							
24			X				Q		
25	X			X					
26		Q				T	C	X	
27	Q		Q	Q				C	X
28		T			Q				
29	T		T						Q
30				T	X				
31						X	C	X	T

Date	Aries	Taurus	Gemini	Cancer	Leo	Virgo	Libra	Scorpio	Sagittarius	Capricorn	Aquarius	Pisces
1	F		f	u	f		U		f	u	f	
2		F		f	u	f		U		f	u	f
3		F		f	u	f		U		f	u	f
4	f		F		f	u	f		U		f	u
5	f		F		f	u	f		U		f	u
6	u	f		F		f	u	f		U		f
7	u	f		F		f	u	f		U		f
8	f	u	f		F		f	u	f		U	
9	f	u	f		F		f	u	f		U	
10		f	u	f		F		f	u	f		U
11		f	u	f		F		f	u	f		U
12		f	u	f		F		f	u	f		U
13	U		f	u	f		F		f	u	f	
14	U		f	u	f		F		f	u	f	
15		U		f	u	f		F		f	u	f
16		U		f	u	f		F		f	u	f
17		U		f	u	f		F		f	u	f
18	f		U		f	u	f		F		f	u
19	f		U		f	u	f		F		f	u
20	u	f		U		f	u	f		F		f
21	u	f		U		f	u	f		F		f
22	u	f		U		f	u	f		F		f
23	f	u	f		U		f	u	f		F	
24	f	u	f		U		f	u	f		F	
25		f	u	f		U		f	u	f		F
26		f	u	f		U		f	u	f		F
27		f	u	f		U		f	u	f		F
28	F		f	u	f		U		f	u	f	
29	F		f	u	f		U		f	u	f	
30		F		f	u	f		U		f	u	f
31		F		f	u	f		U		f	u	f

2025 Retrograde Planets

Planet	Begin	Eastern	Pacific	End	Eastern	Pacific
Uranus	9/1/24	11:18 am	**8:18 am**	1/30	11:22 am	**8:22 am**
Jupiter	10/9/24	3:05 am	**12:05 am**	2/4	4:40 am	**1:40 am**
Mars	12/6/24	6:33 pm	**3:33 pm**	2/23	9:00 pm	**6:00 pm**
Venus	3/1	7:36 pm	**4:36 pm**	4/12	9:02 pm	**6:02 pm**
Mercury	3/14		**11:46 pm**	4/7	7:08 am	**4:08 am**
Mercury	3/15	2:46 am		4/7	7:08 am	**4:08 am**
Pluto	5/4	11:27 am	**8:27 am**	10/13	10:54 pm	**7:54 pm**
Neptune	7/4	5:34 pm	**2:34 pm**	12/10	7:21 am	**4:21 am**
Saturn	7/12		**9:07 pm**	11/27	10:52 pm	**7:52 pm**
Saturn	7/13	12:07 am		11/27	10:52 pm	**7:52 pm**
Mercury	7/17		**9:45 pm**	8/11	3:30 am	**12:30 am**
Mercury	7/18	12:45 am		8/11	3:30 am	**12:30 am**
Uranus	9/5		**9:51 pm**	2/3/26	9:33 pm	**6:33 pm**
Uranus	9/6	12:51 am		2/3/26	9:33 pm	**6:33 pm**
Mercury	11/9	2:02 pm	**11:02 am**	11/29	12:38 pm	**9:38 am**
Jupiter	11/11	11:41 am	**8:41 am**	3/10/26	11:30 pm	**8:30 pm**

Eastern Time in plain type, **Pacific Time in bold type**

	Dec 24	Jan 25	Feb	Mar	Apr	May	Jun	Jul	Aug	Sep	Oct	Nov	Dec	Jan 26
☿				▓			▓							
♃	▓	▓										▓	▓	▓
♀				▓										
♄								▓	▓	▓	▓	▓		
♇						▓	▓	▓	▓	▓	▓			
♆								▓	▓	▓	▓	▓		
♅	▓	▓									▓	▓	▓	
♂	▓	▓												

Egg-Setting Dates

To Have Eggs by this Date	Sign	Qtr.	Date to Set Eggs
Jan 7, 5:11 pm–Jan 9, 8:07 pm	Taurus	2nd	Dec 17, 2024
Jan 11, 11:24 pm–Jan 13, 5:27 pm	Cancer	2nd	Dec 21, 2024
Jan 30, 5:52 pm–Feb 1, 8:10 pm	Pisces	1st	Jan 09, 2025
Feb 3, 10:33 pm–Feb 6, 1:44 am	Taurus	1st	Jan 13
Feb 8, 6:04 am–Feb 10, 12:01 pm	Cancer	2nd	Jan 18
Feb 27, 7:45 pm–Mar 1, 4:52 am	Pisces	1st	Mar 06
Mar 3, 5:37 am–Mar 5, 7:29 am	Taurus	1st	Feb 10
Mar 7, 11:29 am–Mar 9, 6:59 pm	Cancer	2nd	Feb 14
Mar 30, 4:16 pm–Apr 1, 4:26 pm	Taurus	1st	Mar 09
Apr 3, 6:50 pm–Apr 6, 12:34 am	Cancer	1st	Mar 13
Apr 10, 9:12 pm–Apr 12, 8:22 pm	Libra	2nd	Mar 20
Apr 27, 3:31 pm–Apr 29, 2:34 am	Taurus	1st	Apr 06
May 1, 3:23 am–May 3, 7:29 am	Cancer	1st	Apr 10
May 8, 3:06 am–May 10, 3:58 pm	Libra	2nd	Apr 17
May 28, 1:33 pm–May 30, 4:17 pm	Cancer	1st	May 07
Jun 4, 9:38 am–Jun 6, 10:23 pm	Libra	2nd	May 14
Jun 25, 6:32 am–Jun 27, 2:05 am	Cancer	1st	Jun 04
Jul 1, 5:16 pm–Jul 4, 5:33 am	Libra	1st	Jun 10
Jul 29, 1:43 am–Jul 31, 1:25 pm	Libra	1st	Jul 08
Aug 25, 10:08 am–Aug 27, 9:27 pm	Libra	1st	Aug 04
Sep 6, 11:54 am–Sep 7, 2:09 pm	Pisces	2nd	Aug 16
Sep 21, 5:41 pm–Sep 24, 5:00 am	Libra	1st	Aug 31
Oct 3, 10:07 pm–Oct 6, 12:48 am	Pisces	2nd	Sep 12
Oct 21, 8:25 am–Oct 21, 11:42 am	Libra	1st	Sep 30
Oct 31, 7:46 am–Nov 2, 10:39 am	Pisces	2nd	Oct 10
Nov 4, 11:16 am–Nov 5, 8:19 am	Taurus	2nd	Oct 14
Nov 27, 2:24 pm–Nov 29, 8:07 pm	Pisces	1st	Nov 06
Dec 1, 10:13 pm–Dec 3, 9:48 pm	Taurus	2nd	Nov 10
Dec 24, 8:09 pm–Dec 27, 3:02 am	Pisces	1st	Dec 03
Dec 29, 6:57 am–Dec 31, 8:13 am	Taurus	2nd	Dec 08

Dates to Hunt and Fish

Date	Quarter	Sign
Jan 3, 10:21 am–Jan 5, 2:01 pm	1st	Pisces
Jan 11, 11:24 pm–Jan 14, 4:12 am	2nd	Cancer
Jan 21, 11:20 am–Jan 23, 11:29 pm	3rd	Scorpio
Jan 30, 5:52 pm–Feb 1, 8:10 pm	1st	Pisces
Feb 8, 6:04 am–Feb 10, 12:01 pm	2nd	Cancer
Feb 17, 7:19 pm–Feb 20, 7:55 am	3rd	Scorpio
Feb 20, 7:55 am–Feb 22, 6:09 pm	3rd	Sagittarius
Feb 27, 3:46 am–Mar 1, 4:52 am	4th	Pisces
Mar 7, 11:29 am–Mar 9, 6:59 pm	2nd	Cancer
Mar 17, 3:30 am–Mar 19, 4:17 pm	3rd	Scorpio
Mar 19, 4:17 pm–Mar 22, 3:29 am	3rd	Sagittarius
Mar 26, 3:31 pm–Mar 28, 4:36 pm	4th	Pisces
Apr 3, 6.50 pm–Apr 6, 12.34 am	1st	Cancer
Apr 13, 9:54 am–Apr 15, 10:37 pm	3rd	Scorpio
Apr 15, 10:37 pm–Apr 18, 10:12 am	3rd	Sagittarius
Apr 23, 1:07 am–Apr 25, 3:24 am	4th	Pisces
May 1, 3:23 am–May 3, 7:29 am	1st	Cancer
May 10, 3:58 pm–May 13, 4:35 am	2nd	Scorpio
May 13, 4:35 am–May 15, 3:58 pm	3rd	Sagittarius
May 20, 8:28 am–May 22, 12:26 pm	4th	Pisces
May 28, 1:33 pm–May 30, 4:17 pm	1st	Cancer
Jun 6, 10:23 am–Jun 9, 10:56 am	2nd	Scorpio
Jun 9, 10:56 am–Jun 11, 9:55 pm	2nd	Sagittarius
Jun 16, 2:09 pm–Jun 18, 7:08 pm	3rd	Pisces
Jun 24, 11:44 pm–Jun 27, 2:05 am	4th	Cancer
Jul 4, 5:33 am–Jul 6, 6:06 pm	2nd	Scorpio
Jul 6, 6:06 pm–Jul 9, 4:55 am	2nd	Sagittarius
Jul 13, 7:45 am–Jul 16, 12:32 am	3rd	Pisces
Jul 16, 12:32 am–Jul 18, 3:59 am	3rd	Aries
Jul 22, 8:26 am–Jul 24, 11:28 am	4th	Cancer
Jul 31, 1:25 pm–Aug 3, 2:00 am	1st	Scorpio
Aug 3, 2:00 am–Aug 5, 1:04 pm	2nd	Sagittarius
Aug 10, 2:50 am–Aug 12, 6:33 am	3rd	Pisces
Aug 12, 6:33 am–Aug 14, 9:22 am	3rd	Aries
Aug 18, 3:05 pm–Aug 20, 7:17 pm	4th	Cancer
Aug 27, 9:27 pm–Aug 30, 10:04 am	1st	Scorpio
Sep 6, 11:54 am–Sep 8, 2:37 pm	2nd	Pisces
Sep 8, 2:37 pm–Sep 10, 4:03 pm	3rd	Aries
Sep 14, 8:30 pm–Sep 17, 1:20 am	4th	Cancer
Sep 24, 5:00 am–Sep 26, 5:37 pm	1st	Scorpio
Oct 3, 10:07 pm–Oct 6, 12:48 am	2nd	Pisces
Oct 6, 12:48 am–Oct 8, 1:12 am	2nd	Aries
Oct 12, 2:37 am–Oct 14, 6:47 am	3rd	Cancer
Oct 21, 11:42 am–Oct 24, 12:19 am	1st	Scorpio
Oct 31, 7:46 am–Nov 2, 10:39 am	2nd	Pisces
Nov 8, 10:06 am–Nov 10, 12:34 pm	3rd	Cancer
Nov 17, 4:44 pm–Nov 20, 5:26 am	4th	Scorpio
Nov 27, 2:24 pm–Nov 29, 8:07 pm	1st	Pisces
Nov 29, 8:07 pm–Dec 1, 10:13 pm	2nd	Aries
Dec 5, 8:54 pm–Dec 7, 9:48 pm	3rd	Cancer
Dec 14, 10:51 pm–Dec 17, 11:38 am	4th	Scorpio
Dec 24, 8:09 pm–Dec 27, 3:02 am	1st	Pisces

Both tables in Eastern time

Dates to Destroy Weeds and Pests

Date	Sign	Qtr.
Jan 14, 4:12 am–Jan 16, 11:46 am	Leo	3rd
Jan 16, 11:46 am–Jan 18, 10:33 pm	Virgo	3rd
Jan 23, 11:29 pm–Jan 26, 8:43 am	Sagittarius	4th
Jan 28, 2:31 pm–Jan 29, 7:36 am	Aquarius	4th
Feb 12, 8:53 am–Feb 12, 8:07 pm	Leo	3rd
Feb 12, 8:07 pm–Feb 15, 6:45 am	Virgo	3rd
Feb 20, 7:55 am–Feb 20, 12:33 pm	Sagittarius	3rd
Feb 20, 12:33 pm–Feb 22, 6:09 pm	Sagittarius	4th
Feb 25, 12:40 am–Feb 27, 3:46 am	Aquarius	4th
Mar 14, 2:55 am–Mar 14, 2:59 pm	Virgo	3rd
Mar 19, 4:17 pm–Mar 22, 3:29 am	Sagittarius	3rd
Mar 24, 11:25 am–Mar 26, 3:31 pm	Aquarius	4th
Mar 28, 4:36 pm–Mar 29, 6:58 am	Aries	4th
Apr 15, 10:37 pm–Apr 18, 10:12 am	Sagittarius	3rd
Apr 20, 7:22 pm–Apr 20, 9:36 pm	Aquarius	3rd
Apr 20, 9:36 pm–Apr 23, 1:07 am	Aquarius	4th
Apr 25, 3:24 am–Apr 27, 3:17 am	Aries	4th
May 13, 4:35 am–May 15, 3:58 pm	Sagittarius	3rd
May 18, 1:29 am–May 20, 7:59 am	Aquarius	3rd
May 20, 7:59 am–May 20, 8:28 am	Aquarius	4th
May 22, 12:26 pm–May 24, 1:38 pm	Aries	4th
May 26, 1:21 pm–May 26, 11:02 pm	Gemini	4th
Jun 11, 3:44 am–Jun 11, 9:55 pm	Sagittarius	3rd
Jun 14, 7:00 am–Jun 16, 2:09 pm	Aquarius	3rd
Jun 18, 7:08 pm–Jun 20, 9:53 pm	Aries	4th
Jun 22, 10:57 pm–Jun 24, 11:44 pm	Gemini	4th
Jul 11, 1:21 pm–Jul 13, 7:45 pm	Aquarius	3rd
Jul 16, 12:32 am–Jul 17, 8:38 pm	Aries	3rd
Jul 17, 8:38 pm–Jul 18, 3:59 am	Aries	4th
Jul 20, 6:22 am–Jul 22, 8:26 am	Gemini	4th
Jul 24, 11:28 am–Jul 24, 3:11 pm	Leo	4th
Aug 9, 3:55 am–Aug 10, 2:50 am	Aquarius	3rd
Aug 12, 6:33 am–Aug 14, 9:22 am	Aries	3rd
Aug 16, 12:01 pm–Aug 18, 3:05 pm	Gemini	4th
Aug 20, 7:17 pm–Aug 23, 1:24 am	Leo	4th
Aug 23, 1:24 am–Aug 23, 2:07 am	Virgo	4th
Sep 8, 2:37 pm–Sep 10, 4:03 pm	Aries	3rd
Sep 12, 5:38 pm–Sep 14, 6:33 am	Gemini	3rd
Sep 14, 6:33 am–Sep 14, 8:30 pm	Gemini	4th
Sep 17, 1:20 am–Sep 19, 8:23 am	Leo	4th
Sep 19, 8:23 am–Sep 21, 3:54 pm	Virgo	4th
Oct 6, 11:48 pm–Oct 8, 1:12 am	Aries	3rd
Oct 10, 1:12 am–Oct 12, 2:37 am	Gemini	3rd
Oct 14, 6:47 am–Oct 16, 2:06 pm	Leo	4th
Oct 16, 2:06 pm–Oct 19, 12:01 am	Virgo	4th
Nov 6, 10:20 am–Nov 8, 10:06 am	Gemini	3rd
Nov 10, 12:34 pm–Nov 12, 12:28 am	Leo	3rd
Nov 12, 12:28 am–Nov 12, 6:52 pm	Leo	4th
Nov 12, 6:52 pm–Nov 15, 4:44 am	Virgo	4th
Dec 4, 6:14 pm–Dec 5, 8:54 pm	Gemini	3rd
Dec 7, 9:48 pm–Dec 10, 2:20 am	Leo	3rd
Dec 10, 2:20 am–Dec 11, 3:52 pm	Virgo	3rd
Dec 11, 3:52 pm–Dec 12, 11:04 am	Virgo	4th
Dec 17, 11:38 am–Dec 19, 8:43 pm	Sagittarius	4th

Weather, Economic & Lunar Forecasts

An Introduction to Long-Range Weather Forecasting

Vincent Decker

Long-range weather forecasting based on planetary cycles, also known as astrometeorology, has been a field of study for centuries. The basic premise underlying the field is that the main heavenly bodies of our solar system exercise an influence over weather conditions on Earth.

Planets

The heat of summer and the chill of winter can be traced back to the Sun's apparent movement north and south of our terrestrial equator. The Moon, while mostly known for its effect on the oceans' tides, in astrometeorology also affects air tides in its circuit around the earth and serves as a triggering influence on solar and planetary configurations as they form. Under Mercury's domain, we find high pressure or fair weather as well as gentle breezes to hurricane-force winds. Venus is known for gentle showers, moderate temperatures, and snowfall or freezing rain in winter. Mars, the red planet, brings hot summers, mild winters, dry conditions, and fierce storms. Jupiter's trademark is a temperate and invigorating atmosphere under benign configurations. The traditional malefic Saturn engenders cold, damp conditions, and when aggravated by certain configurations, low-pressure systems. Like Mercury, the power of Uranus brings high-barometer and erratic wind velocities. Neptune is the pluvial planet *par excellence* capable of torrential downpours, flooding conditions, and warming trends. Pluto is held by some to be a warm influence while for others it is considered cold. In the forecasts included here, Pluto is considered a warm influence.

Aspects and Influences

The foregoing effects of the Sun, Moon, and planets are modified depending on the aspect that each one makes in relation to the other heavenly bodies. The traditional astrological aspects are employed: the conjunction, sextile, square, trine, opposition, and parallel of declination. Fair weather aspects are the sextile and trine. Disturbed weather is induced by the square and opposition. The kind of weather produced by the conjunction and parallel of declination vary depending on if the celestial bodies involved are of similar or contrary natures.

The signs of the zodiac in which the members of the solar system reside at any given moment also affect the manifestation of weather conditions. Heat and dryness are associated with the fire signs Aries, Leo, and Sagittarius. The water signs of Cancer, Scorpio, and Pisces enhance precipitation. Air signs such as Gemini, Libra, and Aquarius relate to lower temperatures and wind, while the earth signs Taurus, Virgo, and Capricorn are generally wet and cold.

Forecasting

Although the aspects involved in the planetary configurations determine the time that weather processes will be at work (do keep in mind to allow a day or two leeway in all forecasting), it is by the use of key charts that the geographical locations of weather systems are ascertained. When a planet in a key chart is angular, that is to say it is on the cusp of the first, fourth, seventh, or tenth house, the influence associated with that planet will be strongest at that locale. The monthly alignments of the Sun and Moon such as New Moon, Full Moon, and Quarter Moons are examples of key charts. Other important charts include the cardinal solar ingresses and solar and lunar eclipses to name a few. Through setting up these key charts, noting the angular planets, the signs they tenant, and their aspects, as well as the kind of weather typical at the location in question, the long-range weather forecaster makes a judgment as to the type of weather to be expected. By faithfully comparing the forecasts with the actual ensuing weather, the forecaster has an opportunity to improve on method and results.

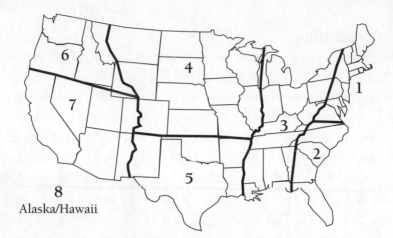

6

4

1

7

3

2

5

8
Alaska/Hawaii

Weather Forecast for 2025

Vincent Decker

Winter

Zones 1 and 2 experience lower temperatures and high barometric pressure when benign planetary aspects predominate. When under adverse configurations, the atmosphere is cold, bleak, and penetrating with increased wind velocities.

Zone 3 shows a mild and humid atmosphere with southerly winds and temperate showers as January begins. A breezy atmosphere with variable winds is indicated for February.

Zones 4 and 5 see more evaporation than usual accompanied by rising temperatures. When planetary configurations are of a contrary nature, turbulent atmospheric conditions ensue.

Heat and dryness are the themes for Zones 6 and 7 when under beneficent planetary alignments. Westerly winds predominate, and fire hazards increase.

Western and central portions of Alaska will see lower temperatures with cloudy and rainy conditions. Eastern areas see warmer conditions with springlike temperatures. Under certain alignments, precipitation can be heavy. Lower-than-average temperatures are indicated for Hawaii with increased cloudiness and rainfall.

New Moon January 1–6

Zone 1: Period begins with fair and possibly breezy conditions, followed by a cold front triggering shower potential. Precipitation likely over the mid-Atlantic area by the 6th.

Zone 2: Fair and mild conditions for starters. By the 4th, windy over the zone, then declining temperatures. Precipitation likely by the 6th.

Zone 3: Fair and mild for western portions. Lower-than-average temperatures for the Great Lakes. By the 2nd, cold fronts trigger storms. Around the 4th, windy over the Great Lakes area and northeast followed by lower temperatures.

Zone 4: Southerly breezes and warmer temperatures trigger storm potential in the west. The 4th–6th, strong winds and storms are indicated. Winds increase centrally around the 4th, then precipitation likely by the 6th. Fair and mild conditions over eastern areas. Northern sections see below-average temperatures.

Zone 5: Southerly breezes and warmer temperatures trigger storm potential in the west. The 4th–6th, strong winds and storms are indicated. Winds increase centrally around the 4th, then precipitation likely by the 6th. Fair and mild conditions over eastern areas.

Zone 6: Coastal areas fair, with high winds likely around the 4th. Southerly breezes and warmer temperatures over the east, then potentially strong winds and storms the 4th–6th.

Zone 7: Coastal areas fair, with high winds likely around the 4th. Southerly breezes and warmer temperatures over the east, then potentially strong winds and storms the 4th–6th.

Zone 8: Alaska: Western areas mild and breezy, then cooler and fair around the 4th. Central areas mild and breezy, then stronger winds around the 4th followed by lower temperatures. Eastern portions are windy around the 4th, then stormy by the 6th. The panhandle starts fair and mild. By the 3rd, strong storm potential increases. Hawaii: Mild and breezy, then cool and fair.

2nd Quarter January 6–13

Zone 1: A cold front pushes through the region producing showers 9th–11th. By the 13th, high pressure brings declining temperatures and some wind.

Zone 2: Some showers indicated around the 9th. Temperatures decline around the 13th under sunny skies and northwest wind.

Zone 3: A stormy period for the mid-Mississippi portion of the zone. The period begins with a front, triggering showers. Around the 9th, a low-pressure area brings a winter storm with strong winds over the Great Lakes.

Zone 4: Western areas see prevailing southerly winds and increased precipitation with some thunderstorm activity over western and central areas. Fair conditions indicated around the 13th. Mid-Mississippi Valley area experiences strong atmospheric disturbance. Northeastern sections see strong wintry storms around the 9th.

Zone 5: Western areas see prevailing southerly winds and increased precipitation with some thunderstorm activity over western and central areas. Fair conditions indicated around the 13th. The eastern section is stormy.

Zone 6: Lower temperatures for western portions. The period begins with a strong front and storms over coastal areas. Eastern sections are stormy around the 7th and 11th. Fair conditions develop toward the end of the period.

Zone 7: Lower temperatures for western portions. The period begins with a strong front and storms over coastal areas. Eastern sections are stormy around the 7th and 11th. Fair conditions develop toward the end of the period.

Zone 8: Alaska: Western and central areas see some shower activity. Eastern sections and Panhandle see increased wind velocities and a strong winter storm around the 8th. Fair conditions develop toward the end of the period. Hawaii: Lower-than-average temperatures. Shower potential increases around the 10th.

Full Moon January 13–21

Zone 1: New England begins cloudy with possible precipitation, then becomes cool and fair. By the 18th, low pressure brings precipitation. The period ends cool and cloudy with gusty winds. A mid-Atlantic storm system develops on the 21st.

Zone 2: Strong storms with sharp winds are indicated throughout the zone during this period. A mid-Atlantic storm develops on the 21st.

Zone 3: Strong storms over the Great Lakes area.

Zone 4: Northwestern zone is damp, chilly with heavy downpours. Other western areas see thunderstorms, rising temperatures, and pleasant conditions by the 16th. Low pressure and precipitation on the 18th over Front Range. Thunderstorms by the 20th. The northern high plains see powerful storms around the 17th.

Zone 5: Western areas see thunderstorms, rising temperatures, and pleasant conditions around the 16th. Low pressure and precipitation on the 18th over Front Range. Thunderstorms by the 20th.

Zone 6: Strong low pressure over Pacific Northwest coast on the 17th. Cool and fair coastal conditions southward. After the 19th, possible precipitation. The period ends with gusty winds. Eastern areas start with thunderstorms, then rising temperatures and pleasant conditions around the 16th. Thunderstorms by the 20th with gusty winds.

Zone 7: Cool and fair coastal conditions around the 17th. Then a front with possible precipitation after the 19th. Gusty winds as the period ends. Eastern areas see thunderstorms, rising temperatures, then pleasant conditions around the 16th. Thunderstorms by the 20th with gusty winds.

Zone 8: Alaska: West sees clouds increase with possible precipitation, especially by the 18th, then fair. Central area is subject to various strong storms. Rising temperatures and generally pleasant conditions for the east around the 16th, then a stronger storm system around the 21st. Hawaii: Increasing clouds and possible precipitation. Conditions are somewhat cooler by the 17th leading to storms on the 18th, then becoming fair.

4th Quarter January 21–29

Zone 1: Fair and cool with moderate-to-gusty winds. Temperatures rise on the 25th. Cold wave, windy, wintry precipitation around the 27th.

Zone 2: Fair and cool with moderate-to-gusty winds. Temperatures over northern areas rise on the 25th. Cold wave, windy, wintry precipitation around the 27th.

Zone 3: Lower ranges of temperatures. Chance of rain over central Mississippi Valley on the 26th.

Zone 4: West and central see rising temperatures and sharp winds. Western zone ends with potential for windy storms. Central sees a cold wave, windy, wintry precipitation around the 27th. Chance of rain over central Mississippi Valley on the 26th.

Zone 5: West and central see rising temperatures and sharp winds. Western zone ends with potential for windy storms. Central sees a cold wave, windy, wintry precipitation around the 27th, then fair over central Texas. Chance of rain over central Mississippi Valley on the 26th.

Zone 6: West is windy around the 23rd. Coastal areas are affected by strong low pressure and fronts bringing wind and rain. Pacific Northwest sees warmer temperatures and clear skies by the 25th. East has thunderstorms with sharp winds around the 23rd. Period ends with potential for windy storms.

Zone 7: West is windy around the 23rd. Coastal areas are affected by strong low pressure and fronts bringing wind and rain. East has thunderstorms with sharp winds around the 23rd. Period ends with potential for windy storms.

Zone 8: Alaska: West is fair, cool, and windy, especially around the 28th. Central and east have southerly winds, rising temperatures, and gentle breezes with precipitation likely. Wind and storms indicated around the 27th. Alaska Panhandle sees sharp winds and thunderstorms on the 23rd. Hawaii: Cool and fair by the 26th. Fair and windy around the 28th.

New Moon January 29–February 5

Zone 1: Below-average temperatures. Storms, strong winds, cold waves.

Zone 2: Below-average temperatures. Storms, strong winds, cold waves.

Zone 3: Below-average temperatures. Storms, strong winds, cold waves, especially over the Great Lakes and Kentucky-Indiana area. Warm and pleasant the 2nd. Colder, possible fog, rain the 4th.

Zone 4: West is warmer, dry, and windy the 4th–5th. Thunderstorms, then warmer and breezy. Central is dry, warm, and windy. On the 1st, rain over high plains. Fair the 2nd. Possible fog or rain the 4th. East is warm and pleasant. Cooler and windy by the 3rd, then possible fog or rain, except for the Great Lakes area where strong winter storms are indicated.

Zone 5: West is warmer, dry, and windy the 4th-5th. Thunderstorms, then warmer and breezy. Central is dry, warm, and windy. Fair the 2nd. Possible fog or rain the 4th. East is warm and pleasant. Cooler and windy by the 3rd, then possible fog or rain.

Zone 6: Strong thunderstorms hit the Idaho area on the 1st. Fair Pacific Northwest the 2nd. Thunderstorms around the 3rd, then warm and fair the 5th.

Zone 7: Thunderstorms around the 3rd, then warm and fair the 5th.

Zone 8: Alaska: West and central are mostly warm and pleasant with a chance of precipitation. East and Alaskan Panhandle see warmer temperatures, higher chance of precipitation. Hawaii: Western areas are warm and pleasant. Eastern portions begin a bit cooler with a chance of rain, especially a strong cold front around the 30th.

2nd Quarter February 5–12

Zone 1: Cold waves, gusty winds, and wintry precipitation.

Zone 2: Cold waves, gusty winds, and wintry precipitation.

Zone 3: Cold waves, gusty winds, and wintry precipitation.

Zone 4: Western areas are warmer and fairer the 7th. A chance of thunderstorms the 10th. East and central have a chance of rain around the 5th. A winter storm over the central and eastern plains around the 12th.

Zone 5: Breezy conditions develop over southwestern Texas the 6th. Western areas are warmer and fairer the 7th. A chance of thunderstorms the 10th–11th with wintry precipitation likely over New Mexico and Arizona. East and central see a chance of rain around the 5th. A winter storm over the central and eastern plains around the 12th.

Zone 6: Low pressure in and around Nevada possibly delivering wintry precipitation the 5th. Around the 9th, cloudy and windy conditions set in. Precipitation develops in eastern areas the 8th.

Zone 7: Low pressure in and around Nevada possibly delivering wintry precipitation the 5th. Around the 9th, cloudy and windy conditions set in. Precipitation develops over eastern areas on the 8th. Thunderstorms the 10th–11th with wintry precipitation likely over New Mexico and Arizona.

Zone 8: Alaska: West and central areas start with clear and fair conditions. Chance of showers is indicated by the 7th, then cloudy and windy by the 9th with low pressure over northern areas. Eastern areas see a chance of thunderstorms the 8th. The Alaskan Panhandle is warm and fair from the 7th on with a slight chance of precipitation. Potential for a winter storm along the southern coast develops by the 12th. Hawaii: Clear and fair weather with a chance of rain around the 7th.

Full Moon February 12–20

Zone 1: Cold front with possible showers the 12th. Cold and windy with possible precipitation the 15th. Increasing winds and storm potential the 18th. A cold front activates thunderstorms the 20th.

Zone 2: Cold front with possible showers the 12th. Cold and windy with possible precipitation the 15th. High pressure and clear skies over the Deep South the 19th. A cold front activates thunderstorms the 20th.

Zone 3: Cold front with possible showers the 12th. Cold and windy with possible precipitation the 15th. High pressure and clear skies over the Deep South the 19th. A cold front activates thunderstorms the 20th.

Zone 4: Clear skies and breezy-to-windy conditions over western and central areas. Low pressure brings rain over Kansas and Oklahoma the 15th. Western thunderstorms over Wyoming the 16th. A chance of thunderstorms across the zone the 17th. Eastern sections cloudy, precipitation, lower temperatures the

13th. North-central states see low pressure bringing wind and precipitation the 19th. Increasing clouds and chance of rain east the 20th.

Zone 5: Clear skies and breezy-to-windy conditions over western and central areas. Low pressure brings rain over Kansas and Oklahoma the 15th. A chance of thunderstorms across the zone the 17th. Eastern sections cloudy, precipitation, lower temperatures the 13th. Increasing clouds and chance of rain east the 20th.

Zone 6: Lower temperatures, gusty winds, and possible storms. Thunderstorm potential across the zone the 16th.

Zone 7: Lower temperatures, gusty winds, and possible storms. Thunderstorm potential across the zone the 16th.

Zone 8: Alaska: West has lower temperatures, windy, with possible storms. Cloudy with precipitation, chilly, easterly winds the 13th. Warmer with increasing winds and possible precipitation the 18th–20th. Central is cloudy with precipitation, chilly, easterly winds the 13th. Storms form along south-central coast the 16th. East is breezy around the 13th. Cool and fair the 14th, then a chance of rain. Alaskan Panhandle is cloudy with precipitation, chilly, easterly winds the 13th, then cool and fair the 14th. Afterward, a slight warming with a chance of showers. Hawaii: Mild and breezy the 13th. Cooler with rain likely the 19th.

4th Quarter February 20–27

Zone 1: Colder, windy, possible thunderstorms over New England the 21st. Rain, increasing temperatures the 23rd. New England sees low pressure, clouds, and easterly winds the 25th. Strong winds, possible thunderstorms the 26th followed by a cold wave and high pressure.

Zone 2: Cooler, breezy conditions over southern areas the 21st. Northern sections see rain, increasing temperatures the 23rd. Storm system from Ohio Valley southward through Florida the 25th. A cold front activates thunderstorms the 26th. Temperatures decline under clear skies the 27th.

Zone 3: Storm system from Ohio Valley southward through Florida the 25th. A cold front activates thunderstorms the 26th.

Zone 4: A stormy period for western sections while fair and breezy east. Storm system over Front Range ejects into the plains the 22nd. A front activates western thunderstorms the 25th.

Zone 5: A stormy period for western sections while fair and breezy east. Storm system over Front Range ejects into the plains the 22nd. A front activates western thunderstorms the 25th.

Zone 6: A stormy period for eastern sections. Dry and breezy conditions over western sections with an increase in temperatures, which continues eastward the 23rd.

Zone 7: A stormy period for eastern sections. Dry and breezy conditions over western sections with an increase in temperatures, which continues eastward the 23rd.

Zone 8: Alaska: Cool and breezy weather over the zone. A system generating wind and thunderstorms traverses the zone the 21st. Alaskan Panhandle is cold with thunderstorms the 21st. Windy, possible storms west the 23rd. Increasing heat leads to eastern storm formation while western areas see low pressure, clouds, and easterly winds the 24th. Low pressure over Alaskan Panhandle the 25th. Strong winds, possible winter storm west and central the 26th. Temperatures over central and eastern sections decline under clear conditions the 27th. Hawaii: Cool and breezy weather. Cooler, windy, possible thunderstorms the 21st. Windy, possible storms the 23rd.

New Moon February 27–March 6

Zone 1: Cold, windy, possible precipitation the 27th. Heavy precipitation over New England followed by cold wave the 3rd.

Zone 2: Warmer with variable winds and increased precipitation. Cold front generates thunderstorms the 3rd.

Zone 3: Lower temperatures, precipitation, and variable winds. Cold with precipitation throughout zone and a storm system over Great Lakes the 28th.

Zone 4: Storm system over Colorado Front Range the 1st. Warm and windy the 3rd–5th with possible thunderstorms. The central area is fair and breezy. East sees lower temperatures, precipitation. Storm system over Great Lakes the 28th.

Zone 5: Storm system over Colorado Front Range the 1st. Warm and windy the 3rd–5th with possible thunderstorms. The central area is fair and breezy. East sees lower temperatures, precipitation. Storm system over Great Lakes the 28th.

Zone 6: West is dry with high pressure and lower temperatures. South winds, possible coastal rains the 1st–3rd. Front triggers storms which move eastward the 2nd.

Zone 7: West is dry with high pressure and lower temperatures. South winds, possible coastal rains the 1st–3rd. Front triggers storms which move eastward the 2nd.

Zone 8: Alaska: West is mild and breezy the 27th. Cold front and precipitation the 28th. Mild and breezy again the 2nd. Heavy precipitation followed by cold wave the 3rd. Fair, breezy the 6th. Central is mild, breezy the 27th with precipitation likely around the 28th. East sees a cold front and precipitation the 28th. Humid, cloudy, possible precipitation the 1st. Windy conditions, possible precipitation the 3rd. Alaskan Panhandle is humid, cloudy, with possible precipitation the 1st. Windy conditions, possible precipitation the 3rd. Warm and breezy conditions the 5th. Hawaii: Mild, breezy the 27th and 2nd. Potential heavy rain, then cooler the 3rd. Fair, breezy the 6th.

2nd Quarter March 6–14

Zone 1: Mostly lower-than-average temperatures, windy, and fair.

Zone 2: Mostly lower-than-average temperatures, windy, and fair.

Zone 3: Fair over western sections. Cold wave, windy the 11th.

Zone 4: West sees an active period for thunderstorms. Dry and breezy the 6th. Front activates thunderstorms the 9th. Central is dry and breezy the 6th. Front activates thunderstorms the 9th. East sees mostly fair conditions.

Zone 5: West sees an active period for thunderstorms. Dry and breezy the 6th. Front activates thunderstorms the 9th. Central is dry and breezy the 6th. Front activates thunderstorms the 9th. East sees mostly fair conditions.

Zone 6: West is clear, with moderate temperatures the 7th. Front triggers thunderstorms the 8th. Strong winter storm over the West Coast the 12th. Eastern front activates thunderstorms the 8th. Cool and fair the 9th.

Zone 7: West is clear, with moderate temperatures the 7th. Front triggers thunderstorms the 8th. Strong winter storm over the West Coast, especially over Southern California, the 12th. Eastern front activates thunderstorms the 8th. Cool and fair the 9th.

Zone 8: Alaska: Zone experiences lower-than-average temperatures and windy conditions with potential heavy precipitation. The period ends cold, fair, and windy. Alaskan Panhandle is dry and breezy the 6th. Cold front with precipitation the 7th. Cold, windy, stormy conditions the 8th–9th. Hawaii: Breezy with a chance of rain the 10th. Lower-than-average temperatures, possible wind, and rain the 7th–12th. Breezy the 13th.

Spring

Eastern portions of Zone 1 are generally under fair conditions. Cooler temperatures give way to warm and dry influences, especially as May begins. Zones 2 and 3 along with the western portions of Zone 1 generally experience lower-than-average temperatures and strong high pressure when under benign planetary influences. When adverse aspects add their influence, then wind velocities increase and storms intensify, such as will be evidenced between April 23–26.

Zones 4 and 5 are inclined to rising temperatures and dry weather. Discordant planetary aspects result in atmospheric disturbance, such as excessive heat, thunderstorms, and destructive winds. In May, the zones will be subject to a breezy atmosphere and variable winds.

Generally, Zones 6 and 7 will see some fair conditions over northwest portions and a breezy-to-windy atmosphere. The season is shown to be an active one weather-wise with its fair share of low-pressure systems over these zones.

Alaska experiences below-average temperatures in April, a potentially stormy south-central coast in May, and rising temperatures and dryness in June. Hawaii sees generally fair conditions with lower temperatures during mid-April and a bit of a stormier time the last two weeks of May.

Full Moon March 14–22

Zone 1: Mid-Atlantic sees low pressure, elsewhere fair and cool the 14th. Ohio Valley sees strong thunderstorms the 17th. Fair, warmer the 18th. Cold front, possible thunderstorms. Strongest over the Delmarva Peninsula the 20th.

Zone 2: Fair, variable temperatures the 14th–18th. Cold front, thunderstorms. Strongest over Delmarva Peninsula the 20th.

Zone 3: Stormy, windy period over the Great Lakes. Strong thunderstorms over the Ohio Valley the 17th. Fair, warmer the 18th. Cold front, thunderstorms the 20th.

Zone 4: West is fair and warmer the 14th and 19th–21st. Potential thunderstorms, especially in Kansas and Oklahoma the 17th. Low pressure over North Dakota the 21st. Stormy and windy over the Great Lakes.

Zone 5: West is fair and warmer the 14th and 19th–21st. Storm system over New Mexico-Texas the 22nd. Potential thunderstorms, especially in Kansas and Oklahoma the 17th.

Zone 6: Western zone is cooler. Windy, possible storms along coast the 15th–18th, then fair and warm. East has thunderstorms the 16th, then fair and warm the 18th.

Zone 7: Western zone is cooler. Windy, possible storms along coast the 15th–18th, then fair and warm. East has thunderstorms the 16th, then fair and warm the 18th.

Zone 8: Alaska: West is fair and warm the 15th. Above-average precipitation and lower-than-normal temperatures the 16th–18th. Cool, breezy the 18th–20th. Fair, warm the 21st. Central is fair with variable temperatures the 14th–15th. Above-average precipitation and lower-than-normal temperatures 16th–18th. Fair and warm the 19th–21st. Rain the 21st. East is fair the 14th. Heavy rain and warm the 16th–19th. Fair the 19th–21st. Rain the 21st. Alaskan Panhandle is fair the 14th. Windy, possible storms the 15th–17th. Heavy rain, warm the 16th–19th. Fair after the 19th–21st. Precipitation the 22nd. Hawaii: Above-average precipitation and lower-than-normal temperatures the 16th–18th. Fair, warm the 21st.

4th Quarter March 22–29

Zone 1: A storm event in the mid-Atlantic brings the potential for heavy rain and damaging winds. New England sees stormy weather move in from the west, then fair.

Zone 2: A storm event takes place over the length of the zone bringing the potential for heavy rain and damaging winds. Temperatures may be lower than average.

Zone 3: A storm event takes place over the east, from the Great Lakes southward, bringing the potential for heavy rain and damaging winds.

Zone 4: Rain likely the 22nd. The eastern section is fair the 25th. Zone-wide potential for a winter storm followed by colder temperatures the 27th.

Zone 5: Rain likely the 22nd. The eastern section is fair the 25th. Zone-wide potential for a winter storm followed by colder temperatures the 27th.

Zone 6: West sees storms with potentially damaging winds the 24th. Windy and stormy system along coast the 27th. Plentiful rain likely in and around Idaho the 28th. East sees storms with potentially damaging winds the 24th. Rain likely the 27th.

Zone 7: West sees storms with potentially damaging winds the 24th. Windy and stormy system along northern coast the 27th. East sees storms with potentially damaging winds the 24th. Rain likely the 27th.

Zone 8: Alaska: Increased wind activity and lower temperatures across the zone. Front triggers precipitation over the area on the 26th and 27th. Alaskan Panhandle sees a very stormy period with potential for heavy precipitation and high wind velocities. Hawaii: Predominantly fair conditions for the zone. A front may trigger showers on the 26th.

New Moon March 29–April 4

Zone 1: A stormy pattern over the mid-Atlantic area resulting in heavy precipitation and strong winds the 29th–31st. Then warmer followed by showers the 2nd. New England is fair with lower-than-average temperatures the 29th. Cloudy and windy with lower temperatures March 30th–April 2nd.

Zone 2: A stormy pattern over the zone resulting in heavy precipitation and strong winds the 29th–31st. Cloudy and windy with lower temperatures and a chance of rain March 30th–April 2nd.

Zone 3: A stormy pattern over the zone resulting in heavy precipitation and strong winds the 29th–31st. A chance of rain the 2nd. Cloudy and windy over northern sections March 30th–April 2nd.

Zone 4: Fair conditions and pleasant temperatures. West and central see potential thunderstorms the 30th. Low pressure over Montana the 3rd. Eastern sections are cloudy and windy with strong low pressure, wind, and rain over Minnesota the 30th. Cloudy and windy with strong precipitation the 4th.

Zone 5: Fair conditions and pleasant temperatures. West and central see potential thunderstorms the 30th. Eastern sections are cloudy and windy the 30th. Cloudy and windy with strong precipitation the 4th.

Zone 6: High barometric pressure and lower temperatures for the period. The West Coast sees low pressure, heavy precipitation, and colder temperatures the 30th. Potential thunderstorms east the 30th. Low pressure over Pacific Northwest brings rain the 2nd. Fair conditions west with a chance of showers east on the 3rd.

Zone 7: High barometric pressure and lower temperatures for the period. The West Coast sees low pressure, heavy precipitation, and colder temperatures the 30th. Potential thunderstorms east the 30th. Fair conditions west with a chance of showers east on the 3rd.

Zone 8: Alaska: High barometric pressure and lower temperatures west and central. Low pressure over west coast the 3rd. East sees low pressure, heavy precipitation, colder temperatures, and windy conditions the 30th. Alaskan Panhandle: A strong winter storm affects the area with lower temperatures, heavy precipitation, and damaging winds the 29th–31st. Lower temperatures, cloudy and windy with possible showers the 2nd. Windy and fair with lower temperatures the 4th. Hawaii: Seasonal temperatures and average precipitation.

2nd Quarter April 4–12

Zone 1: Mid-Atlantic is fair, cool, and windy. New England is fair the 7th.

Zone 2: Fair, cool, and windy. Southern portions warmer.

Zone 3: Fair, cool, and windy the 4th. Fair and warm the 6th, then becoming cooler. Great Lakes are warmer with thunderstorms the 9th.

Zone 4: West sees cooler temperatures and fair conditions. Strong chance of thunderstorms for central portions the 7th. Eastern portions are windy and partly cloudy the 4th. Fair and warm the 6th. Windy the 7th. Central area sees warmer temperatures and thunderstorms the 9th. Fair central and east the 11th.

Zone 5: West sees cooler temperatures and fair conditions. Strong chance of thunderstorms for central portions the 7th. Eastern portions are windy and partly cloudy the 4th. Fair and warm the 6th. Windy the 7th. Central area sees warmer temperatures and thunderstorms the 9th. Fair central and east the 11th.

Zone 6: Fair and breezy conditions for the zone the 4th–9th. Eastern zone warmer with thunderstorms the 9th.

Zone 7: Fair and breezy conditions for the zone the 4th–9th. Eastern zone warmer with thunderstorms the 9th.

Zone 8: Alaska: West, central, and eastern areas begin cool, fair, and windy. East warms up the 5th, then fair the 11th. Alaskan Panhandle is fair, cool, and windy the 4th, then windy and stormy the 7th. Southerly winds and showers the 10th–12th. Hawaii: The zone begins partly cloudy and windy, then fair.

Full Moon April 12–20

Zone 1: Mid-Atlantic sees potential for strong, destructive storms the 14th–18th. Warm, windy, some thunderstorms the 20th.

Zone 2: Potential for strong, destructive storms in and around Kentucky the 14th–18th. Warm, windy, some thunderstorms the 20th.

Zone 3: Potential for strong, destructive storms in and around Kentucky the 14th–18th. High temperatures, humidity, and high heat or thunderstorms over the Great Lakes the 17th–19th. Warm, windy, some thunderstorms the 20th.

Zone 4: Low pressure over Montana the 18th. West and central thunderstorms the 20th. Eastern warmth and humidity with thunderstorm potential or high heat in and around the Great Lakes the 16th–19th.

Zone 5: Strong low pressure over New Mexico the 20th. West and central thunderstorms the 20th. Eastern warmth and humidity with thunderstorm potential the 17th–19th.

Zone 6: Rising temperatures and humidity resulting in showers and thunderstorms.

Zone 7: Rising temperatures and humidity resulting in showers and thunderstorms.

Zone 8: Alaska: West sees possible thunderstorms the 13th. Warm and unsettled the 20th. Central is cool and fair. East sees potential thunderstorms over north coast the 13th. Low pressure over southern coast the 17th. Alaskan Panhandle sees rising temperatures and humidity resulting in showers and thunderstorms. Hawaii: Mostly fair conditions with increasing temperatures around the 17th. Cool and fair the 20th.

4th Quarter April 20–27

Zone 1: Mid-Atlantic storm system the 20th. Warm, atmospheric disturbance, especially over the eastern Great Lakes the 23rd. Severe storms, strong winds, and possible hail the 25th. Strong thunderstorms the 27th. New England sees below-average temperatures. Strong low pressure off coast the 20th. Fair, cool the 23rd. Potential storms the 25th and 27th.

Zone 2: Storm system the 20th. Warm, strong atmospheric disturbance the 23rd. Severe storms, strong winds, possible hail the 25th and 27th.

Zone 3: Storm system the 20th. Warm, strong atmospheric disturbance the 23rd. Severe storms, strong winds, possible hail over the upper Mississippi Valley the 26th.

Zone 4: Warmer temperatures with strong storm systems over the western and central areas, which then move eastward. Strong storms over the upper Mississippi Valley 26th.

Zone 5: Warmer temperatures with strong storm systems over the western and central areas, which then move eastward. More intense storms are shown in and around New Mexico.

Zone 6: Coastal areas see increasing temperatures, breezy-to-windy conditions with precipitation from the 24th on. These conditions then continue eastward with heavy precipitation.

Zone 7: Coastal areas see increasing temperatures, breezy-to-windy conditions with precipitation from the 24th on. These conditions then continue eastward with heavy precipitation.

Zone 8: Alaska: Atmospheric disturbances likely over western area the 23rd and 25th. The central and eastern areas see increased precipitation and storminess during the forecast period. Hawaii: Fair conditions with an invigorating atmosphere. Cold front with possible showers the 23rd.

New Moon April 27–May 4

Zone 1: The period begins warm and fair. Heavy rain indicated for New England the 1st–2nd. Increasing temperatures from the west lead to thunderstorms the 4th.

Zone 2: The period begins warm and fair. Low pressure develops over Georgia and South Carolina the 30th. Warm and fair the 2nd. Increasing temperatures lead to thunderstorms the 4th.

Zone 3: Eastern sections begin warm and fair. Potential for heavy rain from western Great Lakes southward the 1st–3rd. Increasing temperatures lead to thunderstorms the 4th.

Zone 4: The zone begins with fair conditions, continuing fair over western sections. Central and eastern sections have lower-than-average temperatures. Potential for heavy rain from western Great Lakes southward 1st–2nd. Increasing temperatures central and east lead to thunderstorms with strong winds the 3rd.

Zone 5: The zone begins with fair conditions, continuing fair over western sections. Central and eastern sections have lower-than-average temperatures. Increasing temperatures central and east lead to thunderstorms with strong winds the 3rd.

Zone 6: A good chance of rain the 30th. Heavy rain indicated throughout the zone the 2nd. Pacific Northwest is fair the 3rd. Eastern thunderstorms with strong winds the 4th.

Zone 7: A good chance of rain the 30th. Heavy rain indicated throughout the zone the 2nd. Eastern thunderstorms with strong winds the 4th.

Zone 8: Alaska: Western areas begin fair. The south-central coast is generally a stormy area with potential for heavy rain throughout the period. Possible heavy precipitation over western and central southern coasts the 1st–2nd. Western and central areas see increasing temperatures that lead to thunderstorms the 4th. The Alaskan Panhandle starts warm and fair. Cloudy and rainy conditions, sometimes heavy, are indicated the 29th–2nd, then fair. Hawaii: Generally fair for the remainder of April. Potential for heavy rain the 1st–2nd.

2nd Quarter May 4–12

Zone 1: Dry and breezy with potential thunderstorms over the Delmarva Peninsula the 5th. Cold front with showers the 7th. Fair the 9th. Strong, windy storms the 11th.

Zone 2: Dry and breezy with potential thunderstorms over the Delmarva Peninsula the 5th. Strong, windy storms with low pressure over the Carolinas the 11th.

Zone 3: Warm and dry. Strong, windy storms the 11th.

Zone 4: Fair and pleasant. Chance of thunderstorms west, and low pressure around Minnesota and Iowa the 5th. West and central see rain the 8th. Central and east are warm and dry the 10th. Heavy thunderstorms over Colorado and New Mexico push through central region the 11th.

Zone 5: Fair and pleasant. Chance of thunderstorms the 5th. West and central see rain the 8th. Central and east are warm and dry the 10th. Heavy thunderstorms over Colorado and New Mexico push through central region the 11th.

Zone 6: Warm and dry. Eastern thunderstorms the 5th. Storms and lower temperatures the 9th. Strong, windy, coastal storms push eastward the 11th.

Zone 7: Warm and dry. Eastern thunderstorms the 5th. Storms and lower temperatures the 9th. Strong, windy, coastal storms push eastward the 11th.

Zone 8: Alaska: Clear and pleasant across zone the 5th. Cloudy and rainy west the 10th. West and central see strong windy storms the 11th. Alaskan Panhandle: Warm and breezy the 5th. Chance of showers the 7th–9th. Hawaii: Rising temperatures and showers. Western areas see storms with strong winds the 11th.

Full Moon May 12–20

Zone 1: Cool, fair the 13th. Windy, rainy, cooler the 14th–16th. Stronger storms the 17th. Front and thunderstorms the 19th. Warm, fair the 20th.

Zone 2: Cool, fair the 13th. Windy, rainy, cooler the 14th–16th. Stronger storms the 17th. Front and thunderstorms the 19th. Warm, fair the 20th.

Zone 3: Cool, fair east the 13th. Windy, rainy, cooler the 14th–17th. West sees thunderstorms, hail, and wind the 17th. Cold front east, possible showers the 19th.

Zone 4: Warm west and gusty thunderstorms central and east, then fair and cool the 16th. Thunderstorms, hail, and wind the 17th. Cold front east, possible showers the 19th.

Zone 5: Warm west and gusty thunderstorms central and east, then fair and cool the 16th. Thunderstorms, hail, and wind the 17th. Cold front east, possible showers the 19th.

Zone 6: West sees a coastal front and rain the 15th. West and east are fair, breezy the 15th. Warm and dry Pacific Northwest, but strong storms over Oregon and Nevada the 18th. Fair with a chance of thunderstorms west the 20th.

Zone 7: West sees a coastal front and rain the 15th. West and east are fair, breezy the 15th. Warm and dry but strong storms over Oregon and Nevada the 18th. Fair with a chance of thunderstorms west the 20th.

Zone 8: Alaska: West is cool with variable winds. Central storms the 15th. Central and east see thunderstorms, wind, and hail the 17th. Cold front, possible showers the 19th. Alaskan Panhandle is cool and fair the 13th. Cold front, precipitation the 15th. Increasing wind, storm conditions, and lower temperatures the 17th. Above-normal precipitation, misty or foggy the 20th. Hawaii: Windy, rainy, and cooler the 17th. Warm and fair the 20th.

4th Quarter May 20–26

Zone 1: Fair weather. Cooler, gusty winds, and stormy the 23rd.

Zone 2: Fair weather. Cooler, gusty winds, and stormy the 23rd.

Zone 3: Dry, breezy the 21st. Showers west the 23rd. Great Lakes are fair the 25th. Front and possible thunderstorms the 25th. East is cooler with gusty winds and stormy the 23rd.

Zone 4: Thunderstorms over northwestern portions. Dry, breezy the 21st. Warm, fair the 24th. Central is dry, breezy the 21st. Warm, fair the 24th. Warmer, showers the 26th. East is dry and breezy the 21st. Showers the 23rd. Great Lakes are fair the 25th. Warmer, showers the 26th.

Zone 5: West and central are dry, breezy the 21st. Warm, fair the 24th. Warmer with showers centrally the 26th. East is dry, breezy the 21st. Showers the 23rd. Warmer with showers the 26th.

Zone 6: Warm, fair the 22nd. Warmer, showers the 26th. Northeastern portions see thunderstorm activity.

Zone 7: Warm and fair. Southern California is hot with dry winds the 22nd. Warmer with showers the 26th.

Zone 8: Alaska: West is warm with possible wind the 22nd. Central is fair and breezy the 22nd. East is fair, dry, and breezy the 21st. Alaskan Panhandle is fair the 20th, and dry and breezy the 21st. Cooler, gusty winds, and stormy the 23rd. Colder, possible heavy rain the 24th. Fair, warming the 25th. Hawaii: Fair conditions. Cool, gusty winds, and stormy the 23rd.

New Moon May 26–June 2

Zone 1: Warm, windy, and fair the 27th–28th. Gusty thunderstorms the 30th. Cold front, showers the 1st.

Zone 2: Warm, windy, and fair the 27th. Gusty thunderstorms the 30th. Possible thunderstorms the 1st.

Zone 3: East is warm and windy the 27th. Gusty thunderstorms the 30th. Strong thunderstorms for Kentucky, Tennessee, and Alabama the 1st. West has a chance of showers the 30th. All fair the 30th. Possible thunderstorms the 1st.

Zone 4: Stormy period over northwestern sections. Thunderstorms the 28th, a chance of showers the 30th. Central is fair with thunderstorms the 28th. East sees chance of showers the 30th.

Zone 5: Thunderstorms the 28th, and a chance of showers the 30th. Central is fair with thunderstorms the 28th. East sees chance of showers the 30th.

Zone 6: West is fair with moderate winds May 26th–June 1st. Possible gusty thunderstorms over the Pacific Northwest, then fair the 30th. East is fair the 27th. Chance of showers the 30th.

Zone 7: West is fair with moderate winds May 26th–June 1st. East is fair the 27th. Chance of thunderstorms the 28th and chance of showers the 30th.

Zone 8: Alaska: West sees a stormy period. Central is warm and dry. Windy conditions while north and southeast coasts see thunderstorms the 28th. East is warm and dry. Windy conditions the 29th, and thunderstorms the 1st. Alaskan Panhandle is warm, windy, and fairer, afterward thunderstorms the 27th–28th. Fair the 30th. Hawaii: Warm, windy the 27th–28th. Cool, fair the 30th. Cold front, showers the 1st.

2nd Quarter June 2–11

Zone 1: Mid-Atlantic is fair the 4th. Storms with potential for heavy rain the 9th. New England sees lower temperatures with storms. Fair conditions the 6th. Storms with potentially heavy rain the 9th.

Zone 2: Fair the 4th. Thunderstorms increase around the 7th. Storms with potentially heavy rain the 9th.

Zone 3: Fair conditions over the Great Lakes the 4th. Warm and fair the 6th. Storms with potentially heavy rain the 9th.

Zone 4: West sees fair conditions on the 4th, then warmer with a chance of showers north the 6th. Fair, breezy the 8th. Storms with potentially heavy rain the 9th. Central is cool, and north is fair on the 4th. Storms with potentially heavy rain the 9th. East sees thunderstorms the 7th.

Zone 5: West sees fair conditions on the 4th. Fair, breezy the 8th. Storms with potentially heavy rain the 9th. Central has storms with potentially heavy rain the 9th. East has thunderstorms the 7th.

Zone 6: West sees stormy coastal conditions. Mild and pleasant in the Pacific Northwest the 4th. Potential for strong storms and heavy rain the 5th–8th. East is fair the 4th. Potential for strong storms and heavy rain the 5th-8th. Thunderstorms the 9th.

Zone 7: West sees stormy coastal conditions. Potential for strong storms and heavy rain the 5th–8th. East is fair the 4th. Potential for strong storms and heavy rain the 5th–8th. Thunderstorms the 9th.

Zone 8: Alaska: Northwest is fair the 4th. Thunderstorms, potentially heavy rain the 9th. Possible thunderstorms along the south-central coast the 4th. Cooler and stormy the 9th. East is warm and fair the 4th–6th. Possible thunderstorms the 7th. Cooler and rainy the 9th. Alaskan Panhandle has strong storms with winds and heavy rain the 5th–-8th. Southerly winds, rain the 10th. Hawaii: High pressure with lower-than-average temperatures. Chance of thunderstorms the 9th.

Full Moon June 11–18

Zone 1: A stormy period for the zone, especially New England the 11th, 15th, and 18th. Eastern Great Lakes and mid-Atlantic have strong storms the 15th.

Zone 2: Mild, humid atmosphere with showers. Strong thunderstorms and lightning the 15th.

Zone 3: Mild, humid atmosphere with showers.

Zone 4: West has increased moisture and higher-than-average precipitation. Windy conditions the 12th. Central and east have windy conditions north the 12th. Chance of rain the 14th. Rising temperatures with a chance of thunderstorms the 16th.

Zone 5: West has increased moisture and higher-than-average precipitation. Windy conditions the 12th. Central and east see a chance of rain the 14th. Rising temperatures with a chance of thunderstorms the 16th.

Zone 6: West is warm, dry along the coast. Windy coastal conditions the 12th. Low pressure, easterly winds, rain the 13th. Gusty storms the 15th. East sees increased moisture and higher-than-average precipitation. Fair the 11th. Low pressure, easterly winds, rain the 13th. Heavy rain, below-normal temperatures the 15th.

Zone 7: West is warm, dry along the northern coast. Fair the 11th. Windy coastal conditions the 12th. Low pressure, easterly winds, rain the 13th. Gusty storms the 15th. East sees increased moisture and higher-than-average precipitation. Fair the 11th. Low pressure, easterly winds, rain the 13th. Heavy rain, below-normal temperatures the 15th.

Zone 8: Alaska: West sees stormy conditions, then fair the 12th. Rising temperatures, strong thunderstorms, and lightning the 15th. Central and east are fair the 12th. Strong storms over southeastern coast and northeastern areas the 15th. Rising temperatures, strong thunderstorms, and lightning the 17th. Alaskan Panhandle sees rain the 11th. Low pressure, easterly winds, rain the 13th. Strong thunderstorms and lightning, heavy rain, cooler the 15th. Hawaii: Mild with temperate showers. Strong thunderstorms and lightning the 15th.

Summer

Zone 1 generally experiences high barometric pressure, windy conditions, and lower-than-average temperatures under favorable planetary influences. When under contrary astronomical conditions, cold, damp conditions or storms with gusty winds ensue.

Increasing temperatures are shown for Zone 2 along with occasional atmospheric disturbances that spawn severe winds, hail, and intense precipitation.

Conditions over Zone 3 range from a mild and humid atmosphere with southerly breezes and temperate showers to occasional gusty winds.

Zones 4 and 5 when under benevolent planetary alignments see moderate northerly winds and fine conditions accompanied by high barometric pressure. Under more challenging planetary combinations, sudden storms develop. Toward the end of the season, warm and dry conditions are indicated for western portions of the zone.

Zones 6 and 7 most likely experience heavier-than-average precipitation and increased cloud cover. Mild showers push through the zones in July. By August, dryer and warmer weather moves from west to east.

Variable weather conditions are indicated for northwestern Alaska, and warmer-than-average temperatures and dry conditions are shown for central portions. These conditions move eastward during July. By September, a mild pattern moves over western portions, engendering showers.

The Alaskan Panhandle sees below-average temperatures, high pressure, and windy conditions under benign planetary configurations and gusty storms under adverse planetary aspects.

At times, conflicting hot and cold air masses over Hawaii will bring high winds and stormy conditions, especially over eastern portions. The first week of July shows a mild, humid atmosphere with temperate showers. September begins with a breezy atmosphere and variable winds.

4th Quarter June 18–25

Zone 1: Fair, cool in the mid-Atlantic the 18th. Thunderstorms the 21st. Cold front, possible showers over New England the 22nd. Low pressure over Nova Scotia the 23rd. High pressure over eastern Great Lakes the 25th.

Zone 2: Fair, cool in the mid-Atlantic the 18th. Thunderstorms the 21st.

Zone 3: Fair the 18th. Thunderstorms over the Gulf Coast the 21st. Warm with showers the 22nd. High pressure over eastern Great Lakes the 25th.

Zone 4: West sees potentially heavy rain the 18th. Thunderstorm potential the 22nd. Rain the 25th. Central sees potentially heavy rain. Dry, warm, windy the 19th. Thunderstorm potential, heavy rain the 22nd. Heavy rain the 25th. East is dry, warm, and windy the 19th. Thunderstorm potential, heavy rain the 22nd. Low pressure over western Great Lakes the 23rd. Heavy rain the 25th.

Zone 5: West sees potentially heavy rain. Possible heavy precipitation the 18th. Thunderstorm potential, cooler the 22nd. Rain the 25th. Central sees potentially heavy rain. Dry, warm, windy the 19th. Thunderstorm potential, heavy rain the 22nd and 25th. East is dry, warm, and windy the 19th. Thunderstorm potential, heavy rain the 22nd and 25th.

Zone 6: Possible heavy precipitation, windy the 18th. Rain the 25th.

Zone 7: West is warm with showers, especially over northwest coastal areas, the 22nd. East sees possibly heavy precipitation and is windy the 18th. Rain the 25th.

Zone 8: Alaska: West is warm and dry the 18th–20th. Low pressure, rain the 23rd. Central sees rising temperatures and increased precipitation, then fair and warm the 22nd. Low pressure, rain the 23rd. Rain south the 25th. East is fair the 21st. Alaskan Panhandle sees strong low pressure, heavy precipitation the 18th. Rain, cooler the 22nd. Thunderstorms the 25th. Hawaii: Southerly winds and temperate showers. Fair, cool the 18th. Possible showers the 21st. Fair, warm the 22nd.

New Moon June 25–July 2

Zone 1: Cooler and windy with high pressure. Possible thunderstorms the 27th. Thunderstorms west to east the 29th. Precipitation is more than average over New England. Fair the 26th.

Zone 2: Fair with variable winds. Possible thunderstorms over the eastern Great Lakes the 27th. Thunderstorms, especially over the mid-Atlantic the 29th.

Zone 3: Mostly pleasant conditions. Warm, breezy, fair the 26th. Possible thunderstorms over the Ohio Valley the 27th.

Zone 4: West is fair and warm. Central sees thunderstorms the 25th, then fair the 27th. Thunderstorms around the 1st. East is warm, breezy, and fair the 26th. Strong thunderstorms over the northern Mississippi Valley the 29th, then fair the 1st.

Zone 5: West is fair and warm. Central sees thunderstorms the 25th, then fair the 27th. Thunderstorms around the 1st. East sees surging temperatures with possible thunderstorms. Warm, breezy, fair the 26th. Strong thunderstorms over the central Mississippi Valley the 29th.

Zone 6: High pressure and lower temperatures for coastal areas. Coastal storms the 29th. Front triggers coastal showers the 2nd. East is fair and breezy June 26th–July 2nd.

Zone 7: High pressure and lower temperatures for coastal areas. Coastal storms the 29th. Front triggers coastal showers the 2nd. East is fair and breezy June 26th–July 2nd.

Zone 8: Alaska: West is fair the 26th with possible showers the 28th. Central is warm and fair. Thunderstorms the 29th. East is fair June 25th and July 1st. Hawaii: Cool, windy, with high pressure over the Big Island the 26th and 30th. Western and central islands are mild with temperate showers.

2nd Quarter July 2–10

Zone 1: Storm system, possibly tropical in nature the 4th–6th. Fair the 7th.

Zone 2: Breezy with variable winds. Fair the 7th.

Zone 3: Breezy with variable winds. West is fair the 6th.

Zone 4: West and central are fair with rising temperatures. Thunderstorms the 6th and 9th. East is warm with thunderstorm potential. Fair the 6th.

Zone 5: West and central are fair with rising temperatures. Thunderstorms the 6th and 9th. East is warm with thunderstorm potential. Strong thunderstorms over Arkansas. Elsewhere, fair the 6th.

Zone 6: West sees higher-than-average precipitation. Thunderstorms over the Pacific Northwest the 7th. East sees rising temperatures. Thunderstorms the 4th.

Zone 7: West sees higher-than-average precipitation. East sees rising temperatures. Thunderstorms the 4th.

Zone 8: Alaska: West is warm and fair. Central is warm. Sudden showers after the 4th. Thunderstorms, especially over southern areas, the 6th. East is warm. Thunderstorms the 6th. Fair the 10th. Alaskan Panhandle is cool and rainy the 3rd–6th. Fair the 7th. Hawaii: Cool, thunderstorms the 3rd–6th.

Full Moon July 10–17

Zone 1: A windy and stormy period along the mid-Atlantic and New England coasts. Thunderstorms the 10th. Cool, fair the 11th. Chance of thunderstorms the 13th. Cooler, rainy, windy the 15th.

Zone 2: A windy and stormy period along the mid-Atlantic and New England coasts. Thunderstorms the 10th. Declining temperatures with increased precipitation after the 12th.

Zone 3: Declining temperatures with increased precipitation over eastern areas after the 12th. Warm, fair, breezy the 13th. Breezy, chance of rain the 15th.

Zone 4: West is breezy with variable winds. Thunderstorms the 10th. Central sees thunderstorms the 10th. Fair the 14th. East is warm, fair, and breezy the 13th. Breezy with a chance of rain the 15th.

Zone 5: West is breezy with variable winds. Thunderstorms the 10th. Fair the 14th. Central sees thunderstorms the 10th. Fair the 14th. East is warm, fair, and breezy the 13th. Breezy with a chance of rain the 15th.

Zone 6: West sees thunderstorms the 10th. Fair over the Pacific Northwest the 12th. Chance of rain the 14th. Fair over the Pacific Northwest the 16th. East sees higher temperatures with a chance of thunderstorms. Windy the 13th.

Zone 7: West sees lower temperatures and increased precipitation. Thunderstorms the 10th. Lower temperatures with precipitation the 15th. East sees higher temperatures with a chance of thunderstorms. Windy the 13th.

Zone 8: Alaska: West and central are cooler, breezy, with variable winds. Cold fronts trigger showers. East begins warm and fair, then turns cooler with increasing precipitation. Alaskan Panhandle is showery, then colder after the 12th. Hawaii: Generally, fair. Chance of thunderstorms the 13th. Cooler, rainy, windy the 15th.

4th Quarter July 17–24

Zone 1: Warm, dashing showers the 19th. Fair, cool, breezy the 21st. Local showers, then cool and breezy with strong thunderstorms over mid-Atlantic the 23rd. Fair the 24th.

Zone 2: Warm, dashing showers the 19th. Fair, cool, breezy the 21st. Local showers, then cool and breezy with strong thunderstorms over mid-Atlantic and southeast the 23rd. Fair the 24th.

Zone 3: Increasing temperatures the 19th. Rain the 20th. East is fair, cool, and breezy the 21st. Strong thunderstorms zone wide the 22nd. Local showers, then cool and breezy in the east the 23rd. Dry, breezy the 24th.

Zone 4: West is warm and dry the 17th. Possible showers the 19th. Showers or thunderstorms the 22nd. Warm and dry the 24th. Central is fair the 18th and 23rd. East is fair the 18th and 23rd. Chance of rain the 20th. Dry, breezy the 24th.

Zone 5: West is warm and dry the 17th. Possible showers the 19th. Showers or thunderstorms the 22nd. Warm and dry the 24th. Central is fair the 18th and 23rd. East is fair the 18th and 23rd. Chance of rain the 20th. Dry, breezy the 24th.

Zone 6: Low pressure over coastal areas and windy over the Pacific Northwest. Fair, breezy, then possible showers the 18th. Warm, possible showers the 21st. Warmer, showers the 23rd. East is fair the 17th. Warm, possible showers the 21st. Warmer, showers the 23rd.

Zone 7: Low pressure over the northern and central coast. Fair the 17th. Warm, possible showers the 21st. Warmer, showers the 23rd. East is warm with possible showers the 21st. Warmer, showers the 23rd.

Zone 8: Alaska: Low pressure affects northwestern coast. Central is fair the 18th and 20th. Cool, fair over the north-central coast the 24th. East is fair the 18th. Fair, cool the 23rd. Alaskan Panhandle: Increasing warmth the 19th. Fair, cool, breezy the 21st. Warmer with showers the 23rd. Dry, breezy the 24th. Hawaii: Fair the 18th. Possible showers the 19th. Fair, cool, breezy the 21st. Chance of thunderstorms the 22nd.

New Moon July 24–August 1

Zone 1: Warm with thunderstorms the 25th. Windy, stormy, possible tropical system the 31st.

Zone 2: Warm with thunderstorms the 25th. Tropical showers in Florida the 29th. Windy, stormy coast the 31st.

Zone 3: Chance of showers the 25th. Fair the 27th. Warming the 28th. Showers the 31st.

Zone 4: Montana thunderstorms the 26th. Showers the 28th. High pressure the 29th. Warm with showers, then fair with strong storms on the high plains the 31st. Cloudy and rainy the 1st. Central is warm with thunderstorms the 25th. Breezy, fair the 29th. Strong thunderstorms the 31st. Cloudy and rainy the 1st. East is breezy, fair the 29th. Gusty thunderstorms the 31st.

Zone 5: West sees showers the 28th. Breezy, fair the 29th. Strong thunderstorms the 31st. Cloudy, rainy the 1st. Central is warm with thunderstorms the 25th. Breezy, fair the 29th. Fair the 31st. East has gusty thunderstorms the 31st.

Zone 6: West sees coastal showers. Breezy, fair inland the 29th. Eastern showers the 28th. Warm with showers, then fair the 31st. Cloudy, rainy the 1st.

Zone 7: West sees coastal showers. Breezy, fair inland the 29th. Eastern showers the 28th. Warm with showers, then fair the 31st. Cloudy, rainy the 1st.

Zone 8: Alaska: The west coast experiences low pressure the 25th. Windy thunderstorms the 26th. High pressure along the southwest coast the 26th. West coast storms the 1st. Central has windy thunderstorms the 26th. High pressure south-central coast the 29th. Thunderstorms the 1st. East is windy with thunderstorms the 26th. High pressure along the southeast coast the 27th. Thunderstorms the 1st. Alaskan Panhandle is warm and dry. Warm, showers the 28th. Hawaii: Windy thunderstorms the 26th. Western thunderstorms the 31st.

2nd Quarter August 1–9

Zone 1: Lower temperatures, then potentially heavy downpours over the mid-Atlantic the 1st. Front and thunderstorms the 3rd. Windy the 5th. Warm with showers the 7th. Windy the 8th.

Zone 2: Lower temperatures, then potentially heavy downpours the 1st. Front and thunderstorms in the north on the 3rd. Windy in the north on the 5th. Windy in the north on the 8th.

Zone 3: The east sees potentially heavy downpours the 1st. Hot with showers the 7th. Strong thunderstorms over the Mississippi Valley and western Great Lakes the 8th.

Zone 4: West is warm with possible heavy rain the 1st. Front and thunderstorms the 5th. Heat and thunderstorms the 6th. Central is warm with possible heavy rain the 1st. Heat and thunderstorms the 6th. Strong thunderstorms the 8th. East is hot with showers the 7th. Strong thunderstorms over the Mississippi Valley and western Great Lakes the 8th.

Zone 5: West is warm with possible heavy rain the 1st. Front and thunderstorms the 5th. Heat and thunderstorms the 6th. Central is warm with local thunderstorms. East is hot with showers the 7th. Strong thunderstorms the 8th.

Zone 6: West is breezy with variable winds. Thunderstorms the 3rd. Strong coastal thunderstorms the 8th. East is breezy with variable winds. Front and thunderstorms the 5th. Heat and thunderstorms the 6th.

Zone 7: West is warm with thunderstorms the 3rd. Strong coastal thunderstorms the 8th. East is breezy with variable winds. Front and thunderstorms the 5th. Heat and thunderstorms the 6th.

Zone 8: Alaska: The west is warm and fair the 1st. Thunderstorms the 8th. Central sees strong thunderstorms the 1st. Thunderstorms the 8th. Low pressure along the southern coast and central area. Warm, showers the 7th. Alaskan Panhandle sees thunderstorms, possible heavy rain the 1st. Front and thunderstorms the 3rd. Windy the 5th. Warm, strong thunderstorms the 7th. Hawaii: Warm, fair the 1st. Front with thunderstorms the 3rd. Windy the 5th. Showers the 8th.

Full Moon August 9–16

Zone 1: Windy, possible showers the 9th. Warm, fair the 10th. Cooler the 11th. Strong storms possibly tropical the 12th. Warm, dry, breezy the 14th.

Zone 2: Windy, possible showers the 9th. Warm, fair the 10th. Strong storms possibly tropical the 12th. Warm, dry, breezy the 14th.

Zone 3: Windy the 9th. Warm, fair the 10th–13th. Thunderstorms over Louisiana-Mississippi the 14th.

Zone 4: Strong storms in the west the 9th–10th. Central sees strong storms the 9th–10th, then windy the 11th. Warm, fair the 13th. East is windy the 11th. Warm, fair the 13th.

Zone 5: Strong storms in the west the 9th–10th. Central is windy the 9th–11th. Warm, fair the 13th. East is windy the 9th–11th. Warm, fair the 13th. Thunderstorms over Louisiana-Mississippi the 14th.

Zone 6: In the west, a strong front, winds, and storms push eastward the 12th. Storms and wind the 14th. In the east, a strong front, winds, and storms push eastward the 12th. Dry, breezy the 14th.

Zone 7: In the west, a strong front, winds, and storms push eastward the 12th. Storms and wind the 14th. In the east, a strong front, winds, and storms push eastward the 12th. Dry, breezy the 14th.

Zone 8: Alaska: Front and thunderstorms in west and central on the 10th. Fair the 12th. Chance of thunderstorms the 14th. East is fair the 12th. Chance of thunderstorms the 14th. Alaskan Panhandle sees strong storms the 9th. Cooler, fair the 11th. Storms, wind the 15th. Hawaii: Mild with temperate showers. Front, thunderstorms the 10th. Cooler the 11th.

4th Quarter August 16–23

Zone 1: Chance of showers, cooler the 16th. Dry, breezy the 18th. Thunderstorms, cooler the 21st.

Zone 2: Dry, breezy the 18th. Chance of thunderstorms the 20th. Breezy, variable winds the 21st.

Zone 3: Fair, warm, slight chance of rain the 18th. Thunderstorms over Kentucky-Tennessee the 19th. Southerly winds, temperate showers the 20th. Breezy, variable winds the 21st.

Zone 4: West sees chance of thunderstorms the 19th. Fair the 22nd. Stormy central. Fair, warm the 18th. Chance of thunderstorms the 19th. Chance of thunderstorms but fair north the 20th. Storms east. Fair, warm, slight chance of rain the 18th. Southerly winds, temperate showers the 20th. Breezy, variable winds the 21st.

Zone 5: West sees chance of thunderstorms the 19th. Fair the 22nd. Central is fair and warm the 18th. Chance of thunderstorms around the 20th. East is fair and warm with a slight chance of rain the 18th. Southerly winds, temperate showers the 20th. Breezy, variable winds the 21st.

Zone 6: West is cooler, fair the 16th. Dry, breezy the 18th. Chance of thunderstorms the 19th. East is fair.

Zone 7: West is dry, breezy the 18th. Chance of thunderstorms the 19th. East is fair.

Zone 8: Alaska: Western thunderstorms the 19th. Fair the 20th. Thunderstorms, cooler the 21st. Fair the 22nd. Central is fair the 18th. Thunderstorms the 19th. Alaskan Peninsula fair the 20th. Thunderstorms, cooler the 21st. Fair the 22nd. East is fair the 18th. Thunderstorms the 19th. Alaskan Panhandle sees a chance of showers, cooler the 16th. Thunderstorms the 18th. Thunderstorms, cooler the 21st. Hawaii: Slight chance of rain the 16th. Thunderstorms, cooler the 21st. Fair the 22nd.

New Moon August 23–31

Zone 1: Thunderstorms the 24th, then fair the 25th–26th. Thunderstorms the 26th–27th. Fair the 28th. Cold front, thunderstorms the 30th.

Zone 2: Mostly fair with a slight chance of showers the 24th–26th. Thunderstorms the 26th–27th.

Zone 3: Showers the 25th. Strong central thunderstorms the 26th. Thunderstorms northeast of the Great Lakes the 28th.

Zone 4: West is fair the 23rd. Fair, thunderstorms north on the 25th and 28th. Central and east are generally fair.

Zone 5: West sees a stormy period with possible flash flooding. Fair the 25th. Central and east are fair.

Zone 6: West sees a stormy period. Thunderstorms the 26th. Strong thunderstorms over the Pacific Northwest the 27th. Low pressure offshore the 28th. East is fair the 25th. Thunderstorms the 26th.

Zone 7: West sees thunderstorms the 26th. Low pressure offshore the 28th. Thunderstorms over California-Nevada the 29th. East is fair the 25th. Thunderstorms the 26th.

Zone 8: Alaska: Fair but stormy along the southwest coast the 23rd. Warm with thunderstorms the 24th. Possible showers and thunderstorms the 29th. Central is fair the 23rd. Warm with thunderstorms the 24th. Thunderstorms north the 28th. Cold front east with possible showers the 23rd. Fair along the south coast, then thunderstorms north the 28th. Alaskan Panhandle has gusty thunderstorms the 24th. Fair the 25th–28th. Cold front, thunderstorms the 30th. Hawaii: Fair the 23rd. Warm, gusty thunderstorms the 24th. Cold front, chance of showers the 29th.

2nd Quarter August 31–September 7

Zone 1: Lower ranges of temperatures with a stormy mid-Atlantic coast. Storms, high winds the 2nd. Cooler, windy, with possible storms the 5th.

Zone 2: Stormy mid-Atlantic coast. Warmer, possible thunderstorms the 4th.

Zone 3: Thunderstorms the 3rd. Possible showers the 7th.

Zone 4: West is cooler with intense rain the 1st. Fair the 3rd. Cooler with increasing winds the 5th. Central is cooler with intense rain the 1st. Fair the 3rd. Gusty storms the 6th. East sees intense rain the 1st. Thunderstorms the 4th. Gusty storms the 6th.

Zone 5: West is cooler with intense rain the 1st. Fair the 3rd. Cooler with increasing winds. Severe thunderstorms over west Texas on the 5th. Central has intense rain the 1st. Fair the 2nd. Gusty storms the 6th. East has intense rain the 1st. Thunderstorms the 4th. Gusty storms the 6th.

Zone 6: Low pressure offshore affects the Pacific Northwest with intense rain the 1st. Gusty storms the 6th. East has rising temperatures. Warmer with thunderstorms the 4th.

Zone 7: West is cooler with intense rain the 1st. Gusty storms the 6th. East has rising temperatures. Warmer with thunderstorms the 4th.

Zone 8: Alaska is breezy with variable winds. West and central have storms and high winds the 2nd. East is warmer with thunderstorms the 4th. Fair the 7th. Alaskan Panhandle is cooler with intense rain the 1st. Hawaii: Breezy, variable winds. Storms, high winds the 2nd. Cold front and thunderstorms the 6th.

Full Moon September 7–14

Zone 1: Chance of thunderstorms the 10th. Unseasonably cool the 11th. Showers the 12th.

Zone 2: Chance of thunderstorms the 10th. Showers the 12th.

Zone 3: Windy, dry, and warm the 9th. Fair the 12th. Windy with showers the 13th.

Zone 4: Dry with rising temperatures in the west. Thunderstorms the 10th. Central thunderstorms the 10th. East is windy, dry, and warm the 9th. Fair the 12th.

Zone 5: Dry with rising temperatures in the west. Thunderstorms the 10th. Central has strong thunderstorms. Thunderstorms the 10th. Strong thunderstorms in the east. Windy, dry, warm the 9th. Fair the 12th.

Zone 6: Western showers the 9th. Cold front with showers the 13th. East is dry with rising temperatures. Windy, dry, and warm the 9th.

Zone 7: Western showers the 9th. Cold front with showers the 13th. East is dry with rising temperatures. Windy, dry, and warm the 9th.

Zone 8: Alaska: West is mild with showers. Chance of thunderstorms the 10th. Showers the 12th. Central sees possible showers the 11th. Cold front and showers the 13th. East is breezy with variable winds. Fair the 10th. Alaskan Panhandle is cloudy and cooler with showers the 8th. Unseasonably cool the 11th. Fair, breezy the 12th. Hawaii: Fair the 10th. Unseasonably cool the 11th. Showers the 12th.

4th Quarter Moon September 14–21

Zone 1: Wind or windy storms. Cloudy, gusty winds, and cooler the 17th. Cool, cloudy, rainy the 18th. Warm, windy over the mid-Atlantic. Cooler, rainy over New England the 20th. Fair, breezy, cooler the 21st.

Zone 2: Cloudy, windy the 17th. Warm, windy the 20th.

Zone 3: Lower temperatures. Fair, then thunderstorms the 16th.

Zone 4: West is warm and fair the 15th. Thunderstorms the 16th. Windy, possible showers the 18th. Windy, fair, mild the 19th. Rising temperatures, then fair the 21st. Central is warm and fair the 15th. Thunderstorms the 16th. Windy, cooler the 19th. Low pressure, precipitation the 20th. Rising temperatures, fair the 21st. East sees lower temperatures. Fair the 16th. Low pressure, precipitation the 20th.

Zone 5: West is warm and fair the 15th. Thunderstorms the 16th. Windy, possible showers the 18th. Windy, fair, mild the 19th. Rising temperatures, then fair the 21st. Central is warm and fair the 15th. Thunderstorms the 16th. Fair the 19th. Low pressure, precipitation the 20th. East sees lower temperatures. Fair the 16th. Low pressure, precipitation the 20th.

Zone 6: Western front triggers thunderstorms the 14th. Coastal storms the 21st. Eastern front triggers thunderstorms the 14th. Windy, possible showers the 18th. Windy, fair, mild the 19th.

Zone 7: Western front triggers thunderstorms the 14th. Coastal storms the 21st. Eastern front triggers thunderstorms the 14th. Windy, possible showers the 18th. Windy, fair, mild the 19th.

Zone 8: Alaska: West is warm and fair the 15th. Cooler, rainy the 18th. Fair, mild the 19th. Cooler, rainy the 20th. Rising temperatures, mostly fair the 21st. Central is stormy. Cooler, rainy the 18th. Fair, mild the 19th. Rising temperatures, mostly fair the 21st. Alaskan Panhandle is windy and stormy. Hawaii: Variable winds with showery weather. Gusty winds, cooler the 17th. Cool, rainy the 18th. Fair, mild the 19th. Cooler, rainy the 20th. Rising temperatures, mostly fair the 21st. Fair, breezy, cooler the 21st.

Autumn

Zone 1 sees increased temperatures and dryness under beneficent planetary aspects. Dangerous, gusty storms occur under contrary planetary alignments. Conditions for Zones 2 and 3 are generally windy and fair. Periods of rain and wind bring colder nights.

Under positive influences, Zones 4 and 5 see lower temperatures, high pressure, and increased wind velocities over western areas. Negative influences bring windy, rainy, damp conditions. Central and eastern areas fluctuate between cooler temperatures and mild, pleasant conditions. Adverse weather is mostly cold, windy, and stormy.

Western portions of Zones 6 and 7 are mild with temperate showers under benign aspects. Eastern portions see high pressure and lower temperatures. However, difficult planetary alignments bring low temperatures and rainy conditions to all areas.

Western portions of Alaska inclined to fair weather and higher temperatures. Adverse aspects lead to thunderstorm formation. The central and eastern Alaskan zones along with the Alaskan Panhandle experience heat and increasing aridness. Inharmonious celestial influences bring turbulent and destructive weather patterns. The Hawaiian Islands see warmer temperatures and dry conditions under benign planetary aspects. Destructive storms are possible under discordant planetary influences.

New Moon September 21–29

Zone 1: Strong wind and storms the 24th. Fair the 28th. Showers and thunderstorms the 29th.

Zone 2: Fair the 28th. Showers and thunderstorms the 29th.

Zone 3: Breezy the 22nd. Cloudy, easterly winds, rainy the 23rd. Strong winds and storms the 24th. Fair the 28th.

Zone 4: West is fair and windy with a cold wave the 23rd. Declining temperatures the 26th. Central is windy and rainy with possible fog the 23rd. Fair the 26th. Chance of rain the 27th. Showers and thunderstorms the 29th. East is breezy the 22nd. Windy and rainy with possible fog the 23rd. Strong winds and storms the 24th. Fair the 26th. Showers and thunderstorms the 29th.

Zone 5: West is fair and windy with a cold wave the 23rd. Declining temperatures the 26th. Central is windy and rainy with possible fog the 23rd. Fair the 26th. Chance of rain the 27th. Showers and thunderstorms the 29th. East is breezy the 22nd. Windy and rainy with possible fog the 23rd. Strong winds and storms the 24th. Fair the 26th. Showers and thunderstorms the 29th.

Zone 6: West sees a stormy period the 23rd–25th. Fair, declining temperatures the 26th. Rain and wind, then cooler the 28th. East is fair and windy with a cold wave the 23rd. Fair, declining temperatures the 26th. Chance of rain the 27th. Rain and wind, then cooler the 28th.

Zone 7: West sees a stormy period the 23rd–25th. Fair the 26th. Rain and wind, then cooler the 28th. East is fair and windy with a cold wave the 23rd. Fair the 26th. Chance of rain the 27th. Rain and wind, then cooler the 28th.

Zone 8: Alaska: West is fair and breezy the 23rd. Fair the 26th and 28th. Central sees strong wind and storms the 24th. Fair the 28th. East sees strong wind and storms the 24th. Alaskan Panhandle has strong wind and storms the 24th. Warm, fair the 28th. Hawaii: Breezy, chance of showers the 23rd. Fair the 26th and 28th.

2nd Quarter September 29–October 6

Zone 1: Windy, cooler temperatures, possible rain the 30th. Possible thunderstorms, then fair the 2nd. Dry, warm, windy, with possible electrical storms the 6th.

Zone 2: Breezy with variable winds. Windy, cooler temperatures, possible rain the 30th.

Zone 3: Rain, wind, and cooler nights the 30th. Fair, warm the 2nd. Cloudy, rainy, cooler the 5th.

Zone 4: In the west, southerly winds, rain, then fair the 30th. Cold front, thunderstorms the 3rd. Cloudy, rainy, cooler the 5th. Clear skies, moderate temperatures the 6th. Central thunderstorms the 5th. Clear skies, moderate temperatures the 6th. East sees rain, wind, and cooler nights the 30th. Fair, warm the 2nd. Thunderstorms the 5th.

Zone 5: In the west, southerly winds, rain, then fair the 30th. Cold front, thunderstorms the 3rd. Cloudy, rainy, cooler the 5th. Clear skies, moderate temperatures the 6th. Central thunderstorms the 5th. Clear skies, moderate temperatures the 6th. East sees rain, wind, and cooler nights the 30th. Fair, warm the 2nd. Thunderstorms the 5th.

Zone 6: West sees a cold front and thunderstorms the 3rd. Showers the 5th. East sees southerly winds, rain, then fair the 30th. Cold front, thunderstorms the 3rd. Showers the 5th. Cool, fair the 6th.

Zone 7: West sees a cold front and thunderstorms the 3rd. Showers the 5th. East sees southerly winds, rain, then fair the 30th. Cold front, thunderstorms the 3rd. Showers the 5th. Cool, fair the 6th.

Zone 8: Alaska is breezy with variable winds. West is windy with cooler temperatures and possible rain the 30th. Clear skies, moderate temperatures the 6th. Central is windy with cooler temperatures and possible rain, then fair the 30th. Thunderstorms the 2nd. Fair the 6th. East is windy with cooler temperatures, possible rain, then fair the 30th. Thunderstorms the 2nd. Fair the 6th. Alaskan Panhandle sees showers the 30th. Thunderstorms the 2nd. Warm, fair the 4th. Dry, warm, windy, with possible electrical storms the 6th. Hawaii: Breezy with variable winds. Fair the 1st–3rd. Dry, warm, windy, with possible electrical storms the 6th.

Full Moon October 6–13

Zone 1: Fair, breezy over the mid-Atlantic the 7th. Strong, windy storms over New England the 8th. Storm potential increases with possible heavy rain the 9th–13th.

Zone 2: Mild with temperate showers. North is fair, breezy the 7th. Front generates thunderstorms zone-wide the 11th.

Zone 3: Mild with temperate showers. Front generates thunderstorms the 10th.

Zone 4: West is fair and cool. Becoming cloudy, with possible heavy rain over central and eastern areas the 8th–13th.

Zone 5: West is fair and cool. Becoming cloudy, with possible heavy rain over central and eastern areas the 8th–13th.

Zone 6: Lower temperatures over western areas. Thunderstorms over Pacific Northwest and Intermountain West the 8th. Warm, gentle breezes the 9th. Pacific Northwest coast storms the 12th. Sharp winds and possible electrical disturbance over Pacific Northwest the 13th.

Zone 7: Lower temperatures over western areas. Thunderstorms over Intermountain West the 8th. Warm, gentle breezes the 9th.

Zone 8: Alaska: Western areas are generally fair with north winds. Breezy at times. Central and eastern areas see destructive storms, hail, and wind the 7th. Fair, cool the 10th. Alaskan Panhandle: Destructive storms, hail, and wind the 8th. Sharp winds and possible electrical disturbance the 13th. Hawaii: Fair, breezy the 7th. Windy conditions likely the 9th. Thunderstorms the 11th.

4th Quarter October 13–21

Zone 1: The period begins and ends with windy and stormy weather along the coast. Mild, breezy the 14th, 17th, and 20th.

Zone 2: The period begins and ends with windy and stormy weather along the coast. Mild, breezy the 14th, 17th, and 20th.

Zone 3: Mild, possible showers the 18th. Mild, breezy, then possible heavy rain the 20th.

Zone 4: West is cool, fair the 14th. Cold front, showers the 16th. Fair the 17th. Cool, fair the 19th. Windy, showers the 20th. Central showers and thunderstorms the 13th. Cool, fair the 14th. Chance of rain the 18th. Cool, fair the 19th. Possible heavy rain the 20th. Eastern showers and thunderstorms the 13th. Cool, fair the 14th. Mild, possible showers the 18th. Cool, fair the 19th. Possible heavy rain the 20th.

Zone 5: West is cool, fair the 14th. Cold front, showers the 16th. Fair the 17th. Cool, fair the 19th. Windy, showers the 20th. Central showers and thunderstorms the 13th. Fair the 14th. Chance of rain the 18th. Cool, fair the 19th. Possible heavy rain the 20th. Eastern showers and thunderstorms the 13th. Cool, fair the 14th. Mild, possible showers the 18th. Cool, fair the 19th. Possible heavy rain the 20th.

Zone 6: Western coastal areas dry, warm, with sharp winds the 13th. Coastal thunderstorms the 15th. Fair coastal areas the 17th. Dry, warm, windy the 20th. Heavy rain at times for the Intermountain West. Cool, fair the 14th. Showers the 16th. Fair the 17th. Cool, fair the 19th. Dry, warm, windy the 20th.

Zone 7: Western cold front and showers the 16th. Fair northern coastal areas the 17th. Dry, warm, windy the 20th. Heavy rain at times for the Intermountain West. Cool, fair the 14th. Showers the 16th. Fair the 17th. Cool, fair the 19th. Dry, warm, windy the 20th.

Zone 8: Alaska: West is fair the 13th. Moderate temperatures and breezy the 14th and 17th. Central is cool and fair the 14th. Moderate temperatures, breezy the 17th. Fair the 19th. East sees moderate temperatures, breezy the 17th. Alaskan Panhandle is warm and windy the 13th. Thunderstorms the 15th. Dry, warm, windy the 20th. Hawaii: Dry, warm, and windy the 13th. Cool, fair, breezy the 14th. Moderate temperatures, breezy the 17th. Warm and windy the 20th.

New Moon October 21–29

Zone 1: Showers over New England the 21st. Temperatures rise over New England the 23rd. Atmospheric disturbance the 24th. Mid-Atlantic is fair the 22nd. Showers the 26th.

Zone 2: Mild with temperate showers, especially after the 25th.

Zone 3: Stormy over the southern Mississippi Valley. Mild, tem-

perate showers the 22nd. Cloudy, rainy the 24th. Fair the 25th. Mild, possible showers the 27th.

Zone 4: West is fair the 23rd. Cold front, possible showers the 24th. Cool, fair the 25th. Fair, windy the 29th. Central and east see possible rain the 22nd, 24th, and 26th. Fair the 23rd, 25th, 27th, and 29th.

Zone 5: West is fair the 23rd. Cold front, possible showers the 24th. Cool, fair the 25th. Fair, windy the 29th. Central and east are stormy over the southern Mississippi Valley. Possible rain the 22nd, 24th, and 26th. Fair the 23rd, 25th, 27th, and 29th.

Zone 6: Fair, moderate temperatures the 21st. Warm, dry, windy the 23rd and 28th.

Zone 7: West is fair with moderate temperatures the 21st. Warm, dry, windy the 23rd and 28th.

Zone 8: Alaska: West is fair with moderate temperatures the 21st. Warm, dry, windy the 23rd. Cloudy, rainy the 24th. Possible showers the 27th. Warm, dry the 28th. Central and east showers the 21st. Atmospheric disturbance the 24th. Possible showers the 27th. Alaskan Panhandle sees showers the 21st. Temperatures rise the 23rd. Clear, mild the 26th. Hawaii: Fair, warm, and dry. Cold front, wind the 23rd.

2nd Quarter October 29–November 5

Zone 1: Warm, cloudy, with possible showers.

Zone 2: Mild with temperate showers.

Zone 3: Mild with temperate showers.

Zone 4: West is cold and windy the 30th. Thunderstorms the 31st. Cloudy, windy, possible showers the 2nd. Warm, then sultry the 3rd. Severe thunderstorms, wind the 4th. Central and east are cloudy and windy October 29th and November 2nd. Warm, fair October 30th and November 3rd.

Zone 5: West is cold and windy the 30th. Thunderstorms the 31st. Cloudy, windy, possible showers the 2nd. Warm, then sultry the 3rd. Severe thunderstorms, wind the 4th. Central and east are cloudy and windy October 29th and November 2nd. Warm, fair October 30th and November 3rd.

Zone 6: West is cold and windy the 30th. Thunderstorms the 31st. Warm, showers the 2nd. East is cloudy, cold, and windy the 29th. Thunderstorms the 31st. Cloudy, windy the 2nd. Warm, then sultry the 3rd. Severe thunderstorms, wind the 4th.

Zone 7: West is cold and windy the 30th. Thunderstorms the 31st. Warm, showers the 2nd. East is cloudy, cold, and windy the 29th. Thunderstorms the 31st. Cloudy, windy the 2nd. Warm, then sultry the 3rd. Severe thunderstorms, wind the 4th.

Zone 8: Alaska: West, central, and east are cloudy and warm with possible showers. Alaskan Panhandle is fair the 30th. Possible showers the 4th. Hawaii: Cloudy and warm with possible showers.

Full Moon November 5–12

Zone 1: Temperatures rise, showers and thunderstorms the 6th. Thunderstorms the 8th. Fair the 11th. Stormy for New England.

Zone 2: Thunderstorms the 8th. Fair the 11th.

Zone 3: Thunderstorms Great Lakes and southward the 8th. Increasing winds the 9th.

Zone 4: West is windy with thunderstorms the 6th. Fair, windy, colder the 7th. Thunderstorms, colder, windy the 9th. Thunderstorms, windy the 11th. Central and east are warm, humid the 5th. Fair, windy, colder the 7th. Thunderstorms, colder, windy the 9th. Thunderstorms, windy the 11th.

Zone 5: West is windy with thunderstorms the 6th. Fair, windy, colder the 7th. Thunderstorms, colder, windy the 9th. Thunderstorms, windy the 11th. Central and east are warm, humid the 5th. Fair, windy, colder the 7th. Colder, rainy, windy the 9th. Thunderstorms, windy the 11th.

Zone 6: Wind, thunderstorms the 6th. Fair, windy, colder the 7th. Colder, rainy, windy the 10th. Thunderstorms, windy the 11th.

Zone 7: Wind, thunderstorms the 6th. Fair, windy, colder the 7th. Thunderstorms the 9th. Colder, rainy, windy the 10th. Thunderstorms, windy the 11th. Stormy for California.

Zone 8: Alaska: West is warm and fair the 6th. Thunderstorms the 7th. Fair, warmer the 11th. Central and east are warm and fair the 6th. Thunderstorms the 7th. Thunderstorms, windy the 11th. Alaskan Panhandle sees temperatures rise and showers the 6th. Increasing winds the 9th. Showers the 10th. Hawaii: Temperatures rise, showers the 6th. Thunderstorms the 8th. Fair, warmer the 11th.

4th Quarter November 12–20

Zone 1: Lower-than-average temperatures and wind over the mid-Atlantic. Warmer with sharp winds over New England.

Zone 2: Lower-than-average temperatures and windy conditions.

Zone 3: Sharp winds, storms the 12th–15th. Fair the 18th. Cold, windy the 19th.

Zone 4: West is dry, breezy the 12th–14th. Showers the 15th. Cold, gusty winds the 17th. Windy, rainy the 19th. Central is dry and breezy the 12th–14th. Showers the 15th. Fair the 17th. Warm, gentle breezes the 18th. East is dry and breezy the 12th–14th. Fair the 17th. Warm, gentle breezes the 18th.

Zone 5: West is dry, breezy the 12th–14th. Showers the 15th. Cold, gusty winds the 17th. Windy, rainy the 19th. Central is dry and breezy the 12th–14th. Showers the 15th. Fair the 17th. Warm, gentle breezes the 18th. East is dry and breezy the 12th–14th. Fair the 17th. Warm, gentle breezes the 18th.

Zone 6: West is fair, windy the 13th. Showers the 15th. Cold, gusty winds the 17th. Windy, rainy the 19th. East sees cold, gusty winds the 17th. Windy, rainy the 19th.

Zone 7: West is fair, windy the 13th. Showers the 15th. Cold, gusty winds the 17th. Windy, rainy the 19th. East sees cold, gusty winds the 17th. Windy, rainy the 19th.

Zone 8: Alaska: West is fair the 13th. Fair the 17th and 18th. Central and east are fair. Warm, breezy the 17th. Alaskan Panhandle sees fair conditions. Hawaii: Sees fair conditions.

New Moon November 20–28
Zone 1: Fair with chance of showers the 22nd.

Zone 2: Fair with chance of showers north and over Florida-Georgia the 22nd.

Zone 3: Gusty storms the 21st and 27th.

Zone 4: West sees rain and strong winds the 20th. Cold, damp, windy the 23rd. Showers the 25th. Fair the 26th. Gusty storms, then colder and rainy the 27th. Central and east have rain and strong winds the 20th. Fair the 22nd. Showers the 25th. Fair the 26th. Colder and rainy, gusty thunderstorms north the 27th.

Zone 5: West sees rain and strong winds the 20th. Cold, damp, windy the 23rd. Showers the 25th. Fair the 26th. Gusty storms, then colder and rainy the 27th. Central sees rain and strong winds the 20th. Fair the 22nd. Showers the 25th. Fair the 26th. Colder and rainy the 27th. East is partly cloudy, then cooler the 20th. Fair the 22nd. Fair the 26th. Gulf Coast showers, colder and rainy the 27th.

Zone 6: West sees a stormy, windy coast the 21st. Cold, damp, windy the 23rd. Showers the 25th. Fair the 26th. East sees rain, strong winds the 20th. Fair the 22nd. Cold, damp, windy the 23rd. Fair the 26th.

Zone 7: West sees a stormy, windy coast the 21st. Cold, damp, windy the 23rd. Showers the 25th. Fair the 26th. East sees rain, strong winds the 20th. Fair the 22nd. Cold, damp, windy the 23rd. Fair the 26th.

Zone 8: Alaska: Western thunderstorms the 21st. Fair the 23rd. Fair the 26th. Gusty storms south the 27th. Central sees thunderstorms the 21st. Gusty storms the 27th. East is windy and stormy the 20th. Gusty storms the 27th. Alaskan Panhandle is breezy the 24th. Gusty storms the 27th. Hawaii: Thunderstorms the 21st. Fair the 22nd–26th.

2nd Quarter November 28–December 4

Zone 1: Fair with a chance of rain over New England the 29th.

Zone 2: Mild temperatures, calm.

Zone 3: Mild temperatures, calm east. Cooler, west. Thunderstorms the 28th. Fair the 2nd.

Zone 4: West is cold, rainy, windy the 29th. Fair in the north the 1st. Warm, fair the 4th. Central and east see thunderstorms the 28th. Cool, fair the 30th. Warm, fair the 4th.

Zone 5: West is cold, rainy, windy the 29th. Warm, fair the 4th. Central and east see thunderstorms the 28th. Cool, fair the 30th. Warm, fair the 4th.

Zone 6: Colder, rainy, windy November 29th and December 1st. Fair the 2nd. Warmer, possible showers the 3rd.

Zone 7: Colder, rainy, windy November 29th and December 1st. Fair the 2nd. Warmer, possible showers the 3rd.

Zone 8: Alaska: West is cold, rainy, windy. Moderate, breezy the 1st. Fair the 2nd. Central is cold, rainy, windy. Warm, breezy the 2nd. East is cold, rainy the 29th. Warm, breezy the 2nd. Alaskan Panhandle is colder, rainy, windy the 29th. Hawaii: Moderate, breezy the 1st. Fair the 3rd. Possible showers the 4th.

Full Moon December 4–11

Zone 1: Dry with rising temperatures. Thunderstorms the 5th. Strong wind and storms the 8th. Gusty storms the 10th.

Zone 2: Dry with rising temperatures. Thunderstorms the 5th. Strong wind and storms the 8th. Showers the 10th.

Zone 3: Dry with rising temperatures. Thunderstorms the 5th. Strong wind and storms the 8th.

Zone 4: West has high pressure with lower temperatures. Cold, gusty winds the 10th. Central and east thunderstorms the 5th. Fair the 6th. Strong wind and storms the 8th. Possible showers the 10th. Fair the 11th.

Zone 5: West has high pressure with lower temperatures. Cold, gusty winds the 10th. Central and east thunderstorms the 5th. Fair the 6th. Strong wind and storms the 8th. Possible showers the 10th. Fair the 11th.

Zone 6: Stormy, then fair the 6th. Cold, gusty winds the 10th.

Zone 7: Stormy, then fair the 6th. Cold, gusty winds the 10th.

Zone 8: Alaska: West has fine weather with northerly winds. Brief local showers the 8th. Central and east are warm and dry. Thunderstorms the 8th. Gusty storms the 10th. Alaskan Panhandle has seasonal temperatures. Breezy with variable winds. Hawaii: Fine weather with northerly winds. Brief local showers the 8th.

4th Quarter December 11–19

Zone 1: Warm and dry. Squally storms the 14th. Cold, stormy, especially New England the 16th.

Zone 2: Warm and dry. Southeast thunderstorms the 12th. Squally storms, heavy rain over Florida the 14th. Cold, stormy the 16th.

Zone 3: Great Lakes are mostly windy and stormy. Thunderstorms the 15th. Cold, stormy the 16th.

Zone 4: West sees high pressure, lower temperatures. Thunderstorms the 12th. Fair the 13th. Cold, windy, stormy the 15th.

Central thunderstorms the 12th. Warm, squally storms the 14th. Cold, windy, stormy the 15th. Cold, stormy the 16th. East is mild with temperate showers. Great Lakes are mostly windy and stormy. Warm, squally storms the 14th. Cold, stormy the 16th.

Zone 5: West sees high pressure, lower temperatures. Thunderstorms the 12th. Fair the 13th. Cold, windy, stormy the 15th. Central thunderstorms the 12th. Warm, squally storms the 14th. Cold, windy, stormy the 15th. Cold, stormy the 16th. East is mild with temperate showers. Warm, squally storms the 14th. Cold, stormy the 16th.

Zone 6: West is cold, windy, stormy the 15th. Thunderstorms the 19th. East sees high pressure, lower temperatures. Cold, windy, stormy the 15th.

Zone 7: West is cold, windy, stormy the 15th. Thunderstorms the 19th. East sees high pressure, lower temperatures. Cold, windy, stormy the 15th.

Zone 8: Alaska: West sees north winds, fair. Cold, stormy the 16th. Central and east are warm and dry. Fair the 13th. Thunderstorms the 15th. Precipitation, windy the 19th. Alaskan Panhandle is fair the 13th. Cold, stormy the 17th. Hawaii: Lower temperatures, windy. Thunderstorms the 15th.

New Moon December 19–27

Zone 1: Cloudy, rainy the 20th. Lower temperatures and stormy over the eastern Great Lakes the 21st. Fair in New England the 25th.

Zone 2: Cloudy, rainy, heavy over Florida the 20th. Lower temperatures the 21st. Gusty storms the 27th.

Zone 3: Cloudy, rainy the 20th. Stormy over the eastern Great Lakes the 21st. Heavy rain the 23rd. Thunderstorms over the Great Lakes and Deep South the 24th. Gusty storms the 27th.

Zone 4: Heavy rain over Montana the 20th. Warm, dry the 21st. Gusty storms the 27th. Central and east are cloudy, rainy the

20th, then fair the 21st. Rain over Minnesota the 22nd. Thunderstorms over the Great Lakes the 24th.

Zone 5: West is warm, dry the 21st. Gusty storms the 27th. Central and east are cloudy, rainy the 20th. Fair the 21st. Thunderstorms south the 24th.

Zone 6: West is warm, fair the 20th. Breezy over the Pacific Northwest the 21st. Increased precipitation the 24th. Gusty storms the 27th. East is warm, fair the 20th. Increased precipitation, especially in Idaho the 24th. Rain the 27th.

Zone 7: West is warm, fair the 20th. Increased precipitation the 24th. Gusty storms the 27th. East is warm, fair the 20th. Increased precipitation the 24th. Rain the 27th.

Zone 8: Alaska: West and central see potential heavy rain the 20th. Cooler, breezy, coastal rain the 22nd. Fair the 24th. East sees low pressure along southeast coast the 19th. Temperatures decline the 21st. Coastal rain the 22nd. Alaskan Panhandle is. warm, fair the 20th. Temperatures decline the 21st. Fair the 23rd. Increased precipitation the 24th. Rain the 27th. Hawaii: Lower temperatures, breezy. Rain the 24th.

2nd Quarter Moon December 27–31

Zone 1: High pressure and lower temperatures. Cold front, possible thunderstorms the 31st.

Zone 2: Warm, then a cold front, possible thunderstorms the 31st.

Zone 3: Fair, then thunderstorms the 28th. Cold front, possible thunderstorms the 31st.

Zone 4: West is warm. Showers the 28th. Windy the 30th. Central is warm. Windy the 30th. East is fair. Windy the 30th.

Zone 5: West is warm. Showers the 28th. Windy the 30th. Central is warm. Windy the 30th. East is fair. Windy the 30th.

Zone 6: West is cloudy, rainy, windy the 29th–31st. East is warm, showers the 28th. Windy the 30th.

Zone 7: West is cloudy, rainy, windy the 29th–31st. East is warm, showers the 28th. Windy the 30th.

Zone 8: Alaska: West sees lower temperatures and variable winds. Cold front, thunderstorms the 31st. Central sees high pressure and lower temperatures. Stormy over the southern coast. Cold front, possible thunderstorms the 31st. East sees high pressure and lower temperatures. Stormy over the eastern coast. Cold front, possible thunderstorms the 31st. Alaskan Panhandle is cloudy, rainy the 29th–30th. Cold front the 31st. Hawaii: Warm with possible thunderstorms.

Economic Forecast for 2025

Christeen Skinner

Understanding solar rhythms is increasingly imperative. Solar flares have the potential to knock out satellite systems, impairing connectivity—including the distribution of food—on Earth. For over two hundred and fifty years, the sunspot cycle has been monitored and numbered. The cycle has an average length of 11.2 years.

The present cycle has not behaved as expected, and we may yet be surprised by its length. The diminishing number of sunspots in recent cycles led solar scientists to conclude that Cycle 25 would contain lower-than-average sunspots, even as that cycle reached its peak. Yet, there was not one single day in the early part of 2023 when there were no sunspots. Instead, the number was higher than expected. It now appears that maximum was reached in 2024, making this a shorter-than-usual cycle.

We should expect 2025 to be a year of considerable commercial activity, not dissimilar to 2000 before what is now recognised as the dot-com crash. That economic event took place within weeks of an alignment of Jupiter conjoining Saturn when both planets were within a few degrees of right angle to Uranus. Such planetary formations are rare and mark years of financial eventfulness.

In 2025, Jupiter and Saturn will be at heliocentric right angle to one another (Jupiter 90° ahead of Saturn) on January 27. Simultaneously, Neptune lies at the midpoint of Uranus and Pluto. This curious planetary picture suggests a milestone year reminiscent of 2000, 2007–2008, and 2020, when major planetary configurations correlated with significant economic activity.

When the planets are all grouped on one side of the Sun, they have considerable effect on our special star: effectively pulling solar flares from the Sun. It doesn't take long for solar flares or coronal mass ejections from the Sun to reach Earth i.e., there is very little warning of potential catastrophe.

The Carrington Event in 1859 and the blackouts of Quebec in 1989 are two memorable events caused by solar storms. Should a similar event incapacitate the power grid of a major trading city, the result would be catastrophic.

As yet, there is no way of forecasting such an event, though it is wise to note when the planets make an unusual formation. At those times, it seems that there is potential to affect solar behaviour. We should, perhaps, heave a sigh of relief if the end of January 2025 passes without notice.

Major alignments or formations have also coincided with Earth movement, such as volcanic or earthquake activity. In February 2023, and heralded by visible comet C/2022 E3 (ZTF) just three days earlier, Venus, Jupiter, and Chiron were at right angle to Mars from the heliocentric, i.e., Sun-centred perspective. Compounded by a Full Moon with the Moon at maximum declination, activity below the Earth's surface resulted in an earthquake and the loss of over 50,000 souls in Turkey and Syria.

The death toll was terrible, and it will take years for Turkey to recover. Its stock exchange was impacted, yet there were few reverberations across the rest of the world, where indices absorbed the shock and continued on their upward trajectory. This was a markedly different reaction than the Fukushima disaster, when the devastating tsunami brought death and destruction and made economic impact visible across many indices.

Astrologers rely on an ephemeris (a book of tables listing the positions of the Sun, Moon, and planets every twenty-four hours). Using this invaluable tool, we scan the skies for unusual planetary pictures, taking into account lunar rhythms (new, full, and quarter Moons) along the way.

On June 11, 2025, the Moon will be full whilst also at maximum southern declination and at minimum latitude. That same day, Mercury is at maximum declination and Jupiter is on the world axis (0° Cancer). Add Venus at opposition to Vesta to this, and we have a significant planetary picture suggesting singular economic activity, if not Earth movement in the form of a volcano, tsunami, or earthquake.

Eclipses and Their Paths

In any year, there will be a minimum of two solar eclipses with or without accompanying lunar eclipses. In some years there are as many as five solar eclipses. In 2025, there are two solar eclipses, both accompanied by lunar eclipses occurring two weeks before the solar. The order is important. Sometimes a lunar follows a solar. When the lunar occurs first, and if the Moon is at either apogee or perigee or 0 degrees declination, markets have been shown to react strongly.

The first eclipse of 2025, a lunar on March 14, coincides with a stationary Mercury at 9° Aries—the exact degree at which the solar eclipse will take place just two weeks later. It could be that events taking place that day provide the "writing on the wall" for a later crisis. However, this does not have to be of economic significance. With Saturn conjoined the Sun and opposing the Moon in this chart, it may be the death of a leader that captures headlines.

However, that same day Mars transits 19° Cancer. In preparation for my book *Exploring the Financial Universe*, I researched significant economic events over the last 200 years and found that 19° of any one of the cardinal signs of Aries, Cancer, Libra, or Capricorn was being transited at the time of financial significance. This eclipse takes place in the early hours of the morning EDT. If we look at the chart for close of trade on Wall Street, we find the Moon at 0° Libra, the world axis, suggesting global eventfulness.

In March 2023, as Venus transited 19° Aries (a cardinal sign), two banks collapsed in the US. Less than two months later, as Mars transited 18°–19° Cancer, First Republic Bank was rescued.

It is not unreasonable to suppose that there will be yet another bank crisis during this March 2025 lunar eclipse.

For some weeks in the first quarter of 2025, Mars will be out of bounds (i.e., have a declination greater than that which can be reached by the Sun at its maximum declination). The chart for the lunar eclipse is bowl shaped, with Pluto as the lead planet—a shape that was apparent during the pandemic crisis of 2020. Whatever the reason or cause, the planetary alignment at this lunar eclipse suggests sadness and potential loss.

Almost exactly three months following this lunar eclipse—and the Sun having moved on by 90 degrees—on June 11, Venus and Vesta oppose one another within one degree of semi-square to the 19° cardinal axis. Venus moving through Taurus (a sign associated with financial matters) and Vesta (the trader's asteroid) moving through Scorpio (also on the financial axis of the natural zodiac) suggests the potential for currency or foreign exchange rate crisis. A strong possibility is that events taking place mid-March will be the overture to crisis in June.

Solar eclipses are not random and are always part of a sequence. The eclipse on March 29 is the twenty-first of the seventy-one solar eclipses forming Saros Cycle 149.

This particular eclipse is at 9° of Aries (just one degree short of another degree, 8° Aries, often highlighted at times of financial crisis), and indicates the high probability of 2025 proving financially noteworthy. It may be that indices reach significant highs when Jupiter reaches 9° Cancer (90 degrees from the solar position) in July 2025.

This is a partial eclipse visible through much of North Africa and southern Europe. Residents of both Belgrade and Geneva—weather permitting—should witness this special cosmic event. Geneva is home to the headquarters of the Red Cross, formed in 1863, a year in which a solar eclipse could be seen in that city. Solar eclipses have since been witnessed in this city in 1912 (the First Balkan War) and 1961 (Vietnam War). What these years have in common is that the need—and demand—for Red Cross services was considerable. We should anticipate the same in 2025, whether this is the result of climate catastrophe or war.

The path of the eclipse covers vast areas where the euro currency is in operation. Since this eclipse occurs at the midpoint of Jupiter and Pluto (together considered to be a wealth cycle) with Uranus at 45 degrees (an eighth of a circle), we should consider the possibility of sudden moves in its value.

This possibility is underscored by the position of this eclipse relative to the chart for the euro, which was launched amidst considerable fanfare at midnight on January 1, 1999.

In January 2025, Saturn transits the Jupiter position of the 1999 chart: a transit often coinciding with financial restraint. Clients often report this as a period when they feel the need to undertake financial "belt-tightening." The euro might, in the weeks following this eclipse, experience an upsurge in value only to come to another turning point mid-June.

The second solar eclipse of 2025 takes place on September 21 at 29° Virgo within a few minutes of the world axis (0° Libra). A regular exercise for the financial astrologer is to create charts for each equinox and solstice. In this instance, since the solar eclipse and equinox are just a day apart, the charts share an opposition of the Sun to Saturn. An equinox chart is used to forecast likely economic activity for the coming quarter of the year.

A solar eclipse is, of course, a very special kind of New Moon. It suggests new beginnings, the first of which tend to manifest when another planet (usually Mercury, Venus, or Mars) makes major aspect to the eclipse degree, or nine months later when a first quarter Moon again highlights the eclipse degree.

Saturn opposes the solar eclipse position, and at the accompanying lunar eclipse two weeks earlier, Jupiter was at 19° Cancer (accenting a key financial degree). It is reasonable to anticipate that this eclipse will usher in several months of financial turbulence.

It has to be remembered that with crisis comes opportunity. If the past indicates the future, then sectors poised to increase in value include arts and entertainment. It's shares in these areas that could prove to be 2025's "best buys."

The World Axis

As children, we learn how each season is determined by the Sun's position relative to Earth. The equinoxes and solstice points that occur in March, June, September, and December of every year are still regarded as important dates in the astrological calendar marking the Sun's entry into Aries, Cancer, Libra, and Capricorn. These degrees form what is known as the world axis (these degrees would not have the same importance on any planet other than Earth).

In 2025, Jupiter reaches 0° Cancer on June 9. Though it crosses this degree approximately every twelve years, this does not usually coincide with Saturn crossing another of the world axis points. Neptune will also be within a few degrees of 0° Aries. This planetary picture is exceedingly rare but can be compared to 1738 when the two planets were at 0° Cancer (also on the world axis), and when variations on this theme proved turning points in social, political, and economic history.

Importantly, as Jupiter reaches the world axis, Mercury, having crossed 0° Cancer just two days earlier, will be in exact square to Saturn. The Mercury-Saturn conjunction occurs on February 25. It seems reasonable to assume that news stories first intimated in late February will be headline news in June. We should also note Jupiter's position on both the Mars-Pluto and Uranus-Pluto midpoints.

These planetary pictures suggest Earth in sudden and chaotic (Uranus keywords) upheaval, which could be literal. Within days of this event, there may be fissures in Earth's crust that take the form of enormous (a Jupiter word) sinkholes or earthquakes. A further possibility is volcanic activity that pollutes the air and prompts the grounding of aircraft.

This is a realistic possibility given that as Jupiter makes this crossing, both the Moon and Mercury will be at maximum declination. The Moon will be moving through Sagittarius that day and for some hours will cross 4–5 degrees of Sagittarius, a zodiac area that features in charts associated with flight. It may be that those companies working in this sector will experience great fluctuation in share price.

Note that the Moon crosses the world axis four times every month, Mercury and Venus at least four times in any year, and Mars on four occasions every 27 months. (In the case of Mercury, Venus, and Mars, retrograde motion can lead to extra crossings.) Those who work in the field of financial astrology find such dates noteworthy. The bars on a trading chart tend to be of longer length, indicating greater variation in price and, very often, higher volume of trade. The dates for 2025 are given in the quarterly analysis at the end of this article.

Pluto in Aquarius

Pluto completed its geocentric transit of Capricorn in November 2024 and is now moving through Aquarius. It last transited this sign between 1777 and 1797, covering the industrial and French revolutions and the birth of the United States of America. The wording of the Declaration of Independence represents the highest of Aquarian ideals whilst the French ideals of "Liberté, Egalité, and Fraternité" are equally appropriate.

It is entirely reasonable to suppose that in the coming twenty years, politicians in emerging nations will adopt similar phrases. This period should also mark a new industrial revolution. Artificial intelligence will see many tasks automated. Just as in the eighteenth century, new skills will be required. The servicing and development of AI will give rise to new companies, and eventually new sectors will appear.

Pluto's entry into Capricorn in 2007–2008 coincided with the collapse of institutions such as Lehman Brothers, a development that would have been unthinkable just a decade earlier. Until that time, banks were thought of as relatively safe havens. The shock waves as the financial world reacted to the fallout from the subprime mortgage scandals were considerable. As Pluto moves through the early degrees of Aquarius, we should anticipate the underpinning of institutions associated with Aquarius to feel pressure, possibly to the point of collapse.

Whereas Capricorn exemplifies governments, Aquarius is linked to nongovernment agencies. Although their mission statements suggest non-politicisation, as Pluto makes its way through the first ten degrees of this sign (through to 2031), we should expect the unearthing of stories of corruption and misappropriation of funds that, in turn, tarnish the names of high-profile agencies and those who distribute aid. This will undoubtedly send shock waves through the administration departments of humanitarian agencies.

Aquarius is one of the air signs of the zodiac and associated with futuristic ideas and technological breakthroughs and inventions. Aeronautics and electrical machinery are thought of as Aquarian industries. The young altcoins (alternative currencies) and electric cars are also linked to this sign.

A major development as Pluto travels through Aquarius will surely be the rising and eventual dominance of virtual currencies. Cash will no longer be king.

Most people are familiar with Bitcoin: the currency launched in January 2009, six years ahead of its main "rival," Ethereum. Interestingly, the two charts are linked, with their respective Venus positions in direct opposition to one another.

Bitcoin was launched as Mercury, the lunar node, Neptune, and Chiron were moving through Aquarius (the sign Pluto transits in 2025), whereas Ethereum was launched with the Sun in Leo (Aquarius's opposite sign). In 2025, both will surely find the competition from the many other digital currencies in circulation challenging in the extreme.

The first conjunction that the lunar node makes to a natal planet very often describes the trajectory of the business (in this instance, the currency) concerned. In Bitcoin's case, the Lunar Node went on to conjoin Mercury within a few months of launch. Its performance since then has certainly been Mercurial! The trickster planet has seen the value reach a high of over $64,000 in November 2021 and a low of approximately $15,000 just a year later.

Pluto reaches Bitcoin's Mercury position in February and July 2025, and also crosses the progressed Mercury position in January. A limited number of Bitcoins are available, and as with the usual laws of supply and demand, there will always come a time when demand will exceed supply, most likely resulting in the price rising. It is entirely reasonable to expect marked variation in price in the opening weeks of 2025 and again at the start of the third quarter of the year.

Cardano was launched some years after Bitcoin and has a very different cosmic signature to both Bitcoin and Ethereum. It was launched as the Sun conjoined Vesta in the early degrees of Libra. In 2025, Pluto makes good aspect to both, suggesting that it will likely gain strength and value.

The IPO chart for Coinbase will also surely be affected by Pluto transits in 2025. Coinbase launched on April 14, 2012, at 1:24 p.m. local time on Wall Street. That we have the chart—to the minute—means that we can calculate an accurate horoscope. This places 2° Taurus at the Midheaven: 90 degrees away from Pluto's transit position. Coinbase value will surely be shaken (a Pluto keyword), necessitating redefinition of its aims and objectives.

Chiron, in both direct and retrograde motion, passes over the degree held by the Sun at Coinbase's IPO. This, together with Pluto opposing the asteroid Hygiea, is indicative of a challenging year for its executive with the health of the business under scrutiny and affecting its end-of-year value.

It is worth noting that in the chart for the end of the year, asteroid Hygiea opposes Mercury with Saturn and Neptune midway between the two. This rare T-square in mutable signs and connecting with the Galactic Centre does not indicate the year ending on a high; rather, there will be much discussion about losses. Bankers should perhaps not expect bonuses. Another important element in the end-of-year chart is that the Sun lies at the exact midpoint of Venus and Mars, with all three in ambitious Capricorn. Determination to fight losses will surely be great, with the potential for legal challenge exemplified by the opposition of Jupiter to Astraea across the Cancer-Capricorn axis.

First Quarter

This year opens with Chiron transiting 19° Aries. In research for my work *Exploring the Financial Universe*, I showed how 19 degrees of any of the cardinal signs (Aries, Cancer, Libra, or Capricorn) was occupied by a major planet at a period of financial discontinuity (1929 Wall Street crash and 1987 crash included). From 2023 through 2025, Chiron transits 19° Aries: a background indicator for potential correction or crash. With Neptune at right angle to the Galactic Centre, the potential for loss is increased.

The first Full Moon of the year takes place on January 13. When this chart is set for Wall Street, we find Mars in Cancer rising. Mars is not particularly at home in this water sign, and it's placement here suggests that investors may be in fearful mode, anxious to protect existing assets and reluctant to venture into new areas.

Although Chiron and Neptune barely move between the January Full Moon and the New Moon on the twenty-ninth of that month, Mercury will have moved on to form a conjunction with Pluto in an early degree of Aquarius. Those who were initially reluctant to invest in the brave new technical world should then be ready to venture into those areas.

The combination of Mercury and Pluto in Aquarius conjures images of intense scientific research whilst the alignment of Venus and Neptune in neighbouring Pisces suggests artistic vision. For those for whom science fiction holds fascination, this could be the time when a new movie breaks all box office records developing this theme.

The chart for the February 12 Full Moon is of locomotive shape with lead planet, Pluto, and Mars out of bounds. The combined forces of Mars (still in Cancer) and Pluto (currently moving across the early degrees of Aquarius) will likely echo the January theme, prompting investors to withdraw and to focus on preserving savings rather than venturing into new territory.

Many investors will surely feel "all at sea" by the New Moon on February 27. With Saturn, Mercury, the North Node, and Neptune all joining the Sun and Moon in Pisces as Mars continues its transit of Cancer, some investors will surely be overwhelmed, whilst those with a more adventurous spirit will be drawn to oceanics and protection of the oceans. They might also show interest in ship building or the navies of the world and the companies that supply them as well as the extraordinary breakthroughs in the world of medicine that will surely take place this quarter.

The potential for developments in cold fusion technology should also not be forgotten. As Pluto moves through Aquarius, just as the industrial revolution led to (at one time) unthinkable machinery, so, too, could advances in 2025 see new forms of energy become the norm.

This theme continues to play at the Full Moon on March 14, when the emphasis remains on Pisces (Sun, Saturn, and Neptune) but Mercury and Venus conjoin in Aries. This is where the pace should quicken as robotic technology becomes mainstream.

Second Quarter

The Aries Sun in exact conjunction with Chiron at the Full Moon on April 12 is indicative of correction or "woundedness." True, Chiron has associations with the healing profession. In financial terms, however, it should be thought of as an auditor. That Jupiter in Gemini is in loose opposition with asteroid Astraea suggests legal struggle and "fight for truth." We now know that there is a very real danger of artificial intelligence putting words into the mouths of journalists and politicians. How will we know the truth? And how will investors know which balance sheet or profit-and-loss sheet to trust? All this could manifest in many investors shying away from the markets, leaving many company leaders wondering how they can restore capital.

This theme continues to play at the Taurus New Moon on April 27. Whilst shares may not hold as much attraction as in the past, owning precious jewels and metals will surely seem more attractive. Expect to see the value of these increase.

The opposition of Jupiter to Astraea continues through May, with a court case likely to dominate international headlines. However, the conjunction of Uranus and asteroid Hygiea close to the solar position and opposing both the Moon and asteroid Juno could manifest in an alternative headline about the potential merger of two pharmaceutical giants. As the Sun-Uranus-Hygiea configuration is in a sign associated with copper and with sugar, prices in both commodities could experience sharp moves (most likely increase, although technical analysis closer to the time would need to be taken into account).

Two stelliums (large groups of planets and asteroids) in both Aries and Gemini dominate the chart for the Gemini New Moon. This fire and air combination bodes well for energy prices, at least for the consumer. Cheaper alternatives to fossil fuels will surely be widely available, with the companies providing these exceeding expectation in both price and delivery.

By the Full Moon on Wednesday, June 11, Jupiter will have crossed the world axis and moved into Cancer. Those who have invested in companies delivering and providing food and homes (house builders) should begin to show gain. However, the configuration at the Full Moon shows the Lunar Node (in Pisces) positioned halfway between the Sun and Moon. Volume of trade at any Full Moon tends to be higher than normal. At this lunation, with Jupiter in Cancer, it is probable that investors will choose to take profit rather than stay in an unsettled market.

Third Quarter

On July 7, Uranus begins a short stay in Gemini. (It crosses back into Taurus and makes final Gemini ingress in 2026.) We can view this as offering a taste of what's to come. This planet has natural affinity with air sign Aquarius and with scientific and technological breakthroughs. Gemini is viewed as the "great communicator," and we should anticipate product launches showcasing mobile phone technology that increases the ability to communicate with those who do not speak our language.

This is likely to be linked to rapidly expanding artificial intelligence services. Talking to robots should soon be as natural as talking to a neighbour.

What is interesting is that in the chart for the Full Moon on July 10, both Saturn and Neptune are within a degree of the halfway point between Uranus and Pluto. Saturn brings restriction and Neptune dissolution. This combination conjures the type of waves found at the confluence of rivers—requiring experienced navigators to steer through the choppy waters. As the Sun and Moon oppose one another at 18° Cancer—a degree occupied at times of financial drama in the twentieth century—it is not hard to imagine a financial disaster with some left ruined.

Note that Jupiter will be in Cancer too and that there will likely be very real concern about savings, manifesting in investors choosing to leave the market and thus creating a problem that results in reduced stock value—or perhaps even a run on a bank.

The Saturn-Uranus-Neptune-Pluto planetary picture is still in operation at the New Moon later that month. On July 24, the Leo New Moon develops this planetary picture so that the Sun, Moon, Saturn, Uranus, Neptune, and Pluto are each within a degree of 2 degrees of their respective sign positions as Mars moves through the Virgo South Node. Without the Mars factor, one would wonder about scientific breakthroughs and artistic endeavours that herald the new age of connecting. With Mars's position, there may be very real concern about data management and security.

The issue of security, which will surely bring increased interest in precious metals, becomes apparent in the chart for the

next Full Moon (August 9). By then, Mercury will have turned retrograde, and it should be clear that a negative sentiment has gathered momentum.

Extra-ordinary financial developments are probable at the Virgo New Moon. This lunation—at 0 degrees of that sign—is at right angle to Uranus. Political shocks are more likely than not, with those breaches of financial security a common theme across all jurisdictions.

Another financially worrying time is indicated at the Full Moon on September 7. By then the lunar nodes will be aligned with the position of Mars in a chart for the New York Stock Exchange. The potential for dramatic activity is underlined by the presence of Jupiter at 19° Cancer.

True, Jupiter can bring great highs but also great lows. The combined forces here suggest a highly volatile situation with many stock prices falling.

This possibility is emphasised by Pluto, which, by then, will be out of orb (i.e., beyond the Sun's declination). Pluto rules all things underworld (i.e., precious metals, etc.), whose prices could increase.

This quarter closes with a New Moon as well as a solar eclipse within a day of the equinox and with Neptune in opposition. It aligns with the ascendant in the chart for the European Union and likely marks, as most eclipses do, a new beginning. Though it might take until mid-2026 for ideas presented at this eclipse to be realised.

What will likely be important is for member states to agree on how best to cope with multiple crises: from climate disaster to potential financial loss through data mismanagement.

Fourth Quarter

If the chart is set for Wall Street, then Saturn at 27° Pisces and Neptune at 0° Aries straddle the Midheaven at the Full Moon on October 6. This planetary picture conjures up many images, including overt dissatisfaction with those who purport to hold visions of a better future. The share value of pharmaceutical companies may be particularly affected, with a slew of legal actions being taken against them. This planetary picture also suggests the uncovering of fraud on a grand scale.

Court cases in the US especially seem likely to dominate the news cycle at the New Moon on October 21. Again setting the chart for Wall Street, the emphasis is on pharmaceutical companies but perhaps also on the advertising and media sector, which may also be under scrutiny.

Throughout October, Jupiter continues to move through Cancer, and the overarching theme of protection should be apparent. This is set to benefit those providing services to the home-building and repair industries. Those disinterested in equity investment will surely turn to gold, silver, and rare earths to preserve their wealth.

The financial astrologer Arch Crawford identified a "crash cycle" in 1987. He determined that equities tended to ride up into a Mars-Uranus opposition and then quickly fall. This aspect coincides with the Full Moon on November 5, indicating a likely rise in overall indices after the October New Moon but losing strength soon after this Full Moon.

An interesting feature of this chart is that Mars will have moved into Sagittarius to oppose Uranus in Gemini. It may be that it is the communication sector that "rides up" into the opposition and then weakens. Shares in the sector could weaken just a few days after this Full Moon.

This likelihood is amplified at the Scorpio New Moon on November 20 when a retrograde Mercury conjoins the Sun and Moon in the "communications" sector of the Wall Street chart as Saturn and Neptune align at the descendant. Not only might the sectors already listed continue to show signs of weakness, but signs of inflation can be seen as Jupiter in one of the water signs is in trine by element with Neptune in Pisces.

Mercury moves to trine both Jupiter and Neptune around the Full Moon on December 4. This planetary picture is known as a *grand trine* and is generally viewed as a positive signal. By then, a retrograde Uranus will have returned to Taurus, and it could feel to many investors and traders that a positive end to the year is still possible—especially given that the Moon, Mars, and Vesta will all be out of bounds, rendering unrealistic buoyancy and optimism.

All should be on alert to the threat of rising inflation after Jupiter and Neptune both move into fire signs in 2026. This is not the optimum time to take on debt, even if it appears that financial pressures are easing.

Year End

The final New Moon of the year on December 19 aligns with the Galactic Centre. In the chart for Wall Street, this lunation accents an area of the horoscope associated with risk and speculation. With both the Moon and Mars still out of bounds, interest in buying stocks whilst they appear cheap may be considerable and drive prices up. Sectors likely to benefit include those involved in the space age.

This New Moon comes just days before the winter solstice: one of the most powerful dates of the calendar and the chart used by many to forecast the year ahead. Whilst the last few days of 2025 should see indices climbing and optimism returning, it should be noted that this may be short lived. If investing, seek advice and don't assume that an upward trend will continue.

New and Full Moon Forecasts for 2025

Sally Cragin

Sixty years ago, walking in space was all the rage. On March 18, 1965, Soviet cosmonaut Alexei Leonov was the first man to walk in space while tethered safely to his spacecraft. Just eleven weeks later, on June 3, astronaut Ed White became the first American to walk in space. He was the pilot of Gemini 4 and destined to perish in the Apollo 1 tragedy. History does not record these astronauts' impressions of the Moon while they were floating along, but one can imagine they were rightfully dazzled.

For as long as humans have lived on earth, members of every culture have been fascinated with the Moon's constant changeability: first, a crescent, then Cheshire Cat smile, then lopsided peach, and then "the man in the Moon," who gets smaller every day for two weeks. When I teach a class called "Moon Signs" in

New England (which I usually teach between first and last quarter Moons), I guide students to learn what actions to take—and not to take!—as the Moon goes through her phases.

This year, two enormous planetary transitions occur: Jupiter moves from Gemini to Cancer in June, and in late May, Saturn moves into Aries, completing its twenty-nine-year cycle. Readers who are Aries, Cancer, Libra, and Capricorn will experience memorable career transitions, but they will come at a cost (peace of mind or a geographic transition). If one of those is your birthday, mark the days when New and Full Moons are in your Sun sign, as those days could be signposts and help guide you on what comes next. Taurus, Leo, Scorpio, and Aquarius: if you had financial or health shifts (bigger expenses or health challenges), 2025 eases up, so the New and Full Moons in your Sun sign could be harbingers and help you renew your dedication to self-care. For Gemini, Virgo, Sagittarius, and Pisces, 2025's lunar phases should help you develop projects, relationships, and habits that you may have struggled with during 2023–2024. If you reflect on that period and are saying: "I can't believe I got through this," the planets are on your side this year!

A few words on how to use this piece: mark the days when the Moon is new and full in your Sun sign in your brand-new 2025 daybook or journal. Mark the days when the Moon is new and full for loved ones in your book as well, perhaps in a different color. That New Moon during your natal month signifies a new beginning for a project or state of being and can be a deeply powerful and useful interval. This means that the Full Moon that occurs during your natal month, two weeks later, of course, is opposite your Sun sign. "Opposite" makes for an uncomfortable angle, but an angle that could prompt action. That Full Moon may indicate a time when you decide to take an uncalculated risk or gamble.

Some folks may feel "at their best" when the Moon is full—or are most productive just before and after the Full Moon. Others may want to burrow under their covers because they feel overwhelmed. And some may find the time of the New Moon is most helpful: they feel hope, optimism, and possibility. Others may feel anxiety, depression, or a sense of uselessness—that "why bother?" feeling.

Lunar Cycles and the Female Body

Many women may find tracking their menstrual cycles with the cycles of the Moon helps give them a sense of familiarity with their own body's rhythms. The lunar month is approximately 29.5 days (slightly short of a calendar month save for February), and most women's cycles are between 28 and 31 days.

Yes, we are definitely "in tune with the Moon," which should be a cause for celebration. Half the world's population is in sync with our closest satellite, which also governs the ocean tides and growing cycles. My hope is that this piece will help us all to have a better understanding of how we operate in the world as thinking, feeling organisms who are part of the world and affected by the eternal cadence of Luna.

The New Moon to Second Quarter

Where's the Moon? Oh, there it is—a thin silver crescent in the shape of a capital letter "D," which increases in size. Yes, we love the Full Moon, but don't discount the usefulness of this seven-to-eight-day-long phase. Expand and enlarge on projects and activities that may emerge at the New Moon. Stay open to new experiences and people. Who's showing up in your life? Do you feel encouraged? You should—if not, what's missing?

Key words: Build, emerge, grow
Useful phrase: "That sounds interesting; I need to learn more."

The Second Quarter to Full Moon

Now we really see the Moon—that sliver enlarges to a smile and then to the gleaming silver orb that makes our night skies so enchanting. Many cultures developed stories about what the maria represent (the lava flows that make the dark area of the Moon). One ancient Chinese story claims that a gifted archer named Hou Yi shot down nine of the ten suns. He was given an elixir of immortality to drink. But, like many of us, he didn't want to drink alone and wanted to share immortality with his wife, Chang-e. However, his treacherous apprentice, Feng Meng, tried to steal the elixir, and then Chang-e drank it all. Miserable and immortal, she spends eternity on the Moon, where she lives with her companion, a rabbit. I'm waiting for the opera on this theme, to be frank.

The Full Moon is as big of a celestial event as we get in a month. For many years, friends, clients, and students who work in health care, education, and geriatrics have reported higher levels of agitation during this lunar phase. Be prepared for this dramatic time of the month by not overextending yourself, if you can. Some supervisors may pile on the work during this phase—or shorten deadlines.

Key words: Accelerate, expand, enlarge
Useful phrase: "I'm feeling rushed. How important is it that everything be completed right now?"

The Full Moon to the Fourth Quarter

Our view of Luna changes throughout the days and weeks. That beautiful Full Moon becomes a lopsided peach, and then we see just half of the Moon. We call these "quarters" because they represent one-fourth of the entire phase. When the Full Moon makes you feel overexposed or pulled in too many directions, this weeklong phase is useful for sorting out what's crucial and must be done. What happened during the Full Moon that was helpful or lovely? What people came along to improve your lot in life?

Abandoning one plan and choosing another—or looking for another—is a state of affairs I've heard a lot about during the Full Moon. Think of the "Full Moon" as not just a day, but the day or so before and after.

Key words: Focusing, narrowing, consolidating
Useful phrase: "Let's take a breath and evaluate progress. What is going to happen next? What is the most obvious course of action to take?"

The Fourth Quarter to the New Moon

All of a sudden, our beautiful silver Moon vanishes—or seems to vanish. The last quarter phase through New Moon is a fragile, delicate time of the month. When I speak to clients during this phase, they often don't know what they're thinking, but they feel uncomfortable. They feel torn between a couple of choices but then feel they have no energy. It's hard for them to hear me say, "The last quarter Moon until the New Moon should be a time of rest and reflection. Do not force a decision. Wait until after the New Moon, when everything is more clear."

I've also seen people reverse course. During the last quarter Moon phase, they lose faith or interest in something that occupied the previous three weeks. The energy to go-go-go is gone, and urgency gives way to lassitude. Ride this phase out: rent a four-hour movie; let your mind drift. Focus is not your friend right now.

Key words: Simplifying, removing, refining
Useful phrase: "Let's think about things and take a breath. What's the rush?"

Monday, January 13, Full Moon in Cancer

Happy New Year—keep the hospitality going! The Moon herself rules Cancer, sign of bakers and nurturers. With Venus in Pisces

making a beautiful angle to the Moon, friendships can deepen. Sensual pursuits—wine tasting, massage, taking a cooking class with a loved one—beckon. However, Cancer Moons can be fierce and bring out one's defensive side. Libra, Capricorn, Aries, Aquarius, and Sagittarius might be easily irked. In tune with the Moon and showing their loving side are Cancer, Leo, Scorpio, Pisces, Gemini, Taurus, and Virgo.

Wednesday, January 29, New Moon in Aquarius

A superb time for new ideas, new company, and new plans—the wilder the better. Is there some trend, game, or nutrition plan calling your name? If you're feeling the effects of a short attention span (Look! A squirrel!), you're in tune with this Aquarius Moon. Luna is also synced up with Pluto, master of the underworld, so an insidious "why bother?" feeling could bedevil a good mood. Sagittarius, Capricorn, Aquarius, Pisces, Aries, Gemini and Libra: underdogs need you—stand by them. Beware of "overdoing it" (taking on assignments you don't have time to do, for example) if you're Taurus, Leo, Scorpio, Cancer, and Virgo.

Wednesday, February 12, Full Moon in Leo

Publicize everything—even small stuff. Leo Full Moons bring people together for impromptu good times. However, this Moon also revs up the disgruntled and those committed to being on the other side of the desk in the "complaint department." Gemini, Cancer, Leo, Virgo, Libra, Sagittarius, and Aries: others look to your leadership, but don't follow their schedule of urgency. A useful phrase right now is "What's the rush?" Taurus, Scorpio, Aquarius, Pisces, and Capricorn: set plans could get a right turn (or a right hook, sending you straight to the mat). Don't dig in your heels if others promise and don't deliver.

Thursday, February 27, New Moon in Pisces

This Moon dares us to find the middle ground between self-discipline (finishing a project) and artistic impulses (adding frills and furbelows to aforementioned project). Pisces Moons can prompt nostalgic brooding and a likelihood of wallowing in "what could have been." However, you can protect yourself: keep your sense of humor, and care for another person. That will bring that "fish swimming in opposite directions" internal compass into alignment with true north. Capricorn, Aquarius, Pisces, Aries, Taurus, Scorpio, and Cancer: expect lightning bolts of genius—when you're most distracted. Gemini, Leo, Virgo, Libra, and Sagittarius may need to hear things twice to understand.

Friday, March 14, Full Moon in Virgo

The spring equinox awakens dormant feelings of "must do this." But with Jupiter at odds with the Moon, being "overly generous" could get us into financial difficulties. And for the next three weeks, while Mercury is in retrograde, double-check all written communication. Focus on a health overhaul, plus a little spring cleaning. (How ancient are those condiments in the fridge door?) However, if you have a perfectionistic side, this Full Moon helps you see the best course of action. Cancer, Leo, Virgo, Libra, Scorpio, Taurus, and Capricorn: take the initiative, and keep your standards high. Sagittarius, Pisces, Gemini, Aries, and Aquarius: hold back on decisions—you don't have all the information.

Saturday, March 29, New Moon in Aries

Out with the old, in with the new. Stick to folks with clear, firm voices about "the right thing to do." Aries Moons can coax us into burning the candle at both ends—and the heck with burning your fingers! If others are rushing you, take your time. Mercury is still retrograde, so reversals of action are likely. And if you'd rather go shop for a new spring hat than get those needed groceries, you're in tune with the Moon. Aquarius, Pisces, Aries, Taurus, Gemini, Leo, and Sagittarius: focus on building something from scratch; it's okay to discard what doesn't work. However, Mars is putting tension on this New Moon, so holding back is recommended for Cancer, Virgo, Libra, Scorpio, and Capricorn.

Saturday, April 12, Full Moon in Libra

With an emphasis on partnership and harmony, this Full Moon prompts affection from all kinds of folks—even those who'd prefer to "go it alone." Social activities—the more the better—are a natural fit for this weekend. Libra Moons can bring out everyone's gossipy side, and confiding in others, sharing secrets, and having a good laugh helps us find common ground. Leo, Virgo, Libra, Scorpio, Sagittarius, Gemini, and Aquarius: expand a project—or gather more folks around your ideas. Capricorn, Pisces, Aries, Taurus, and Cancer: are you asking for favors? Maybe wait a few days—it's always okay to change direction at the Full Moon.

Sunday, April 27, New Moon in Taurus

Friendship among mentors and students is highlighted, as is gardening. Taurus Moons encourage us to make our home or office environment more elegant and comfortable. But this Moon may also bring out territoriality in some: if you're hearing resistance from others about your opinions, nod politely and move on to another topic. Pisces, Aries, Taurus, Gemini, Cancer, Virgo, and Capricorn: look for investment opportunities. Leo, Aquarius, Scorpio, Libra, and Sagittarius: stubbornness doesn't become you, and others may need to set limits with you. Try not to take this personally.

Monday, May 12, Full Moon in Scorpio

Some Full Moons bring clarity, but Scorpio emphasizes complexity and complication, particularly where sexual relationships and self-identity are concerned. But it's a fine time for weeding, which could refer to those unwanted plants in the garden as well as that clutter on your desk. Mars and Uranus are at odds with this Full Moon, so emotions (explosions) could be on the horizon. Virgo, Libra, Scorpio, Sagittarius, Capricorn, Pisces, and Cancer: indulge your sensual side. Aquarius, Taurus, Leo, Aries, and Gemini: have you tried to hide something? The truth will come out.

Monday, May 26, New Moon in Gemini

Memorial Day gatherings with far-flung friends and family bring joy to all. This is an excellent time to see "both sides," as the twins

(like Libra's scales) can encourage everyone to hold seemingly contradictory thoughts. And with Jupiter also in Gemini, new friendships among folks who love to talk but who have different philosophies are favored. Aries, Taurus, Gemini, Cancer, Leo, Aquarius, and Libra: your persuasive abilities are top-notch. Virgo, Pisces, Sagittarius, Scorpio, and Capricorn: you could get grumpy if others are trying to get you to commit to a course of action.

Wednesday, June 11, Full Moon in Sagittarius

This Moon says go-go-go, which could rile up the slow-and-steady folks. Enormous changes at the last minute are likely, particularly in matters involving travel or higher education. However, justice will prevail, and if someone hasn't played fair with you, the universe will catch up with them. Libra, Scorpio, Sagittarius, Capricorn, Leo, Aries, and Aquarius are full of charm and persuasiveness. Virgo, Pisces, Gemini, Taurus, and Cancer: you may misinterpret others—they're giving you space, perhaps freedom, but you may feel indifference or lack of interest.

Wednesday, June 25, New Moon in Cancer

This could be the "reset" button for the entire year, as Jupiter, the planet of generosity (and overindulgence) is also in Cancer (through June 2026) and in harmony with the Moon. Look for opportunities to build security for yourself, whether in your home or your online activities. This is an excellent interval for fishing and planting, and since Mars shifted into Virgo on June 17, upgrading your technology is a smooth move. Taurus, Gemini, Cancer, Leo, Virgo, Scorpio, and Pisces: your intuition is sparking—follow your instincts on a new relationship. Aries, Libra, Capricorn, Sagittarius, and Aquarius: are slowpokes getting in your way? Find another route versus going around them.

Thursday, July 10, Full Moon in Capricorn

This Moon encourages us to move slowly and steadily, no matter what pressure you're feeling from others. Capricorn Moons are also excellent for laying foundations (for a building or a business). Make time for awkward friends or those who seem neglected by others; your efforts will be deeply appreciated. Scorpio, Sagittarius, Capricorn, Aquarius, Pisces, Taurus, and Virgo: that "worker bee" impulse serves you well—do more than you were planning because others will notice. Aries, Cancer, Libra, Leo, and Gemini: commitment isn't indicated—keep yourself above (and definitely beyond) a local fracas.

Thursday, July 24, New Moon in Leo

Since Mercury retrograded on July 18 (through August 11), messages could be garbled, particularly those relating to cooking and childcare. This New Moon could bring out tantrums in some folks but childlike wonder in others. Since Leo's energy can bring out everyone's hidden egomaniac, you may have more to say than you thought you did. Aries, Gemini, Cancer, Leo, Virgo, Libra, Sagittarius: your need for affection could be met by a pet versus validation from other humans. Taurus, Scorpio, Aquarius, Capricorn, and Pisces: you may get miffed if others blow their own horn. Keep petty resentments contained if you can.

Saturday, August 9, Full Moon in Aquarius

No time for the status quo; Aquarius Moons bring out revolution in the masses—and a need for us to feel independent. However, short attention spans could be an epidemic. Save your "big speech" for another week in case others are likely to interrupt your brilliance! Sagittarius, Capricorn, Aquarius, Pisces, Aries, Libra, and Gemini: honesty counts, particularly if you've been on the fence with some matter. Taurus, Leo, Scorpio, Virgo, and Cancer: feeling contrary and impatient with your more free-spirited buddies? You're in tune with the Moon.

Saturday, August 23, New Moon in Virgo

Slow and steady in conversations with loved ones, as Virgo's inclination for precision—or pickiness—could throw a monkey wrench into an otherwise anodyne conversation. Emotions may not run high during this lunar phase, but logic will be a refuge, as could decluttering. (Start in the bathroom—items connected to health and beauty that have expired must go!) Cancer, Leo Virgo, Libra, Scorpio, Capricorn, and Taurus: indulge your curiosity about others. This is an excellent time for fact-finding. Sagittarius, Pisces, Gemini, Aquarius, and Aries: you may think you're being direct, but others could hear whining.

Sunday, September 7, Full Moon in Pisces

This watery Moon is the last Full Moon of the summer and gives us all the impulse to take a deep dive and bring long-buried feelings bubbling to the surface. Thanks to generous Jupiter moving through harmonious Cancer, the lunar energy could come with a desire to overindulge in consumerism or "feeling less than" if you perceive coldness or rudeness from another. Capricorn, Aquarius, Pisces, Aries, Taurus, Scorpio, and Cancer: you'll have X-ray vision when it comes to reviewing text or casual comments. For those who write poetry, this is the "golden hour," and being elegant in communication brings joy. Gemini, Virgo, Leo, Libra, and Sagittarius: procrastination isn't a bad thing, especially if the straight path you are on turns into a labyrinth.

Sunday, September 21, New Moon in Virgo

This is the perfect time to address health concerns, consult with a physician, or at the least, stand up and stretch those muscles! Virgo Moons encourage "fine-tuning," so if you tend to be a "big picture" person, you'll be able to see the details. Cancer, Leo, Virgo, Libra, Scorpio, Capricorn, and Taurus: helping others is a theme. Your generosity could help others who couldn't help themselves without your guidance. Sagittarius, Pisces, Gemini, Aries, and Aquarius: are you getting irked at others for not following the standard you set for yourself? Not a good recipe for serenity; check that inclination toward fussiness.

Monday, October 6, Full Moon in Aries

Excellent ingredients are in place to move in a new direction—or find something you can complete quickly and just get it done. Aries Moons favor innovation or projects that take very little time (barbecue vs. the slow cooker). Aquarius, Pisces, Aries, Taurus, Gemini, Leo, and Sagittarius: your charisma is bubbling over, and others can't get enough of your company. They will want to follow your lead. Cancer, Libra, Capricorn, Virgo, and Scorpio: getting irritated by trifles or careless comments slows you down. Be kind to yourself.

Tuesday, October 21, New Moon in Libra

Easy does it—Libra Moons favor partnership, and New Moons are all about fresh starts, so if there's been a rocky patch with a workmate or companion, clarity prevails now. The Moon is in sync with Uranus, which could accelerate everyone's appetite for surprises, such as the shrinking violet transforming into a chatterbox. Leo, Virgo, Libra, Scorpio, Sagittarius, Aquarius, and

Gemini: sociability and sense of purpose are strong; let others know your views. Capricorn, Cancer, Aries, Pisces, and Taurus: are you listening to others you wouldn't normally give the time of day?

Wednesday, November 5, Full Moon in Taurus

Acquisitive tendencies are strong, but so is a spirit of generosity. A yearning for elegance could be a wardrobe upgrade or a stylish new scarf or necklace. Taurus Moons accent one's ability to work long and hard at a project that needed more time than planned. Pisces, Aries, Taurus, Gemini, Cancer, Virgo, and Capricorn: others follow your lead; take all the time you need to do things right. Leo, Scorpio, Aquarius, Libra, and Sagittarius: have faith that wheels are turning in your favor.

Thursday, November 20, New Moon in Scorpio

This is one of the high points of the year for intrigue: sex, betrayal, moving money around—all the great themes of noir movies! Since Scorpio rules surgery, ask yourself what projects, situations, or relationships need pruning or reduction. Virgo, Libra, Scorpio, Sagittarius, Capricorn, Pisces and Cancer: you may be on a team, but going it alone could be the best choice. Trust your instincts. Aquarius, Taurus, Leo, Aries, and Gemini: beware of impulses to be sharp or cutting—unkind words will rebound in your direction.

Thursday, December 4, Full Moon in Gemini

Venus and Mars are opposing this Moon, so "opposites attract" could surprise us all. And Gemini Moons bring out the chitchat and gossip; make sure those "funny stories" you're sharing aren't going to ricochet. Chance rules over planning, and Aries, Taurus, Gemini, Cancer, Leo, Libra, and Aquarius have excellent social instincts. Virgo, Sagittarius, Pisces, Scorpio, and Capricorn: you may desire emotional depth from others, but they don't have the time right now.

Friday, December 19, New Moon in Sagittarius

Unlike this month's Full Moon, Venus and Mars are back in sync with the Moon, prompting feelings of fondness and desire for emotional connection. The sign of the archer rules education; ask yourself if you are as well-trained in your current position as you should be. Libra, Scorpio, Sagittarius, Capricorn, Aquarius, Leo, and Aries: your appetite for excitement brings you and others joy. Indulge! Pisces, Gemini, Virgo, Cancer, and Taurus: are you being rough with others who are less focused than you? Why is that? For all: this month concludes the first quarter of the twenty-first century—a period that, like the first quarter of the nineteenth century, saw technological and industrial innovation.

2025
Moon Sign Book
Articles

Lunar Maria

Elizabeth Barrette

The Moon is among the most important of heavenly bodies in astrology. It figures into many major applications such as natal charts, but interpreting it can be tricky because it has such an extensive range of possible connotations. Using the features of the Moon, such as lunar maria, can help with interpretation by suggesting which of the myriad meanings most likely apply in the present moment. These can be used in various ways alongside other things such as houses and signs to add nuance to the Moon.

What Are Lunar Maria?

As seen from the earth, the Moon has a mix of light and dark areas on the side facing us. A *mare* (pronounced MAR-ay; plural *maria*, pronounced MAR-ee-uh) is one of the dark spots. It's Latin for "sea" because early astronomers mistakenly thought they were bodies of water. Maria are actually flat plains of dark basalt, formed by asteroid impacts. The highlands of the Moon consist of different material that reflects much more light.

Maria are large basalt plains. There is also one giant plain, called Oceanus Procellarum, meaning Ocean of Storms. There are many smaller plains variously called *lacus* (lake), *palus* (marsh), or *sinus* (bay). Although smaller than maria, they have the same origin and traits. These basalt plains cover around 16 percent of the Moon, most of them on the side facing the earth. The far side has only a few maria, which are not relevant to this discussion.

To find the locations of the maria, look at a map of the Moon with its features labeled. Start reading the map in the upper left corner and zigzag down it or start in the center and spiral outward until you find the feature you are looking for.

Interpreting Maria in Astrology

Astrology is a complex art based on many moving parts. This often provides different ways that those parts can interact, and thus, different options for interpretation. People may argue over which is the "right" or "best" way, but just explore your options and do what works for you. In the case of lunar maria, you have a variety of choices.

The main point to consider is whether an influence is behaving usually, behaving unusually (like having a negative instead of positive effect), or has been blocked so it has no effect at all. With lunar maria, the Moon's phase determines this. When a mare is lit, it is active, expressing its energy in the usual way. When it is unlit, it can be interpreted as inactive, or it can be interpreted as blocked or hidden. To use the blocked interpretation, compare with difficult aspects such as opposition or square, where two things interfere with each other's energy and influence. The mare's energy may express itself very little or may create conflict. To use the hidden interpretation, compare with how a Sun sign describes a person's obvious, outer personality while the Moon sign describes the subtle, inner nature. The mare's energy may enter through the subconscious rather than the conscious mind and have influence that is harder to pinpoint.

The next important point is to consider how the parts influence each other. Here we have some easy options because the Moon moves through the houses and the signs in ways that are straightforward to track. Note which maria are lit and active at the time the Moon passes through each house or sign. The energy of each mare will then interact with the energy of the house or sign, much as does the Moon itself. This not only tells you what is going on with the mare's own sphere of influence, but can also help you figure out which of the Moon's many possible meanings or influences are most salient in that position, because the maria function as facets of the Moon's own nature. So the closer to full the Moon is, the more activity the maria generate, while the closer to new the Moon is, the less impact they have.

Finally, consider interaction with individual bodies such as planets or asteroids. The Moon can form aspects with any of these, and when it does, the maria also interact with them. The simpler approach is to apply the same aspect to any lit mare, essentially treating the Moon and its maria as a single point. With this approach, the maria just tell you which bits of Moon energy are more influential at a given time and should get more attention as you interpret its interactions in a chart.

The more complicated approach is to imagine the Moon more like a clock face against the background of the sky. In this case, a mare at the top of the Moon will be closer to celestial bodies high in the sky while a mare at the bottom of the Moon will be closer to things low in the sky, so that they may have different relations to each other. When the mare is lit, then it interacts with other heavenly bodies that it is facing toward (from the lit side), but not those it is facing away from (on the dark side). Thus, when the Moon is full, all the maria are active and can interact with anything around them; when the Moon is new, all the maria are inactive (or blocked or hidden). When the Moon is waxing, lit maria on the right side interact with other bodies toward the right of the sky; conversely, when the Moon is waning, lit maria on the left side interact with other bodies toward the left of the sky.

Maria and Their Meanings

Traditionally, the maria take their names from several sources. Mare Frigoris, Mare Humorum, Mare Imbrium, Mare Insularum, Mare Nubium, Mare Spumans, Mare Undarum, Mare Vaporum—as well as Oceanus Procellarum—all relate to sea features. Mare Australe, Mare Cognitum, Mare Marginis, and Mare Orientale match to sea attributes. Mare Crisium, Mare Serenitatis, and Mare Tranquillitatis refer to states of mind. Because the Moon corresponds to the element of water, these watery names for maria help sort out the different traits that can come from both Moon and water, making it easier to determine which is most relevant to your current work. There are also a few other maria whose names don't fit the pattern for various reasons, like Mare Humboldtianum, Mare Moscoviense, and Mare Smythii. They are thus not particularly helpful for this project.

Mare Frigoris (Sea of Cold): This mare relates to both physical and metaphorical cold. It can refer to winter or susceptibility to chills. It could imply frigidity of emotions, reserve, or withdrawal. While this might seem negative, it can be very useful in counterbalancing an excess of fire or hot-tempered feelings. This is particularly handy if you use astrological concepts as a focus for meditation.

Mare Humorum (Sea of Moisture): This is one of several maria that explicitly refer to water sources, so it tends to enhance other instances of water but conflicts with fire. It also relates to feelings and personality through the old idea of "humors" as bodily fluids influencing a person's nature and emotions, the "flow" of moods.

But it is less fractious of an influence than some other examples like the Oceanus Procellarum.

Mare Imbrium can be translated as Sea of Showers or Sea of Rains, making it one of the explicit water maria. This mare is connected to grief and loss, which makes it very helpful if you use astrology to find your way through life challenges.

Mare Insularum (Sea of Islands): Islands relate to isolation, which can imply loneliness or difficulty forming connections. However, this sense of separation can also mediate between two conflicting bodies, allowing their energies to manifest separately instead of interfering with each other. It works well in meditation to separate thoughts from feelings.

Mare Nubium (Sea of Clouds): Cloud is a subtle aspect of water and air. It excels at hiding or blurring things, creating a "cloudy" view, and it can relate to bad weather or other bad events, as in a "cloudy forecast." If you use the interpretation of unlit maria as having hidden actions, then this one can be very powerful.

Mare Spumans (Foaming Sea): This is one of the more active facets of lunar energy, because foam is a busy combination of water and air. This mare stirs things up and makes things happen—but it can be either positive, as in "bubbly joy," or negative, as in "foaming mad," depending on what it's interacting with.

Mare Undarum (Sea of Waves): Wave energy can manifest as gentle and rhythmic, connecting this mare to the cyclic nature of lunar energy. However, it can also turn fractious, in the sense of waves "rocking the boat" to destabilize a situation. On a positive note, it can break up stagnation caused by too much earth or other fixed energy.

Mare Vaporum (Sea of Vapors): This has a similar clouding effect as Mare Nubium. It also suggests emotional overwhelm from the Moon's strong impact on feelings.

Oceanus Procellarum (Ocean of Storms): This is by far the biggest mare and covers over 10 percent of the total lunar surface. Thus it spends the most time active of all the maria. It relates strongly to the tempestuous and unpredictable part of the Moon's energy, causing mood swings or conflict in general. In its hidden form, it seethes under the surface. Blocked, it represents a storm building to a sudden cloudburst.

Mare Australe (Southern Sea): This mare corresponds to the direction south and shares those correspondences like fire, summer, adulthood, and purification.

Mare Cognitum (Sea of Knowledge): This mare embodies the Moon as a source of knowledge, wisdom, and inspiration. It relates to all matters of the mind.

Mare Marginis (Sea of the Edge): It corresponds to boundaries and liminal states. It can be challenging in the sense of "edgy."

Mare Orientale (Eastern Sea): This mare is barely visible from earth. It corresponds to the direction east and shares those correspondences like air, spring, childhood, and psychic work.

Mare Crisium (Sea of Crises): It represents the peak of disturbance or a problem coming to a head. In its hidden form, it indicates a problem you can't find to fix. Blocked, it builds pressure until suddenly released. This mare lies northeast of Mare Tranquillitatis, and a change between calm and crisis is often marked when the terminator line (the division between the currently lit and unlit parts of the Moon) crosses between those two maria.

Mare Serenitatis (Sea of Serenity) and Mare Tranquillitatis (Sea of Tranquillity): These maria share the same meaning of peace and calm. They embody the restful quiet of the Moon. They exert a soothing influence when interacting with other bodies.

Conclusion

Lunar maria offer a new way to look at the Moon's influence in astrology. By exploring them, you can sort out the many possible meanings so they don't tangle together as much. If you use astrology for meditation or inspiration, then the maria provide a wider set of focus points. Try out the different approaches to interpreting them and see which you prefer.

Eggplant: Culinary Hero

Mireille Blacke, MA, LADC, RD, CD-N

Growing up with Sicilian maternal grandparents, I was truly blessed. When it comes to food preparation and culinary wizardry, I didn't fully appreciate the skills of my beloved grandmother, who was magic personified in her kitchen. (And make no mistake, it was *her* kitchen.) I took much of this for granted in my childhood and early adulthood. Much later in my professional life as a registered dietitian and addiction counselor, my clients shared a wide variety of cultural experiences from their own lives, many of which centered upon food and its significance to them. I found myself reflecting back in a similar fashion and noticing the profound role certain foods played throughout my entire life. For example, eggplant was common in a number of dishes my grandmother regularly prepared and served, and was even grown en masse in her own backyard garden. For many people, though,

263

and perhaps even some of those reading this article, eggplant is untried, unappealing, or even avoided at all costs.

Some of you reading this know people who avoid eating or even tasting the entire food group of vegetables. My best friend, Tara, considered an "honorary Italian" and member of my family since we first met in middle school, is one of those people. For a reference point (but not to expose anyone's exact age), we belong to Generation X, whose members were born roughly between 1965 and 1980. Growing up, we had no internet, social media, or mobile phones. We had to entertain ourselves for the most part. After school, Tara and I would walk around our various neighborhoods and overanalyze any current school drama, or dream of seeing our then musical icons performing live. On some days we'd end up in my grandparents' garden, covered in dirt, and surrounded by thriving tomatoes, cucumbers, zucchini, and eggplant.

These many decades later, Tara is a stellar registered nurse (RN) and general doll of a person who nevertheless frustrates me to no end because she still avoids eating vegetables at all costs. This is particularly intolerable to me for two reasons. First, as a registered dietitian (RD), I love to stuff people with vegetables: hello, overwhelming health benefits! Second, I love my best friend to death but would prefer to avoid that eventuality for at least a few more decades, particularly considering certain illnesses that run in her family.

After all, this is the person who took the best friend's vow of "beating anyone over the head with a shovel if they ever hurt you." For legal reasons, I'll clarify that neither of us have ever needed to "shovel" anyone before or since obtaining our respective licenses. However, I'll also state for the record that I have no problem practicing culinary deception when it may benefit someone's health. (I've often recommended this nutrition plan when clients have a child or spouse that's a picky or fussy eater. Being mindful of potential allergies, switch out one or more unhealthy ingredient(s) in a dish with healthier, and ideally undetectable, options. (Many examples of this practice exist online: search for "black bean brownies" or "chocolate avocado cupcakes.") With Tara, though, I'd really need a solid game plan. It took me more than two decades before I could convince her to consume *one, single cooked floret of broccoli*. And she knew most of the dishes made across various generations of my family like the back of her hand.

Enter the unlikeliest of heroes: the eggplant.

Let me give you some reasons why you should try eggplant for yourself, if you haven't already. One cup (99 grams) of cubed eggplant (known as *aubergine* to the British and French) provides a mere 20 calories. Eggplant is also low in saturated fat, cholesterol, and sodium, and is a good source of potassium, manganese, dietary fiber, and vitamin C, though in relatively small quantities compared to other fruits and vegetables. Potassium is a mineral that regulates the heart and blood pressure. Manganese helps in bone-building, thyroid gland functioning, and assists other vitamins in functioning. Dietary fiber is necessary for smooth and regular bowel movements and keeping cholesterol and blood sugar at healthy levels. It also increases feelings of fullness to aid digestion and weight loss. Vitamin C is an antioxidant that assists the body with tissue growth and maintenance.

Antioxidants in eggplant may help to reduce the risk of colon and liver cancers and help in stroke prevention. Nasunin is an antioxidant and phytochemical in the purple pigment of the eggplant's skin (also seen in blueberries) that reduces free radicals, reducing inflammation throughout the body and decreasing risk of various diseases. Another compound found in eggplant is chlorogenic acid, an anti-inflammatory with links to tumor growth inhibition. Like Tara, if you're genetically predisposed to certain illnesses, adding eggplant to your meal planning (or in a plot for culinary deception) might make sense for you too.

By cultivation and use, the eggplant is a vegetable, though botanically it's classified as a fruit. Eggplant is also an edible member of the nightshade (Solanaceae) family, related to tomatoes, chili and bell peppers, potatoes, and ground cherries, as well as some poisonous and addictive plants, such as belladonna, tobacco, and black nightshade. Eggplant and other nightshade plants also contain nicotine, though to a much lesser extent than tobacco. Don't be worried about developing a nicotine addiction from eating eggplant! You'd need to consume 22 pounds (10 kilograms) of eggplant to absorb the nicotine equivalent of one cigarette.

Registered Dietitian (RD) Eggplant Rundown

If you need more convincing, here are a few more reasons to try eggplant:

- The eggplant's low calories and saturated fat make it an excellent substitute for meat in weight loss efforts. I've found the eggplant's bulk and texture easy to work with and almost imperceptible as a meat substitute in vegetarian or vegan meals. Just be careful not to negate these benefits by adding extra cheese, oils, and other calorie-laden ingredients to your eggplant dishes! In full disclosure, my grandmother had versions of eggplant dishes that involved additional cheeses (e.g., ricotta), and if you have a heavy hand, the calories and fat grams will certainly add up. For example, in the included recipe, it's up to you whether you want to choose low-fat versions of mozzarella cheese or not.

- As a member of the nightshade family, eggplant may trigger sensitivities or allergies in some individuals, such as symptoms of arthritis or oral allergy syndrome, which can potentially lead to anaphylaxis if left untreated. Though studies about nightshades and such conditions have been

inconclusive thus far, contact a health care professional if you detect similar symptoms after ingesting nightshades.

- You'll want to avoid eating raw eggplant, due to its bitterness. The bitterness is due to the eggplant's nicotinoid alkaloids and can be addressed during the early preparation process. Try degorging to address this: salt, rinse, and drain the eggplant to reduce overall bitterness. (Degorging is step 3 in the recipe included below.) Salting your eggplant will also reduce the amount of oil absorbed from cooking.
- Open your mind to eggplant's multicultural versatility, and consider the broad range of dishes one can make from eggplant: ratatouille (France), moussaka (Greece), baingan bharta (North India), baba ghanoush (Middle East), and caponata (Sicily). Even if you don't like eggplant, think about serving it to guests who may enjoy culturally diverse foods like those mentioned above. Note: If you're pressed for time, consider grabbing premade eggplant hummus at your local grocery store. Most of them will have it!

- Interested in growing your own? Because eggplants are extremely sensitive to cold, plant seedlings after the danger of frost has passed (in temperate climates). The highest-quality eggplants are harvested at ⅔ their full size. Avoid eggplants with hard seeds, overly bitter flesh, and dull skin. Alternatively, purchase eggplants all year in your local grocery stores.

- In the United States, eggplant is available year-round, with peak season in August through October. Store fresh eggplant at room temperature to maintain better texture and flavor, and use within a few days to avoid softening and wrinkling. Don't consume eggplant leaves, as they're toxic! But do add this diverse plant to your recipe arsenal for better health.

There Goes My Hero

Since the genetic and learned abilities to cook creatively were concentrated in my maternal grandmother and mother but zipped right past me, I asked my mother to assist with the eggplant fake out, using my grandmother's generations-loved recipe, which is basically one of her versions of eggplant Parmesan. Eggplant can be baked, fried, stewed, or added to soups and casseroles, and this versatility helps in culinary trickery. The culinary use for eggplant is only limited by your own creativity, and it can be a heart-healthy substitute for meat or cheese (e.g., sandwich stuffing) or added to grilled skewers or kabobs and dips (e.g., hummus). Although Tara had been an honorary member of my family for decades, even she would not ultimately know what hit her in the taste buds.

Grandma Calvo's Knockout Eggplant Parmesan

For the following recipe, please note cooking times and temperatures may vary based on your particular oven. It's worth reading through this recipe a few times prior to attempting it, as you will notice it's lengthy and detailed. It's very "assembly line" procedurally, so it can become a family group activity if you like. Allow yourself plenty of time.

Base Ingredients

1 large glossy and firm globe eggplant (about 2 pounds),

3 eggs

32-ounce homemade or store-bought tomato sauce

1 pound shredded low-fat mozzarella

Canola oil, enough for frying eggplant slices

Pinch of salt

Breading Mixture

1½ cups Italian-seasoned bread crumbs

¾ cup grated Parmesan (or Parmesan and Romano) cheese

1 teaspoon Italian seasoning

½ teaspoon parsley flakes

½ teaspoon onion powder

½ teaspoon garlic powder

Preheat the oven to 350°–375°F.

Wash, pare, and slice the eggplant into ½-inch thick round or lengthwise slices. Make sure the slices are as uniform as possible.

Soak the slices in salted, cold water for 30 minutes to remove as much bitterness as possible. The water will turn brown, so keep replacing the water until it runs clear. Usually one replacement of the water will do.

Pat the slices a bit to remove excess water using paper towels. Put slices aside.

Put the breading mixture ingredients together in a square or oblong tray with sides, such as a glass lasagna baking dish.

Beat the eggs, adding a little water if desired, and place in another dish similar to the one holding the breading mixture.

Heat a pan with a thin layer of canola oil. (We use an electric frying pan at about 375°–400°F.) While the pan is heating up, dip the eggplant slices into the egg and then into the breadcrumb mixture until evenly coated, and place as many as will fit into the frying pan. Add canola oil to the frying pan as needed (try not to use too much), and repeat the process until all the slices are dipped, breaded, and fried. They will brown on both sides fairly quickly, so it may help to do all of the breading, or most of it, first so they are ready to fry.

Once golden brown, drain the slices between multiple layers of paper towels. It's helpful to arrange the layers on a large cookie sheet.

Somewhere along the way, heat the tomato sauce so it's ready once it's needed.

Cover the bottom of a 9 × 13 glass lasagna dish with tomato sauce. Then, start layering the slices one layer at a time. Layer one: tomato sauce, eggplant, Parmesan cheese, a thin layer of mozzarella. Layer two: tomato sauce, eggplant, Parmesan cheese, mozzarella, etc. Repeat until all ingredients are used up. Finish with a topping of Parmesan and mozzarella over sauce.

Cover the dish with nonstick foil and bake for about 60 minutes. If the dish is particularly full, you may need to extend the baking time.

Throw out any extra unused breading mixture, because any raw egg it contains makes it inedible.

Number of servings depends on preferred portion size.

Deception Reception

So, I admit it. In the end, I successfully deceived my best friend with a long-guarded family recipe, which has been written and printed here for the first time. This dish was created at the complicit hands of my own mother. It was odd to prepare the dish for Tara, knowing that most of my family has just happily, obliviously eaten it without question for decades. I revealed the eggplant sham to Tara shortly after she ate it. I checked in on her by text, as part of me was feeling guilty about it. I'd told her it was a new dish I'd been trying out for a "healthy deception" nutrition class, which I was doing frequently at that time. I'd given her several portions of the eggplant, so she could have more over several days. The reaction was actually exactly as you see it below because I saved the text thread and emailed it to myself to keep. It was that important to me.

Me: "Hi, did you try it yet?"
Tara: "YES, TELL ME WHAT IT WAS!!!"
Me: "Don't kill me. Eggplant."
Tara: "OMG that eggplant ??? was insanely good!!! Would have licked the container if I could have. I am a convert. It was sooooooooo delicious."

Vegetable mission accomplished, even if the eggplant is technically a fruit. The way I saw it, the eggplant was a superhero that day.

Gratitude for Culinary Heroes in Our Lives

My grandmother didn't make eggplant for its numerous health benefits, though I'm sure on some level she was aware that it was extremely nutritious. In short, she herself had grown up with eggplant and was familiar with it; it was part of her heritage and culture, just as it became part of mine. I just wish that she knew that her "simple" cooking and dedication to keeping her family fed and cared for served as the glue to our family's strength as a unit. I know she didn't feel how much we all appreciated her efforts at the time. If any of this resonates with you, please take the time to thank your parents, grandparents, or other influential relatives while they're still here, so they understand the positive impact they've had on you. If you're lucky enough to have that type of person in your life, they'll most likely shrug your comment off, ask you if you're hungry, and try to feed you regardless of your answer.

Reflecting back on the long road Tara and I have walked together, I'm actually more shocked about the two aging Generation Xers easily texting so often than the fact that Tara now regularly tastes a new vegetable every few months or so. I'm thrilled whenever she proudly reports trying and enjoying a new one! But somewhere along the road to adulthood, it dawned on me that maybe that garden of hateful vegetables scared her when we were kids, and I told her that I deserved a "good shoveling" myself for not considering it before. Luckily, Tara mostly remembers laughing with my grandparents, seeing rabbits and chipmunks in the garden, and of course, the dirt. But because she's my best friend and knew I felt guilty, she told me to eat some broccoli instead, and all was forgiven. And because I'm her best friend, I happily obliged.

The Many Faces of Venus

Bernadette Evans

What do you think of when you hear the name *Venus*? Visions of love, romance, and beauty are usually what permeate everyone's thoughts. Did you know that Venusian energy is also about finances and what you value?

Venus, like all the other planets, cycles through the zodiac, meaning it will go through all twelve signs at one time or another. The planet of love, beauty, and finances also goes retrograde approximately every eighteen months.

Venus in the Signs

Let's take a look at how Venus manifests while she's in each astrological sign.

When the goddess of love is in the sign of Aries, a cardinal fire sign, you may be more impulsive. Aries is ruled by Mars, an action-oriented planet. Something or someone catches your eye, and you go for it! For example, shopping could be high on your list. If you're attracted to someone, you don't waste time. The thinking is, why let the grass grow under my feet? An archetype of Mars is the warrior. When Venus is coupled with this energy, she is passionate, likes fun and spontaneity, and can be a fiercely loyal lover. Venus in the sign of Aries values being straightforward and taking action. The shadow side of Venus in Aries is being impulsive (and regretting it), whatever the circumstances. Try to remember that other people also have wants and needs; consider their opinions before you shut them down.

Venus is at home in the sign of Taurus, because this fixed earth sign is ruled by it. When she is here, there is a distinct feeling of slowing down after the transit of Venus in Aries. Beauty, whether it's a piece of art, clothing, or a flower, is something to slow down and admire. Venus in Taurus values a leisurely pace, one where all five senses are steeped in beauty. You're more likely to take your time when it comes to making any decisions about matters of the heart or the wallet. Why not enjoy the dating and romance piece as long as you can! When Venus is in Taurus you could have a fairly nice bank account if you're not filling up your home with stuff. The shadow side of Venus in Taurus is that material things could be extremely important in your life, making you reluctant to ever let anything go.

When Venus goes through the sign of Gemini getting out to play and mingle with others is the name of the game. Gemini is a mutable air sign, ruled by Mercury, the planet known for its communication. When Venus is here, you're interested in sharing your ideas with others and are curious about what they think. You could be pivoting from one area of amusement to another! The shadow side of Venus in Gemini is that if you get bored, you may find it easier to just quit a job or move on to another area of inter-est. This also applies to romance. Financially, Venus in Gemini could be quick and easily distracted, making investments difficult to pin down. Money may fly out just as quickly as it flies into your account. I don't think you'll give it too much thought though; you know tomorrow is another day, and something interesting could be on the horizon.

When Venus glides into the sign of Cancer, you could feel a noticeable slowing down of energy. It may be time to have a family get-together or cozy up with a good book. Cancer is a cardinal water energy and is ruled by the Moon. Sensitivity and intuition can be heightened, so pay attention to your hunches, as well as what feels nurturing for you. You may feel like lavishing your friends and family with hugs and home-cooked meals; just be sure you don't smother them with all your good intentions. Remember to carve out time to pamper yourself. Beautifying your home may become a priority. Maybe you want to renovate or redecorate. You don't have to spend a lot. You'll be happier and feel safer if you have some savings set aside for a rainy day. The shadow side of Venus in Cancer is that you can feel more sensitive and could get your feelings hurt. Try not to shut the door on anyone; instead, have a discussion and explain how you feel. This

can lead to more growth and a deeper connection between both parties.

When Venus enters the sign of Leo, it's time to set the stage for a party and have a good time! Leo is a fixed fire sign, and it is ruled by the Sun. You appreciate fun and like to play on a big scale. Now is the time to bring some friends together and do it up right! When it comes to beauty, this sign likes sparkle and shine and clothing with patterns that stand out and say, "Here I am!" As for love and romance, you enjoy being appreciated as much as the next person … okay, maybe just a tad more. With Venus in Leo, you'll want to experience all the rush of a new and exciting love. You may have to be careful and watch your finances when Venus is in this sign. I know you enjoy lavishing your loved ones, but try not to overdo it. The shadow side of Leo is being dramatic. You have been generous with friends but could feel you weren't thanked properly and feel unappreciated. Try not to let your pride stand in the way of a friendship.

Virgo is a mutable earth sign, and it's ruled by the planet Mercury. When Venus visits here, you can bet she will be practical, meticulous, and hardworking. You'll want to do your very best; you may even be a bit of a perfectionist when Venus is in Virgo. Romance is great and so is sex, but you're likely to be more impressed by someone who is putting in a long work week or helping you out around the house. The shadow side of Venus when it's in Virgo is expecting others to do things just the way you'd do them Try not to be too hard on other people; it may not go over well. Since Virgo is an earth sign, you'll probably want to get your garden and house tidy and in order.

When Venus pays a visit to the sign of Libra, you'll probably want to get out and socialize. Libra is a cardinal air sign, and it's ruled by Venus, which makes this a comfortable placement for this planet. Going to an art gallery or shopping for a beautiful piece of clothing or jewelry would be appropriate. Your eye will be drawn to articles that are exquisite and probably expensive. When it comes to romance, you'll be attracted to someone who is good looking, intelligent, and easy to talk to and share ideas with. Getting along with others and socializing is how Venus in Libra operates. The shadow side of Venus in Libra is going out of your way to be nice to others and losing yourself in the process.

Things could get hot and steamy when Venus moves into the sign of Scorpio. The sign of Scorpio is a fixed water sign and is ruled by Pluto. Beauty is important to everyone, but with this placement, imagine something that has a more mysterious feel to it. When Venus is in this sign, you feel more passionate and could express yourself in an intense manner. Emotions are felt deeply and keenly but are not always easily expressed. It could take some prodding to get you to open up and say what is bothering you. Your likes and dislikes are pronounced; there is no halfway mark. Venus in Scorpio is all about extremes. In the romance department, you will want to feel unmistakable chemistry toward anyone you're interested in. Sex and passion are undeniably exciting, but make sure you also have some substance in the relationship. When it comes to finances, you could be shrewd and examine all the potential ups and downs of any endeavor. The shadow side of Venus in Scorpio is feeling jealous and possessive and being manipulative.

When Venus is in the sign of Sagittarius, life can become more playful. The sign of Sagittarius is a mutable fire sign and is ruled by Jupiter. Think fast movement, lively, fun, and freedom. The siren call of far-off lands and adventure beckon to you as Venus dances through this sign. You could be longing to escape and visit new places to learn about other cultures, customs, and beliefs. When it comes to romance, it may be harder to commit to a relationship, as you could want more freedom. Money may be harder to hold onto because you're feeling generous and playful and not worrying or even thinking about saving for a rainy day.

The shadow side of Venus in Sagittarius is not sticking to your commitments.

Venus has a more serious air about her when she enters the sign of Capricorn. The sign of the goat is a cardinal, earthy energy and is ruled by Saturn. There's a focus on building a career and making plans for the future. Presenting yourself as someone who knows what they're talking about and commanding respect are important. Being dependable and practical may not be glamourous, but everyone appreciates when the work is correct and done on time. Venus is still Venus though, and she still enjoys romance. You'll want someone you can discuss important matters with. When Venus is in Capricorn, you're apt to be attracted to someone who is stable, reliable, and loyal. Find someone who is either already established or someone who will be supportive of your endeavours. An older person may be very attractive now. When it comes to finances, you will be careful how and where your hard-earned dollars go. As for the shadow side of Capricorn, you may not come up for any air. You're too busy working and making money to have any fun.

Aquarius is a fixed air sign ruled by the planet Uranus. When Venus enters this sign, she appreciates a variety of friendships. She values community and differences. You'll value independent thinking and people who view life through a unique lens. Getting together to share ideas with individuals from all walks of life excites you! If you're in the market for romance, when Venus is in this air sign, you could be attracted to someone more for their mind than anything else. Venus in Aquarius wants space and freedom to explore and talk to an assortment of diverse people. The more conversations and ideas, the better. Beauty is in the eye of the beholder, and when Venus is here, you may be attracted to objects that are more avant-garde. The value this Venus placement puts on money is that it is a tool that allows you to enjoy a variety of experiences. The challenge when Venus is in Aquarius is being stubborn and not seeing another person's viewpoint. When problems arise, you could detach from emotions and want to think your way out of an emotional problem.

When Venus takes her place in the sign of Pisces, she relaxes and exudes empathy and sensitivity. Pisces is a mutable water sign ruled by Neptune. Venus in Pisces values intuition, spirituality, creativity, and being compassionate to others. In the romance department, if you find yourself falling for someone, you'll probably be all in. Just beware ... the rose-colored glasses you're wearing could be skewing your perception. When Venus is here, you feel called to extend your compassion and empathy toward others. Be loving and generous, just don't burn yourself out trying to be there for everyone. Remember to take time out to nurture yourself too. Finances can be a little trickier when Venus is here because your feelings could inspire you to make some purchases that may be more flash than substance. Take all things into consideration when spending and planning your budget. Make sure your finances are balanced with some fun and beauty as well as practicality. If you need to, talk with a friend who will be honest with you and help you stay on track. The shadow of Venus in Pisces is being too giving and letting your feelings take over.

Venus Reflections

As you can see, Venus enjoys playing in a variety of ways as she travels through the different signs. When she moves into another sign, pay attention to how you feel when Venus lights up different areas of your life. This will give you a glimpse of how you may respond when Venus changes signs. Remember, Venus is one of the benefics. Everyone will experience her blessings in distinctive and fascinating ways. Enjoy the many faces of Venus!

Grape Glory in Your Backyard

Penny Kelly

One of my earliest memories as a little girl of about three or four years old is of lying in the grass under my grandfather's grape trellis and looking up at the sky through clusters of leaves and grapes. Not only was it a moment of becoming aware of my own presence in the world, it was also a moment of pure delight in seeing the world from a whole new angle—something I've never forgotten!

As things turned out, that was only my first encounter with grapes. Little did I know that I would grow up to buy a farm with two small vineyards on it, or that I would end up growing grapes for Welch Foods, maker of the famous grape juice.

Today, I have only a few grapevines in my backyard, but they are a delight to my soul and provide an abundance of grapes for eating and making jelly or juice. Grapes are easy to grow and full of nutrition. Besides vitamins A, B, C, E, and K, and minerals like potassium and manganese, they are loaded with flavonoids, polyphenols, anthocyanins, and other antioxidants. These help keep tissues, arteries, and veins youthful and flexible, keep inflammation at bay, help the cardiovascular system stay healthy, and play a role in avoiding dementia or other forms of cognitive decline.

Getting Started

Grapes are not only beautiful and tasty, they attract birds to the trellis, they can be trained up to shade an area, and they can form part of a plan to live in a self-sufficient manner.

Before planting grapes, consider what you might like to do with them. Do you just want a few to eat? If so, plant a variety that will have thin skins, firm flesh, and deep flavor. Are you thinking of making some wine? Wine grapes have thicker skins and a higher sugar content (as measured by the Brix scale). What about grape juice? You haven't really had grape juice until you've had real, homemade juice using a fruit press or steam extraction!

If you just want a few to eat and share with family or neighbors, investigate the seedless varieties. Some excellent choices are Concord seedless, Reliance, red seedless, Thompson seedless (aka sultana), Niagara, Somerset, and Lakemont.

If you're thinking of making wine, are you more interested in red wine or white wine? You can make an excellent rosé or Cabernet from red or blue grapes with or without seeds. Varieties to consider would be Concord, red seedless, Red Prince, Muscat Beauty, Merlot, Frontenac, or Cabernet Sauvignon. If you want to make white wine, then you might want to try a combination of white grapes such as Pinot Gris, Riesling, Pinot Noir, Niagara, or Marquis seedless.

If it's jam, jelly, or juice you want, then seeded varieties will bring you deeper, more intense flavor, although any of the varieties will make excellent juice. You can even plant several varieties

of red and white grapes and make delicious juices and jellies from two or three varieties mixed together.

As a last consideration, you may want to dry them into raisins that will store wonderfully well for very long periods of time. This helps provide food in those seasons when things do not grow well because it's too hot or too cold. If drying grapes to make raisins is part of your goal, then Thompson seedless or one of the Muscat varieties such as Alexandria is a good choice. Those varieties that produce big, fat, round grapes are the best, as they will dry to a nice size and remain chewy.

Consider Your Hardiness Zone

Next, consider the area you live in. Grapes grow all over the world, but your backyard is located in a particular zone with temperature ranges, humidity, and weather that has known effects on *viticulture*, the technical term for grape growing. Some varieties simply will not survive the frigid temperatures of the North, and other varieties will close up shop and stop producing in the wilting heat of the South.

I live in an area known locally as the Fruit Belt of Michigan. It is a thirty-five-mile-wide strip along the entire western coast of Michigan. When it comes to fruit and vegetable production, this area is in the top ten fruit growing areas of the US. Because of the wide temperature swings that plants here must endure, the fruits and vegetables are much sweeter and more flavorful. Why? Because plants must develop a sophisticated kind of chemistry to survive these temperature swings, and this gives the fruit grown here a unique flavor and sweetness known as a *bouquet*. When it comes to grapes, that bouquet is known as the *Lake Michigan appellation*. A lot of grapes are grown here because of that unique bouquet, so when you purchase your grape plants, be aware that you will get the best flavor and bouquet if you match the variety to your growing zone.

When it comes to grapes, the shining stars of the viticulture world are Concord grapes. Concords are native to North America and were grown by the American Indians, although credit is due to Ephraim Bull, a farmer from Concord, Massachusetts, who developed the cultivar we enjoy today. Concords are extremely hardy in the face of cold weather and are also fairly tolerant of heat as far south as Arkansas. They grow vigorously, putting out canes that easily reach 20 feet and produce heavy crops. Concords are good for eating, wine, juice, and jellies. The original Concords had seeds, but a seedless variety has been developed.

Here are some good varieties for the backyard, the zones they grow best in, when they ripen, and what they are used for. Keep in mind that there are many other varieties out there, but these are some of the tried-and-true varieties that are dependable producers.

Name	Zone hardiness	Ripens in	Used for
Black Muscat	5–9	Late August	Table, juice, raisins, wine
Concords, seedless	5–9	Mid-September	Table, wine, juice, jelly

Name	Zone hardiness	Ripens in	Used for
Concords, seeded	5–9	Late September	Table, wine, juice, jelly
Frontenac	3–7	Mid-September	Wine
Joy Grape Vine	6–8	Mid-August	Table
Lakemont	5–8	Late August	Table, juice
Marquis seedless	5–8	September	Table, juice, jelly
Muscadine (Fry)	7–9	September	Table, juice, wine, raisins
Muscadine (Cowart)	7–9	Mid-September	Table, juice, raisins, wine
Niagara	5–8	Mid-September	Juice, jelly, wine
Reliance	5–8	August	Table, juice, jelly
Somerset	4–8	August	Table, juice, jelly

Laying Out Your Planting Area

If you are only planting three or four vines, you will need to think carefully about where to plant them. They need full sun. They should also not be planted at the bottom of a dip in the landscape, as they will be vulnerable to sudden cold snaps in spring or to moist, stagnant air in summer that allows mildews and black rot to destroy their fruit.

If you are putting in a tiny vineyard, plenty of space is needed for all of the varieties. If you are planting in rows, use a 6 × 9-foot grid. The rows should be 6 feet apart, and the grapevines in the rows should be planted 9 feet apart. Think twice about putting the rows closer together, because the next thing to consider is equipment.

Have some idea of the equipment you will use to put up your trellis and take care of your vines. When it comes to putting up the trellis, you will save yourself a lot of backbreaking work and stress if you use a small tractor with a posthole digger. Renting one

is worth every dime you spend. When it comes to taking care of your small vineyard, the 6 × 9-foot row spacing will allow you to use an orchard-sized tractor or a four-wheel vehicle if you need to.

It is a good idea to put your trellis up first and then plant your vines. Keep in mind as you build your trellising system that it needs to be very strong and sturdy. Grapes are prolific in the number and length of canes they put out each year, and the grape crops can be very heavy. You will need trellis wire and sturdy 4-inch diameter × 6–8 foot posts to build a trellis. Your end posts should be 6 inches in diameter and supported by a guide wire or brace that prevents them from gradually leaning into the row, causing the wires to sag. Put the posts a good 1½–2 feet deep in the ground. Wrap the wire around the end post several times, then use big, U-shaped staples to secure the wire to the end posts and the posts in the row.

Once the grapes have been planted, feed and water them as necessary. They like an acidic soil with a pH between 5.5 and 6.5, so it's a good idea to add compost or peat moss to the soil and mix it in before planting.

In the first year, each plant will typically produce four or five canes about 3–4 feet long. It's a good idea to put a stake in the ground near the plant, choose one of those canes, and begin training it up toward the trellis. By the second year, it will reach the trellis, and at that point, cut it off so it is just below the trellis wire, and this will cause the plant to send out lateral canes. Once you have 2–5 lateral canes, you have to make a decision regarding how you will trim the plant each year. A good method is the cordon system.

Using the cordon system, you select one lateral cane that will go to the left and another that will go to the right. The best canes are as big around as a pencil and have a nice chocolate color. Gently and loosely tie the two lateral canes to the wire, then cut each one off at about 4½ feet. You now have a vine that stretches 9 feet along the trellis wire. The entire plant is shaped like a "T" and will thicken into a sturdy trunk with two arms. The two arms will produce numerous canes every year, and you will then trim these canes to have 3–5 nodes on each cane.

The Cordon System for Trellising Grapes

Grapes will grow only on one-year-old canes, so be aware that to have grapes at all, you will have to trim the plant pretty heavily every year, deciding how much of that one-year-old cane growth to leave in place in order to allow for your grape crop. Trimming grapes is an art and can be done for a light crop, a heavy crop, or vine renewal. Once in place, grapevines will continue to produce for decades if they are trimmed correctly. They should be trimmed in early spring each year before their sap comes up. The sap begins coming up at the same time the first dandelions appear.

Grapevines will not produce grapes the first year and will not get to full production for 3–4 years. You will see them come to life in the spring after trimming, and if you're paying attention, you will soon be able to recognize the stages of growth: bud swell, bud break, leafing out, clusters form, bloom, fruit set, fruit growth, veraison (coloring), sweetening, and harvest.

If mildew appears, you may have to spray or dust the grape clusters with something that will stop the mildew. Ditto for black rot, which can cause the berries to turn dark and shrivel into little, bitter mummies. The absolute best spray treatment is full-strength raw milk, because it ends the mildew or black rot immediately and also nurtures the plant. Your vines may smell like sour milk for a few days, but that will end with the next rain, and it's a small price to pay for a healthy crop.

Once the grapes are able to make enough sugar, they will not have to fight black rot or many of the other problems that come up. The secret to helping them get to full sugar quickly is to feed them, add minerals in the form of montmorillonite green clay, and water regularly. This helps to avoid stress on the vines, and they do the rest! Your reward will be clusters of amazing sweetness coming right out of your own backyard!

Tuning In to Nature with Phenology

Lupa

I have been living on my friends' farm for almost a decade now. It's the first time I've lived in a rural area since moving away from home over twenty years ago, and I've never been happier. While I loved the cities I lived in—Pittsburgh, Seattle, Portland— there is something within me that does best when immersed in a wilder, more open place.

One of the best changes has been that it's much easier for me to track the seasons by what's going on outside. Sure, I could do that to an extent in urban areas. The cherry, maple, and linden trees outside my Portland apartment showed off their annual displays of leaves, flowers, and fruit, and while many of the birds that showed up at my feeders were year-round residents, I also got to enjoy a changing roster of migratory species in spring and fall. And, of course, there were the rolling patterns of temperature, precipitation, and other environmental changes as the months turned one after another.

But out here on the edge of the continent, all of those changes are more vivid and large. I live in a meadow surrounded by mixed conifer forest, with a freshwater lake within view and the Pacific Ocean a few minutes' walk away. Because this landscape isn't completely dominated by humans, the wild animals don't need to sequester themselves away in the last remaining private pockets, and there are species one would never see in a city. The plants, too, are much more diverse, and the many species of fungi have made it easy to hone my mushroom-hunting skills. I am immersed in nature's cues year-round.

Paying attention to the cycles of nature used to be a universal phenomenon. Before we became increasingly urbanized, we necessarily had to be aware of when certain foods were available, when migration routes were open or closed off, or when the mosquitoes that carried disease were most likely to be active. And even those of us who have spent the bulk of our time closed off in boxlike houses and offices can reacquire that sensitivity, given enough time in a more balanced natural setting.

What Is Phenology?

Those who study the natural sciences use the term *phenology* to refer to the study of when things happen in nature. *Phaino* is a Greek word meaning "to bring to light," "to uncover," "to show"—or, literally, "to shine." Phenology is literally shining a light on cyclical events in nature as they appear. This is an active participation; in order to reveal nature's happenings, we have to be paying attention to them. Other animals are also aware of the changes around them, whether they're looking for cues that will bring them food, mates, or a route to migration. So phenology is simply an organized way for us to get back in touch with that grand, ancient animal experience.

The term was first coined by Belgian botanist Charles François Antoine Morren, who defined it as the "specific science which has the goal to know the *manifestation of life ruled by the time*" (Demarée and Rutishauser 2011, 758). Plants are the easiest organisms for year-round phenological study. Once they're rooted in place they can be watched day after day, and they have several visible changes that can be easily followed even by the most casual observer. Many fungi spend most of their time as mycelial networks permeating soil or rotting wood, and most people never get to see them outside of a brief period each year when they produce their visible fruiting bodies—mushrooms— for a few days to spread spores before rotting away again. Animals, of course, have their own cycles, but it can be tough to follow the movements of an individual animal on the move throughout its territory.

Today, phenology is an incredibly important science. It's one of the best ways to understand the habits and life cycles of living beings we share this planet with. At a time when species are going extinct at an accelerated rate, phenology helps us better understand how to help the remaining members of an endangered species, whether that's knowing when to collect seeds from a rare plant to be propagated and reintroduced to its range, or understanding what time of year a highly threatened butterfly species performs its mating flights so fertilized eggs can be kept in a safe place until they're ready to hatch.

Anthropogenic climate change has had a marked impact on the phenology of many species. Depending on weather fluctuations due to the damage climate change has done to the jet stream and other climatological forces, certain plants may flower earlier or later than usual, which may leave their pollinators without food at a crucial time. Migration patterns of birds and other animals may also be thrown off course, which means the food and other resources they have been using for thousands of years are not ready or are already gone by the time they arrive at important resting points along their route.

As we work to protect our local habitat, the ability to understand the phenology of beings around us not only helps us to know our natural neighbors better, but it also allows us to make more informed decisions that affect the world around us. We can also become better communicators with other people, sharing our observations with friends, family, and even scientists and decision-makers. Watching the changing of the seasons in your neighborhood may not seem like a very important act on a grand scale, but the more people paying attention, the more voices there are speaking for change for the better.

I'd like to share a few ways that you can become a citizen phenologist—an everyday person who studies the cycles of the nature you encounter in your everyday life.

Choose a Touchstone Plant

I no longer get to see my old cherry, maple, and linden trees except when I occasionally visit Portland, but the big twinberry honeysuckle (*Lonicera involucrata*) right outside my kitchen window has become my new touchstone plant. This mature bush has been here for about two decades, and it is a very visible reminder of seasonal changes going on literally just outside my door.

As I write this, numerous native bees—particularly the fuzzy-horned bumblebee (*Bombus mixtus*)—are drinking nectar and carrying pollen as they visit its small pairs of yellow, trumpet-shaped flowers. Now and then an Anna's hummingbird (*Calypte anna*) joins them for a sip. Song sparrows (*Melospiza melodia*) and black-capped chickadees (*Poecile atricapillus*) are among the small songbirds that hide in its greenery.

By mid-August to early September, the flowers will have given way to pairs of round, shiny black berries. Cedar waxwings (*Bombycilla cedrorum*) are among the many birds who make use of this sweet feast. As fall wheels through the land, the leaves begin to turn reddish-brown and fall to the ground, where they will decay and enrich the soil. It won't be until next April when the first buds will start to give the twinberry a green hue again.

Your touchstone plant doesn't need to be so large or active, but you'll do best to choose a perennial rather than an annual or biennial. That way you can follow it for years. If you do choose an annual species, make sure it's in a patch where new generations will reliably appear each year. Ideally it should be one you can see from inside your home so that you can observe it even on days when you may stay indoors.

Make a little time each day to observe this plant, even if that's just glancing out the window or walking past to see what stage it's in. Pay attention if you notice any significant changes. For the first few weeks, it may seem like nothing much is going on, especially if you start this in winter. But as time passes, you'll start to notice how your touchstone plant adapts to the seasons, whether that's by producing flowers, fruit, or cones, by displaying fresh new growth, or dropping old leaves or needles. See how the plant changes when there's rain versus during a dry spell. If you are fortunate enough to observe a young plant for a few years, you'll have the opportunity to see how it grows!

Expand Your Horizons

Your touchstone plant is a good beginning point, but at least once a week, try focusing on other living beings in your area too. You might start with animals that interact with the plant, such as insects that climb on its stem, trunk, or branches, or feed on its leaves or flowers. Or you could see what other plants grow around it and whether any fungi pop up nearby, especially after it rains.

You have a couple different ways you could focus these observations. You might choose a few species in particular to monitor over time. This is easier done with plants than with more ephemeral animals and fungi. On the other hand, you can also just see what species are around each week when you check in and notice how the local cast of characters changes throughout the seasons.

There's no limit on how far you can take these observations. Maybe you want to wander around your neighborhood every week and check in on a number of locations along your route. Or perhaps you'll make a monthly visit to a more far-flung natural place; if you live in a city, maybe there's a park or hiking trail further out that you'd like to go to on a more seasonal basis and watch as the seasons change it too. But don't feel that you have to do more just because. Even if you only ever visit your touchstone tree and its immediate neighbors, you're still making the effort to connect and observe.

Keep a Nature Journal

Nature journaling is a great way to keep track of the changes in your touchstone plant and other neighborhood nature. This can be as simple as written entries describing what you see with each visit, but you're also welcome to be more elaborate too. Some people enjoy expressing themselves through poetry, while others use drawing, painting, and other visual art to mark the seasonal changes.

One rather twenty-first-century way to record your observations is through phone apps and other online resources. Nature's Notebook is a website that encourages you to record observations of phenological changes in the animals, plants, and fungi around you. They've even created a phone app so it's easier to record on the go! Other apps that save your observations of various living beings include eBird (for birds only) and iNaturalist (any living being you can photograph.) Scientists can use the data saved through these apps to study the phenology of various species; every observation you enter is a potential data point for a study. This helps scientists monitor migration routes, flowering and fruiting dates, and other important phenological milestones.

A Couple of Reminders

It is important to make sure that you're paying attention to the actual behaviors and patterns of living beings, rather than folk wisdom that may or may not ring true. For example, woolly bears—the caterpillars of the Isabella tiger moth (*Pyrrharctia isabella*)—have long been assumed to predict the severity of the coming winter. Do your best to simply record what an animal or other being is doing without trying to overlay it with human biases.

You might read up on that species later to see how your observations match with scientific knowledge—sometimes what those organisms are actually up to can be very surprising! For example, when people see a swarm of honeybees on the side of their house, they assume they're about to be attacked and want to call an exterminator. However, the bees are just on the lookout for a new place to live, and they'll likely move on soon thereafter. This is also the time when bees are *least* likely to sting, because they don't have a hive to defend yet. (If you do see a swarm of honeybees, call your local beekeeper, not an exterminator! Many beekeepers are always happy to take on a new batch of bees and will happily come take them off your hands so they can give the bees a new hive to live in.)

People's fear of animals like spiders and snakes can make them avoid observing these beings, even though they're important parts of their ecosystems. It may be difficult for you to sit and watch an animal that you're afraid of, but do the best you can. You just might find that as you watch this species go through its day-to-day life it's really not as scary as you once thought.

Most importantly, it is crucial that you not interfere too much in the day-to-day lives of the living beings around you, especially the animals. First and foremost, never, ever kill an animal or other species just for existing. If you identify it as an invasive species that is harmful to native species, then that's the one exception. But don't squash a spider just for being a spider.

It may be tempting to put out food to get animals to spend more time where you can see them. Birds may visit a feeder without becoming completely dependent on it because they are used to natural sources of food, like seeds, insects, and berries, being seasonal. If one source dries up, they just migrate locally to find another. As long as you keep your feeders squeaky clean to avoid disease transmission, your local birds should come to no harm.

Wild mammals, on the other hand, are much more prone to becoming habituated to humans, losing their fear of us and becoming dependent on us for food. That lovely deer or adorable

raccoon may seem like a great subject for study when it crosses your yard, which could tempt you to feed it so you can see it on a regular basis. However, even seemingly gentle mammals can become pushy and aggressive when seeking food, and when they are no longer afraid of humans, they are at greater risk of injury or death at our hands.

You also don't want to interfere with the very cycles you're trying to observe. Florida scrub jays (*Aphelocoma coerulescens*), a threatened species of corvid, are an important exception to the bird-feeding allowance. Well-meaning people would put out peanuts and other food for them year-round. This caused the birds to begin nesting earlier and earlier in the year, to the point where their young were hatching before caterpillars had hatched in large numbers. Many species of bird require the bulk of their diet to be insects in the first few weeks of life, and Florida scrub jays are no exception. Because there weren't enough caterpillars, and peanuts aren't a suitable substitute, entire nests full of jays died of malnutrition, putting this imperiled species at risk.

Should you notice that feeding or other activities on your part are having a negative effect on the species you're trying to observe, discontinue what you're doing. It's best to prioritize the health, safety, and wildness of the beings around you, even if that means you don't get to see them as often.

Reference

Demarée, Gaston R., and This Rutishauser. "From 'Periodical Observations' to 'Anthochronology' and 'Phenology'—The Scientific Debate Between Adolphe Quetelet and Charles Morren on the Origin of the World "Phenology."" *International Journal of Biometeorology* 55 (June 2011): 753–761. https://link.springer.com /article/10.1007/s00484-011-0442-5.

Solar-Lunar Aspects

Charlie Rainbow Wolf

The way the Sun and Moon interact in your natal astrology chart has a big influence on your life, because the Sun represents your character. The Sun is the center of the solar system, and it's also the center of your world, for you naturally see things from your own perspective. It's usually a good indication of your strengths and challenges in life.

The Moon represents your feelings and your emotional responses to situations and people around you. Examination of the Sun-Moon aspect in your chart brings insight into how you cope with situations. Entire books have been written on this topic; it can't all be covered in this article, but it is interesting to explore.

Natal Sun in Aries

Aries is the first sign of the zodiac. These people are achievers; they're passionate and motivated. They are full of vibrancy and like to be on the cutting edge of things. They are great starters but often get bored before completion. Aries Moon is strongest in this placement, adding vitality and confidence and perhaps a bit of conceit. Taurus Moon amplifies determination, although laziness might occur at times. Gemini Moon brings out curiosity and a sparkling—although sometimes superficial—personality. Cancer Moon is spontaneous but a bit moody or neurotic. Leo Moon boosts fire and passion and is perhaps a bit of a show-off. Virgo Moon is precise and organized, and they're not afraid to criticize. Libra Moon turns up the beauty and charm, and sometimes the secrecy too. Scorpio Moon intensifies passion, although true feelings are often kept hidden. Sagittarius Moon is optimistic and free spirited with an active mind, but they may find persistence elusive. Capricorn Moon is sometimes frustrated, divided between head and heart. Aquarius Moon is opinionated and brings loyalty but demands independence. Finally, a Pisces Moon adds a lighthearted and creative (but sometimes oversensitive) energy.

Natal Sun in Taurus

Taureans are known for their stubbornness and tenacity. They are the doers, the worker bees. Underneath that hardheadedness is someone who is devoted and loyal. They like what money can buy, and they're not afraid to work hard to get it. They are practical and reliable. Aries Moon adds responsibility and sincerity, but flattery may be used to get a desired outcome. Taurus Moon is strongest here, intensifying kindness and patience, but is sometimes a bit too laid back. Gemini Moon brings out the conversationalist; they're easygoing but sometimes impatient. Cancer Moon is delightful and playful, someone who is very expressive but prone to moodiness. Leo Moon turns up the charisma and is delightfully entertaining; they love to be the center of attention. Virgo Moon magnifies hard work and organization skills but might be bossy. Libra Moon creates a helpful and diplomatic energy and dislikes conflict of any kind. Scorpio Moon is resilient and patient, although lasting relationships may be a challenge. Sagittarius Moon brings a "people person" energy and lots of spontaneity, although overindulgence could be an issue. Capricorn Moon adds reliability and tenacity, although they may take a while to warm up to people. Aquarius Moon is curious, fiercely independent, and often unconventional. Finally, Pisces Moon adds creativity; these people may be artistic or good with their hands but could be oversensitive at times.

Natal Sun in Gemini

Geminis are the social butterflies of the zodiac. They are the thinkers; they are the writers. They love variety and look to entertain or be entertained. Adaptable and energetic, they're great motivators but sometimes lack self-discipline. Aries Moon adds a competitive edge, enthusiasm, energy, and an enjoyment of social activities. Taurus Moon is warm and sensual, more laid back but sometimes hard to get to know. Gemini Moon is strongest in this natal position: social and charming and capable; they are friendly but might find it hard to settle down. Cancer Moon adds compassion and a deep understanding of others but gets bored or moody easily. Leo Moon intensifies inventiveness and charm; they are naturally social but may be a bit high strung. Virgo Moon is curious, loves to learn, and is frequently critical. Libra Moon is gracious and charming, outgoing and friendly, and sometimes manipulative. Scorpio Moon is intense and mysterious, hard to get to know but loyal once a rapport is established. Sagittarius Moon may be frivolous; they are amicable and goal driven but often temperamental. Capricorn Moon is practical and pragmatic, torn between caution and excitement, usually only taking calculated risks. Aquarius Moon magnifies intellect and makes self-discipline challenging at times. Finally, a Pisces Moon brings a dreamy quality to plans and ideas; socializing may be easy, but long-term commitments might be problematic.

Natal Sun in Cancer

I see Cancerians as the natural carers of the zodiac. They are the homebodies. They have an innate ability to nurture, whether it is a garden or a home or a relationship. They require their own needs be met or they become quite downcast and withdrawn. Aries Moon brings charm and congeniality; emotions run deep but are sometimes hidden. Taurus Moon is family oriented and loyal but sometimes struggles to stay grounded. Gemini Moon is adaptable and kind with a good sense of humor, although feelings get easily hurt. Cancer Moon is strongest in this position, bringing deep emotions and strong intuition, but they are easily overwhelmed. Leo Moon is sensitive and creative; they're expressive and can be too open or trusting. Virgo Moon is practical, caring, and nurturing, and needs to find a balance between familiarity and newness. Libra Moon is both open and vulnerable, independent yet needs others, diplomatic yet hiding insecurities. Scorpio Moon is mysterious and reserved, self-reliant but prone to taking things too personally. Sagittarius Moon is dynamic, generous, gregarious, and too outspoken at times. Capricorn Moon brings competence and determination, usually thoughtful even when apparently tactless. Aquarius Moon is humanitarian and devoted to fairness; they're unconventional and sometimes extreme. Finally, a Pisces Moon is very emotional and sensitive, extremely intuitive, and nostalgic, but that may give way to melancholy.

Natal Sun in Leo

Leos are the showoffs of the zodiac, but in the best possible way! They make great leaders and love to be the center of attention. Any vanity is usually overlooked because of their gregarious and warm personality. People are drawn to them, which usually results in a full social life and good career prospects. Aries Moon adds to their vitality with warmth and cheerfulness, but excessive risks may be taken in the pursuit of pleasure. Taurus Moon turns on the charm with amiability and enjoyment but sometimes a bit too much drama. Gemini Moon brings great conversation, confidence, and amiability, but can be a bit vain at times. Cancer Moon is compassionate, generous, sensitive, and perhaps a bit too self-sacrificing. Leo Moon is strongest here; they are focused and goal driven, someone who acts first and thinks later and to whom reputation is extremely important. Virgo Moon is pragmatic and a bit of a perfectionist; they may be judgmental when stressed. Libra Moon is engaging, loves the good things in life, wants to be adored, and is prone to self-indulgence. Scorpio Moon is energetic, impressive, and passionate, which makes them prone to emotional outbursts. Sagittarius Moon loves to try new things; they're optimistic and generous, although often impulsive. Capricorn Moon likes to be in charge; they're confident and inspiring

as a leader, but they can be a bit bossy. Aquarius Moon is idealistic and humanitarian; they genuinely desire the best for everyone but might struggle with close relationships. Finally, a Pisces Moon is romantic and charming, expressive and loving, but they may not always be grounded in reality.

Natal Sun in Virgo

Virgos are the organizers of the zodiac. With mental dexterity, they plan and coordinate, and they do it with precision and style. Because Virgos see clearly how things can be done, they might come off as bossy or controlling when trying to explain things to others. They're not; many Virgos are quite lacking in confidence. Aries Moon brings resourcefulness and enthusiasm; they are able to plan and execute things well but can be impatient and blunt at times. Taurus Moon is sensuous and appreciates the finer things in life, which leads to overindulgence at times. Gemini Moon promotes wit and intelligence and a natural acumen for storytelling, but there is potential stress regarding close relationships. Cancer Moon is loyal to loved ones and genuinely wants to help, but is often misunderstood. Leo Moon turns on the charm with an ability to lead by example, although theatrical at times. Virgo Moon is strongest here and blends Virgos' natural organization abilities and their need to try to fix things with their difficulty in separating logic from feelings. Libra Moon is delightfully alluring and naturally diplomatic with high standards, although infidelity may be an issue. Scorpio Moon is passionate and uncannily perceptive and may not always let their feelings show. Sagittarius Moon is benevolent with a good balance between logic and feelings but gets discouraged when things aren't perfect. Capricorn Moon pursues success and recognition; they're dedicated and a bit of a perfectionist, and they may also be a workaholic. Aquarius Moon loves to learn and wants to do things quickly yet methodically; they struggle to understand emotions. Finally, with a Pisces Moon there's compassion and understanding, creativity, and a good balance between head and heart, but they are easily disappointed.

Natal Sun in Libra

Librans are the natural mediators and peacemakers of the zodiac. In their effort to make the right choice, they can be extremely indecisive. They look for the easiest path and the fastest way to reach a goal, which may make them seem lazy. They love company and know how to get what they want, although they may manipulate others to do so. An Aries Moon adds warmth and is sometimes mischievous or unreliable but usually likable. Taurus Moon promotes physical attractiveness and sensuality with a touch of materialism. Gemini Moons are chatty and witty, sociable and expressive, but potentially indecisive or naïve. Cancer Moon is supportive and caring; they have a genuine need to be appreciated and sulk when they aren't. Leo Moon hungers for attention and knows how to get it; they appear independent but are sometimes insecure. Virgo Moon likes precision, seeks beauty through perfection, criticizes often, but still expresses themselves well. Libra Moon is strongest in this placement; they're best with a partner, although they know how to manage on their own. Scorpio Moon is warm and engaging, and they are usually gentle and polite but will eventually erupt if pushed far enough. Sagittarius Moon appreciates travel and socializing; they are vivacious, optimistic, and willing to learn from mistakes. Capricorn Moon is excellent at planning and doing; they are idealistic but practical, with a tendency to take things too seriously. Aquarius Moon is humanitarian and idealistic; they value fairness and equality and sometimes come across as being opinionated. Finally, Pisces Moon is creative, tender, and quietly beguiling, but they can be easily hurt.

Natal Sun in Scorpio

These people are the passion powerhouses of the planets. They are independent, able to take charge, and their tenacity gets things done. They feel things deeply but might not show their emotions easily—that is, until things come to a head with an unforeseen outburst. Ambitious and intuitive, there's an air of mystery around Scorpios that makes them compellingly attractive. Add an Aries Moon, and there's additional drive and purpose, independence, and just a touch of stubbornness. Taurus Moon is practical and determined, loyal, romantic, and fond of finery. Gemini Moon is witty and charming, a disciplined worker, and a good raconteur, with just a touch of eccentricity. Cancer Moon is intense, intuitive, and sensual; they are charming but challenging to get to know and often jealous. Leo Moon is a natural leader, confident and complex with a strong yet emotional personality. Virgo Moon is the worker: ambitious, perfection seeking, perhaps a workaholic. Libra Moon is likable and empathic with a deep connection to others; they are romantic yet may be vengeful if wronged. Scorpio Moon is strongest here, and they can't help but be mysterious and powerful; they'll sacrifice themselves for their beliefs and can be very secretive. Sagittarius Moon enjoys socializing and learning, needs to be liked, and may have many lovers. Capricorn Moon usually finishes what is started and seeks success, sometimes to the point of ruthlessness. Aquarius Moon has a very active mind that is curious and intrigued by the world and its inhabitants but can also be very calculating. Finally, Pisces Moon is insightful and compassionate; they are always looking to improve but may belittle themselves too easily.

Natal Sun in Sagittarius

Sagittarians are natural philosophers. They enjoy learning about themselves and others. They're witty and charming, although prone to a bit of tactlessness. Independent and free-spirited, they hate to be tied down. They often seem unreliable, but that's only because their mind is going in many directions simultaneously. Aries Moon is confident and optimistic, even though there's a touch of arrogance. Taurus Moon is thoughtful and intelligent, with high ideals and lofty ambitions, but not always practical. Gemini Moon is adventurous and loves to learn through travel and socializing but is prone to nervous energy. Cancer Moon is imaginative and hopeful and needs to be surrounded by kindness and positive energy to avoid disappointment. Leo Moon is strong and fiery and passionate; they are fun and full of good intentions, although sometimes a bit pretentious. Virgo Moon is practical and pragmatic, hungry to learn yet critical of what is found. Libra Moon is friendly and diplomatic, a natural mediator but prone to gossiping. Scorpio Moon is feisty, a powerhouse of mystery and independence; they are straightforward and not always tactful. Sagittarius Moon is strongest in this placement; they are high-spirited and courageous, seek new experiences, and are romantic but don't like being tied down. Capricorn Moon is a natural leader who needs to be busy to feel fulfilled; they're practical and sometimes pessimistic. Aquarius Moon crusades for any worthy cause; they are ambitious and driven and often perceived as a bit eccentric. Finally, Pisces Moon is insightful with high ideas; they may be spiritual and are easily disappointed.

Natal Sun in Capricorn

Capricorns are the backbone of the zodiac. They know what they want and how they want it, and they have a hard time trusting someone else to do things correctly. They have the self-discipline to get things done. They may come across as cold, but they're actually quite sympathetic, although overserious at times. Aries Moon brings determination and purpose; they are an excellent leader who may appear aloof at times. Taurus Moon appreciates money and what it buys, needs to feel valued, and often takes things too personally. Gemini Moon is quick witted with a bawdy, earthy sense of humor that's frequently acerbic or sarcastic. Cancer Moon is warm and affectionate but might be shy; they are good at hiding their feelings. Leo Moon has a big personality; they are natural leaders who like to be in charge but can potentially be domineering. Virgo Moon is usually cheerful and sincere, good at handiwork, protective and sensitive, and sometimes withdrawn. Libra Moon loves to learn and follows rules but often questions them; they appear detached at times. Scorpio Moon adds intensity and a radical edge and can be occasionally manipulative. Sagittarius Moon is optimistic, determined, and successful, although sometimes unpredictable. Capricorn Moon is strongest here, highlighting the responsible and dependable Capricorn energy, which can be too serious at times. Aquarius Moon is intellectual and curious, unconventional in many ways but rarely impulsive; they may be too independent. Finally, a Pisces Moon brings creativity and an active imagination as well as deep feelings with emotions that may not be easily expressed.

Natal Sun in Aquarius

Aquarians are the rebels of the zodiac. They're the freethinkers, those who will not be tamed. They value independence, and while they rarely seek to draw attention to themselves, their unique nature often does just that. Humanitarian and quirky, they definitely think outside the box. Aries Moon is freedom loving and willful; they have a potentially eccentric outlook and a resentment for being told what to do. Taurus Moon is usually practical and easygoing; they are social and unique, a natural leader who is often idealistic. Gemini Moon is individual and open minded, someone who is sociable but resents being tied down. Cancer Moon is sincere, intuitive, and potentially a bit unconventional. Leo Moon is warm and upbeat, genuine, and likes attention; they are a good leader, although there's a tendency to be bossy. Virgo Moon brings a perfectionist streak; they are a good problem solver who stresses easily. Libra Moon likes unconventional people and activities; they are social but able to hide feelings well. Scorpio Moon emphasizes passion in many ways; they are rebellious, intriguing, and frequently hard to get to know. Sagittarius Moon is optimistic and playful, rises to a challenge, and sometimes seems indifferent. Capricorn Moon is influential, methodical, and reasonable; they can be a bit of a workaholic and tire easily. Aquarius Moon will be strongest in this placement; they are very humanitarian, often uncomfortable with close attachments. Finally, a Pisces Moon is creative and inspirational, an abstract thinker who is frequently misunderstood.

Natal Sun in Pisces

Pisceans are the "sensitive souls" of the zodiac, and they're often very spiritual in some way. Their feelings run deep, and they need an expressive outlet. Their surroundings should be a haven of peace, a retreat for when the world feels too harsh. Aries Moon is classy and hardworking, even if a bit extravagant at times. Taurus

Moon is loyal, likes to help others, and makes friends easily but gets hurt easily too. Gemini Moon is intuitive and discerning, loves to learn, and has deep feelings, though expressing them may be difficult. Cancer Moon is caring and sensitive, often taken for granted, and sometimes gullible. Leo Moon is emotional and enthusiastic but frequently daydreams. Virgo Moon is self-sacrificing, a natural people pleaser; they are good at hiding their feelings and are easily overwhelmed. Libra Moon dislikes conflict and tense atmospheres; these people place others first, sometimes with disappointing outcomes. Scorpio Moon is sensitive and understanding, mysterious and deep; they make good spiritual leaders but are prone to vanity. Sagittarius Moon is easygoing and warm, unconventional, philosophical, and often brutally honest. Capricorn Moon is protective of themselves and others; they are stern but gentle, even if a bit controlling at times. Aquarius Moon is individualistic and romantic, unconventionally charming, and outspoken about their beliefs. Pisces Moon is strongest in this natal placement; they're very sensitive souls, intuitive, intensely emotional.

Conclusion

Of course, nothing about astrology can be summed up in a line or two. If this has piqued your interest, I encourage you to explore the relationship between the Sun and Moon in the natal birth chart in greater depth. There are many books written on the subject, or you could book an astrological consultation with a reputable astrologer. Astrology has the potential to unlock many doors; this article has simply given you a key to one of them!

Further Reading

The Compleat Astrologer: The Practical Encyclopaedia of Astrological Science by Derek Parker and Julia Parker (London: Mitchell Beazley Ltd., 1971): This was my introduction to astrology all those years ago, and it includes a very good lunar ephemeris and information on Sun-Moon aspects.

Moon Signs: The Key to Your Inner Life by Donna Cunningham (New York: Ballantine Books, 1988): Donna takes a complex topic and makes it easy to understand more about how Moon signs influence compatibility.

Sun Sign, Moon Sign by Charles Harvey and Suzi Harvey (Wellingborough, UK: Aquarian Press: 1994): In this book, the Harveys walk you through the 144 Sun-Moon combinations and help you to understand their strengths and their challenges.

About the Contributors

Elizabeth Barrette has been involved with the Pagan community for more than thirty-four years. She served as managing editor of *PanGaia* for eight years and dean of studies at the Grey School of Wizardry for four years. She has written columns on beginning and intermediate Pagan practice, Pagan culture, and Pagan leadership. Her book *Composing Magic: How to Create Magical Spells, Rituals, Blessings, Chants, and Prayers* explains how to combine writing and spirituality. She lives in central Illinois, where she has done much networking with Pagans in her area, such as coffeehouse meetings and open sabbats. Her other public activities feature Pagan picnics and science fiction conventions. She enjoys magical crafts, historic religions, and gardening for wildlife. Her other writing fields include speculative fiction, gender studies, social and environmental issues. Visit her blog *The Wordsmith's Forge* (https://ysabetwordsmith.dreamwidth.org/) or website PenUltimate Productions (http://penultimateproductions.weebly .com). Her coven site with extensive Pagan materials is Greenhaven Tradition (http://greenhaventradition.weebly.com/).

Mireille Blacke, MA, LADC, RD, CD-N, is a registered dietitian, certified dietitian-nutritionist, and licensed alcohol and drug counselor residing in Connecticut. She has written numerous articles for Llewellyn's annuals series since 2014 and has also been published in *Today's Dietitian*. Mireille worked in rock radio and the music business for two decades before shifting her career focus to behavioral health nutrition and addiction counseling. She spends considerable time renovating her Victorian home, pining for the city of New Orleans, and entertaining her beloved Bengal cats. Someday, Mireille plans to complete a doctorate in behavioral health nutrition when such a program actually exists. She can be reached at mireilleblacke@gmail.com.

Pam Ciampi was a professional astrologer from 1975 until her passing in 2019. She served as president of the San Diego Astrological Society and was President Emeritus of the San Diego Chapter of NCGR. Pam was the author of the Weekly Forecasts for Llewellyn's best-selling *Daily Planetary Guide* since 2007. Her latest contribution was an astrological gardening guide titled *Gardening by the Light of the Moon*. In its fourth printed edition, it is now available in a calendar format.

Sally Cragin is the author of *The Astrological Elements* and *Astrology on the Cusp* (both from Llewellyn Worldwide). These books have been translated and sold in a number of countries overseas. She does readings (astrological and tarot). She also serves as a city councilor at large for the Fitchburg (MA) City Council and is the only professional astrologer serving in public office in the Commonwealth. Visit "Sally Cragin Astrology" on Facebook or email sallycragin@gmail.com.

Vincent Decker, a native New Yorker, has been actively studying planetary influences on the weather for over thirty years. His forecast method relies on the work of the main modern and ancient contributors to the field of astrometeorology. At the same time, Vincent has incorporated many new techniques discovered from his own rewarding and fruitful study of planetary influence on weather patterns. His analyses of important past weather patterns have appeared in several astrological magazines.

Shelby Deering is a lifestyle writer from Madison, Wisconsin. She specializes in writing about home décor, natural wellness, and mental health, contributing to publications like *Better Homes & Gardens*, *The Pioneer Woman*, *Naturally, Danny Seo*, and more. When she's not writing, you'll find her hiking Wisconsin's many trails, shopping flea markets, or going on road trips around the country.

Bernadette Evans has worn many hats—or toques (she's from Canada)—over the years, from daughter to mother and now grandmother, as well as being a clinical counselor, astrologer, and writer. Her daily and monthly forecasts were a mainstay on Conscious *Community Magazine*'s website for four years. When she is not working with clients or writing, you can find her with her nose in a book, going to the movies, singing around the house, or taking a class. Her new love is playing with her grandson. You can contact her at bernadetteevansastrology.com or email her at bbevans001 @gmail.com. You can also follow her on Facebook and Instagram.

Penny Kelly is a writer, teacher of intuition, author, publisher, consultant, and naturopathic physician. After purchasing Lily Hill Farm in southwest Michigan in 1987, she raised grapes for Welch Foods for a dozen years and established Lily Hill Learning Center. Today, she teaches online, posts regularly on Patreon, YouTube, Rumble, Spotify, Google Podcasts, Apple Podcasts, and iHeart. She is the mother of four children, has co-written twenty-three books with others, and has written twelve books of her own. Penny lives, gardens, and writes in Lawton, Michigan.

Lupa is an author, artist, and naturalist Pagan in the Pacific Northwest. She has written several books on nature-based Paganism and is the creator of the Tarot of Bones. A lifelong creative, her more recent efforts involve rediscovering her love of traditional illustration. Find out more about Lupa and her work at http://www.thegreenwolf.com.

Kim Rogers-Gallagher has been a professional astrologer, writer, and lecturer for over twenty years. Based in Florida, Kim is the author of *Astrology for the Light Side of the Brain* and *Astrology for the Light Side of the Future*. Her monthly, weekly, and daily columns appear in *Dell Horoscope* and other astrological websites. She served on the board and edited the quarterly journal for the

International Society for Astrological Research and was a Steering Committee Member of AFAN (Association for Astrological Networking).

Christeen Skinner, D.F.Astrol.S., FRSA, is a director of Cityscopes London Ltd., a future casting company based in the UK. She is author of several books, including *Exploring the Financial Universe*, *The Beginner's Guide to the Financial Universe*, and *Navigating the Financial Universe*. The latter was published in 2019 and correctly forecasted the pandemic of 2020. She is a trustee of the Urania Trust and a director of the Alexandria iBase project, which, together with the Urania Trust, seeks to preserve material that might otherwise be lost. A free monthly newsletter is published and available at www.financialuniverse.co.uk.

Charlie Rainbow Wolf is an old hippie who's been studying the weird ways of the world for over fifty years. She's happiest when she's got her hands in mud, either making pottery in the "artbox" or tending to things in the yarden (yard + garden = yarden). Astrology, tarot, and herbs are her greatest interests, but she's dabbled in most metaphysical topics in the last four decades because life always has something new to offer. She enjoys cooking WFPB recipes and knitting traditional cables and patterns, and she makes a wicked batch of fudge. She lives in central Illinois with her very patient husband and her beloved Great Danes.

Moon Sign Book Resources
Weekly Tips provided by Penny Kelly, Shelby Deering, and Lupa
"The Methods of the *Moon Sign Book*" by Penny Kelly
"Gardening by the Moon" by Pam Ciampi

Notes

Notes

Notes

Notes

Notes